China in the 1990s

Edited by

Robert Benewick and Paul Wingrove

MACMILLAN

First published 1995 by
MACMILLAN PRESS LTD
Houndmills, Basingstoke, Hampshire RG21 2XS
and London
Companies and representatives
throughout the world

ISBN 0–333–60137–8 hardback
ISBN 0–333–60138–6 paperback

A catalogue record for this book is available
from the British Library.

10 9 8 7 6 5 4 3 2 1
04 03 02 01 00 99 98 97 96 95

Printed in Malaysia

Contents

List of Figures and Tables

Figures

Tables

Acknowledgements

We wish to thank Joan Astill and Stephanie Hemelryk of Sussex University for their valuable assistance in the preparation of the manuscript and Steven Kennedy, our long-suffering publisher, for his advice and wisdom.

R.B.
P.W.

List of Contributors

Robert Benewick University of Sussex, UK
Marc Blecher Oberlin College, Ohio, USA
Shaun Breslin University of Newcastle, UK
Donald C. Clarke University of Washington, USA
Elisabeth J. Croll School of Oriental and African Studies, University of London, UK
John Dearlove University of Sussex, UK
Rosemary Foot St Antony's College, Oxford, UK
David S. G. Goodman Institute for International Studies, University of Technology, Sydney, Australia
Jude Howell University of East Anglia, UK
Penny Kane University of Melbourne, Australia
Joe C. B. Leung University of Hong Kong
Simon Long BBC, UK
Nicola Macbean Great Britain-China Centre, UK
Shirin M. Rai University of Warwick, UK
Tony Saich Ford Foundation, Beijing, PRC
John Thoburn University of East Anglia, UK
Anne Wedell-Wedellsborg University of Aarhus, Denmark
Gordon White Institute of Development Studies, University of Sussex, UK
Paul Wingrove University of Greenwich, UK
Xiao-zhuang Zhou University of Chicago, USA
Godfrey Kwok-yung Yeung Institute of Development Studies, University of Sussex, UK

List of Abbreviations

APEC	Asian Pacific Economic Cooperation
ASEAN	Association of South-east Asian Nations
CCP	Chinese Communist Party
CMC	Central Military Commission
CPPCC	Chinese People's Political Consultative Conference
EPZ	Export processing zone
GNP	gross national product
NGO	non-governmental organisation
NPC	National People's Congress
PLA	People's Liberation Army
PRC	People's Republic of China
RMB	Renminbi (People's Currency)
SEZ	Special Economic Zone
SOE	State-owned enterprises
TVP	Township, village and private enterprise
¥	yuan (unit of currency, translated as $)

Introduction

Robert Benewick and Paul Wingrove

Themes

The most striking feature of the development of the People's Republic of China since its founding in 1949 is the rapid and uneven pace of change. Having undertaken the most successful land reform in history almost immediately after seizing power, the Chinese Communist Party (CCP) leaders became embroiled in a power struggle over the future direction of China's development. Mao Zedong (Mao Tse-tung) launched the Great Leap Forward towards the end of the 1950s. However mixed in intentions the consequences were disastrous. This was soon followed by the upheavals of the Cultural Revolution in 1966–69 and the subsequent myriad of radical experiments. During the three years 1976–79, following the Cultural Revolution decade, Mao Zedong and Zhou Enlai died; Hua Guofeng assumed power; but after arresting 'the Gang of Four' Hua was himself deposed by Deng Xiaoping. Deng and his associates set about 'reforming the revolution': the countryside was decollectivised, the 'open policy' towards the outside world was adopted; and, somewhat more hesitantly, urban industrial reforms were embarked upon.

During the years 1978–89 China managed to create an image (however inaccurate) as the more human face of communism, as an innovator introducing radical transformation of the old Stalinist system, as an attractive location for investment, even as a highly desirable tourist destination. Particularly in the mid-1980s China seemed to be avoiding the scepticism and opposition that beset a similar attempt at market modernisation being undertaken by Mikhail Gorbachev in Moscow. And, more to the point, this seemed to be a bold economic transformation that had the great

1

merit of being successful. Not only did there seem to be little resistance to the new policies, but they achieved remarkably high rates of growth in the early stages, especially in agriculture where a flourishing peasant economy seemed to have been unleashed by the new course. The outside world watched with awe as China seemed to be transforming itself into yet one more of those East Asian, high-growth, stable authoritarian regimes.

Yet the 1980s reform decade had its failures, most notably in the realm of political reform and human rights. Generally, the first forty years of the PRC suffered from the absence of a period or opportunity for political consolidation and stability. These failures, combined with more immediate factors such as spiralling urban inflation, help to account for the urban protests which led to the Tiananmen massacre and crackdown.

The Tiananmen 'crackdown' of June 1989 obliterated newly formed images of China. Particularly in the West there was horror, outrage and revulsion. But that was not all that changed. Academics, journalists, China-watchers, and even foreign governments woke up to find that the student-led clash with the Communist party-state had changed much of their understanding and interpretation of China. In particular, since almost nobody had predicted this outcome, a great deal of China expertise seemed undermined. This is probably unfair, since future events are subject to all sorts of random influences – nonetheless, the Sinological community became aware of the limits of its expertise. The lenses through which China had previously been perceived needed to be refocused.

Further, the Tiananmen crackdown exposed the nature of the Chinese party-state to a new generation, and particularly exposed the failure of institutionalisation (see Benewick, Chapter 1). The years leading up to the 50th anniversary of the PRC (1999) and to the millennium promise to be no less breathtaking than the preceding four decades as the 'socialist market economy' accelerates and China becomes further enmeshed in the global economic system while human rights and political reforms remain low on the agenda.

China in the 1990s can boast impressive rates of economic growth; significant increases in industrial output and in fixed capital investment; and rising standards of living, particularly in the coastal and southern provinces. Unlike that in Russia, much of what counts as 'reform' is from the bottom up. On the debit side are mounting urban inflation, increasing unemployment, reports of rural unrest, allegations of corruption, rising crime and an environmental policy which in some areas of China is interpreted as providing recreational facilities for foreign investors. These are manifestations of more fundamental issues such as growing inequalities, central–local conflicts and rudimentary legal and welfare systems. Moreover, these concerns must be fitted into a political context of contest, conflict, control and compromise.

China in the 1990s will be tested on its ability to balance change and stability, and that is the theme of this book. For China today a great deal is at stake with, at one rather dramatic extreme, its unity as a nation. Change and the management of stability are complex processes. Our objective in this book is to provide the student and reader with an introduction to, and understanding of, these processes. This requires a multidisciplinary and multifaceted approach, which is best achieved by bringing together leading scholars in the field to examine, assess and evaluate the achievements and failures in their areas of expertise. The challenge for this book, which we hope we have met, has been to translate this scholarship for a wider audience.

Content

The major transformations which characterise post-Mao China are naturally a central focus of this book, and a number of chapters therefore consider the key issues of agriculture (Blecher, Chapter 9), industry (Zhou, Chapter 12), the 'Open Policy' (Howell and Thoburn, Chapter 14), political reform (Saich, Chapter 3) and population policy (Kane, Chapter 16).

In addition, some of the consequences of these transformations present themselves as barely manageable dilemmas for the Chinese leadership, and these are treated in separate chapters. The tortuous metamorphosis of ideology, for example is discussed by White, Chapter 2; the possible emergence of 'civil society' by Howell, Chapter 6; new, perhaps unanticipated, central-local relationships by Breslin, Chapter 5; and contemporary questions of gender by Rai, Chapter 15.

However, it has always been our intention to go beyond some of these key issues, and to give a broader account of this emerging, new society. Through the many chapters in this book we hope to provide a broad conspectus of the reform process as it has worked its way through all levels and institutions of Chinese society. Thus, Goodman, Chapter 11, assesses the nature and role of the new economic elites that have emerged; Croll, Chapter 17, and Leung, Chapter 18, discuss the complexity of the evolving social security system; Macbean, Chapter 8, examines youth and the management of young offenders; Dearlove, Chapter 10, shows how reform permeates down to the village level; Clarke, Chapter 7, considers the new understandings and practices of the legal system; Yeung, Chapter 13, points to the changed role of the People's Liberation Army; Wedell-Wedellsborg, Chapter 19, traces the transformations in literature and film; and Long, Chapter 4, sketches the present leadership position and the prospects for the future. Finally, China's international position – as world and regional power – is examined in separate chapters, 20 and 21, by Foot and Wingrove.

1

The Tiananmen Crackdown and its Legacy

Robert Benewick

'Killing the chickens to scare the monkey'

There is no shortage of literature recording the brutal suppression of the urban protests of May–June 1989 in China. The thirty or so books include instant on-the-scene reporting from Tiananmen Square, eye-witness accounts, the published experiences of leading participants and supporting intellectual dissidents, postscripts to work in press at the time and subsequently more measured, substantial and systematic analyses. What these works share is a condemnation of the serious violation of human rights and life on the part of the Chinese state.

The reasons for the almost universal humanitarian response in a world where transgressions of human rights are familiar are not difficult to discern. The opening of China raised expectations of changes in its world view, particularly among those seeking its market for trade and investment. China experts were divided between those who applauded the market reforms introduced by Deng Xiaoping and his close associates and those who remained critical of the excesses of forty years of Communist Party rule. In Beijing, at the time of the crackdown, there was a relatively large community of foreign students and scholars in residence and able to bear witness. There was also a considerable media presence for the visit of the President of the USSR, Mikhail Gorbachev, which was swiftly augmented for the news bonus of a student hunger-strike in Tiananmen Square, guaranteeing a world-wide television audience. The celebrated open door was violently, if temporarily, banged shut.

In summary, the literature divided the Tiananmen Square adversaries into two more or less homogeneous and stereotyped camps: the student democracy movement, backed by dissident intellectuals, attracting support from a progressively disenchanted urban population, versus a totalitarian state ruled by an isolated and insulated gerontocracy, fearing an Eastern Europe-styled societal breakdown and embattled in internal élite rivalries. The context was the growth of economic difficulties and corruption consequent upon the rapid but uneven pace of reform.

Pitted against this view is the reality of China five years later. The democracy movement's moral crusade has been reduced within China to a whisper. Its leaders are underground or abroad, while a number of those imprisoned have been released at periodic intervals either in response to external pressures or as the state gains in confidence and control. The market economy ethic has persisted and has been enshrined in the constitution. Associated reforms have regained momentum since the victory of the market reformers at the Fourteenth Party Congress in October 1992. Despite the evidence of widespread corruption which substantiates one of the grievances of the 1989 protesters, students are now eager to seek their fortunes in the market rather than pursue, for example, an economically unrewarding, and thereby status-demeaning, academic career. Nor have the lessons of the Tiananmen crackdown been lost upon the party-state, for the conceptualisation of the socialist market economy has been amended to include political control and stability (Saich 1992). As for the damaged image of the People's Liberation Army (hereafter PLA) having been transformed from the people's friend to the state's instrument of repression, its need for a more professional and modernised military machine has been reasserted at the likely cost of a more circumscribed political role. Condemnation of its human rights record notwithstanding, China is no longer regarded as a pariah, particularly by those nations anxious to exploit economic opportunities.

The view from the state

It is both opportune and necessary to reassess the Tiananmen crackdown. The nature of the protest movement has been the subject of fresh studies (Wasserstrom and Perry 1992). However, what the earlier work avoided or failed to take on is the more troublesome and vexed question of the state which, throughout the history of political thought, is invested with the right and duty to maintain internal order and defend itself against external threats. Even when its legitimacy and credibility are in question, or undermined, it is also expected that the state will protect itself against assaults on its survival (Constitution 1982: Article 28). Yet normative in approach, the early Tiananmen studies accepted as morally wrong the ruling élite's priority to secure its own survival, ignoring the reality that China is by no means unique in employing the military against its own citizens.

This chapter is not a revisionist exercise nor an attempt to redress a balance nor is it an invitation to lower one's voice against the indecent behaviour of a state. Instead it switches the focus prominent in the literature on the Tiananmen crackdown from the activities of the student-led protest movement to those of the party-state. In doing so, it poses the still unpopular question of why politically unidentified students were allowed to occupy and remain in Tiananmen Square, an action formally in contravention of both the state constitution and the municipal regulations of Beijing. Bluntly stated, if British students and their supporters were to occupy Parliament Square prior to the visit of an American President, how long would they be allowed to remain there before being removed by force, even excessive force, if deemed necessary by the state? If anything, Tiananmen Square is more important as the symbolic centre of the Chinese nation.

The mystery deepens when the nature of the demands are taken into account. In the first instance, they were parochial and open to negotiation and concessions; for example, there were student requests to present their grievances to the state and party leadership. There was then an escalation to political demands, most notably against the rising tide of corruption which could be contained, if not satisfied, through a more convincing party-state recognition of this discontent and identifying it with their own (albeit inadequate) anti-corruption measures. The recognition of this demand, however, was soon overtaken by a claim for recognition by those making the demand, in particular the Federation of Autonomous Student Unions in Beijing Universities and Colleges (hereafter, Federation of Autonomous Student Unions). Acknowledgement of these new bodies became a matter of accepting conditions for negotiations. What followed were universal slogans and themes, many of which were only half-understood but inspired political mobilisation. These ranged from calls for the resignation of Premier Li Peng, and the retirement of Deng Xiaoping, to the establishment of a multi-party system. These can be credited, at least in part, to the internal dynamics of crowds but the party-state's responses must also be considered. In short, the political inexperience of the demonstrators was apparently matched by the political ineptitude of the party-state. How then was a transient movement able to reduce the state to intransigence, denying its self-interest by risking its opening to the international economy and world order? Why also was the state unable to implement effective public order measures short of embarking on a massacre? The mobilisation of protest was relatively predictable given the lack of alternative locations to Tiananmen Square as a meeting-place. The access routes were long and well-charted and the Square was easy to police. As is well-known, the demonstrations were allowed to broaden beyond their student base, protest was converted into a protest movement, and disruptions to public order were transformed into perceived threats against the state.

The argument presented here is that there was a failure in political institutionalisation and that this failure is endemic to post-Liberation China and is equally fundamental to post-Mao China. Consequently, the personalisation of power, inherited from the Maoist era, has persisted. The post-Mao leadership headed by Deng Xiaoping recognised and promulgated political reforms of some significance but was unable or unwilling to synchronise them with the rapid economic reforms and the swift pace of societal change. Political institutions in China, not discounting their ritualistic value, have not as yet acquired authority or effective executive or legislative powers. This approach moves the discussion beyond élite rivalries and the lack of public order training and resources to whether there was an authoritative chain of command in a position either to facilitate negotiations with the protesters, or to take and implement the decision to clear Tiananmen Square in an orderly and non-violent manner at an earlier stage. It is accepted that direct action or non-institutionalised political activity is a problem for most, if not all, states and also that this problem is exacerbated by weak institutions. The Chinese party-state then was unable to fulfil one requirement of governance; in management of public order and the resolution of conflict through institutionalised channels based upon agreed and recognised rules and procedures. Through the use of excessive force, however, they were able to fulfil another requirement of governance; the rulers were able to preserve the party-state and at least for that moment ensure their own survival.

The following section addresses issues of constitutionalism, institutionalisation and the personalisation of political power. This is followed by an examination of the salient events leading to the Tiananmen crackdown, based on the official state version, drawn primarily from the report of the Mayor of Beijing to the Standing Committee of the National People's Congress (hereafter, the Mayor's Report). The Mayor's Report incorporates elements of the statements of other party-state leaders and reporting from the party-state media. For present purposes the issue is not the accuracy of the account but the extent to which the official version personalises rather than institutionalises responsibility. The concluding discussion points to the relationship between institutionalisation and stability particularly as it relates to two key aspects of market reforms: decentralisation and the opening of China to the international economy and world system.

The issues

In addressing levels of institutionalisation and personalisation of power in Chinese politics, questions are raised about the nature of the Leninist party-state and the Chinese bureaucracy. Without denying the importance of political leadership, it is necessary to recognise, as in the cases of both Mao Zedong and Deng Xiaoping, that high levels of personalisation can substitute for and undermine political institutions. Nor is it a form of institutional decay peculiar to authoritarian states. What is notable about Chinese politics is that the personalisation of power need not be institutionally based. The Mayor's Report on the Tiananmen crackdown shows how far the formal decision-making process was devalued, allowing responsibility to be shifted and blame personalised.

Although a high level of institutionalisation seeks to manage and minimise direct action and confrontation, a low level encourages it by the absence of procedures and channels for processing demands, needs and grievances, thereby personalising and privileging political access to decision-makers. Just as the protesters had no institutionalised channel independent of party organisations to express their discontents, the leadership had no recognised and established arrangements by which peacefully to respond without weakening the party. And just as the occupations of Tiananmen Square were a *de facto* recognition of the right to protest as a form of access to political leaders, which has continuities in Chinese history and is formally acknowledged in the Constitution (1982: Article 35), the crackdown was a *de facto* acknowledgement that the state will protect itself. The occupations were also a more dramatic manifestation of the transformations of Chinese society during the 1980s and the political demands being made upon the party-state. By not being able rapidly to accommodate these demands, procedurally or substantively, the reforming leadership, which had all but abandoned the Maoist strategy of political mobilisation for the party-state, was faced with a mobilisation against the party-state escalating to a popular uprising.

To enhance our understanding of the party-state in relation to the crackdown, it is helpful to assess the (low) level of political institutionalisation achieved relative to the pace of the economic reforms of the 1980s. The process of institutionalisation has been uneven but, for the purposes of an analysis of the Chinese party-state since 1949, can be divided into three parts: formulation, implementation and legitimisation. Formulation involves the process of constitution-making and the drafting of laws and regulations that are ideally in accord with that constitution. The constitution enshrines the objectives of society and the rights of the citizens, describes the institutions of the state and defines the relationships between them and society. In a more democratic mode, the Chinese political scientist and leading dissident, Yan Jiaqi (Bachman and Yang 1991: pp 19–22, 151–154), stresses the need of the people to influence the choice of the decision-makers and the political responsibility of decision-makers. Even though constitution-making may be regarded as a formality and the constitution as a formalistic document both have symbolic value and record the changing directions as defined by its leaders. For example, citizens' rights are accorded a more prominent position in the current constitution than in previous ones.

The constitution may enshrine the institutions of government but these institutions only acquire continuity and stability through effective implementation of decisions and policies. Operationalising institutions creates experience and a political class that relies upon process and procedures which can be judged within a recognised framework. This was recognised at the highest level when Qiao Shi on the eve of his recent appointment as Chair of the National People's Congress (hereafter NPC) 'spoke of the inadequacy of specific systems to ensure implementation of the constitution' (quoted by Kaye 1993).

The NPC provides an interesting case, for the state constitution sanctions it as the 'highest organ of state power', yet it functions primarily as an endorsing and ratifying body. In recent years, however, the NPC has progressively attempted to exercise its muscle (O'Brien 1990), so that attempts to convene it during the crackdown were blocked and its Standing Committee circumvented. The lack of legitimacy for state institutions in China then is particularly acute in view of the legacy of Mao Zedong, the pre-eminence of the Communist Party, and an entrenched and powerful bureaucracy. As a first step the state constitution must gain precedence over the party constitution.

China acknowledges the need for a state constitution and in its short history has promulgated four: 1954, 1975, 1978, 1982. The same number were enacted between 1909 and 1949. Added to the frequency of turnover, is the ease by which the constitution can be amended by the NPC. In 1993 Article 15 was amended to read 'the state practises a socialist market economy replacing economic planning on the basis of socialist public ownership'; Article 8 to provide constitutional recognition of the replacement of the communes and agricultural producers' cooperatives by the responsibility system; and Article 98 extending the term of office of the People's Congress at county level from three to five years.

In one sense the frequency of constitutional change reflects the scope and pace of change in China and suggests the transitional nature of the state. It also signifies a process of impositional constitution-making with little direct meaning for the population. The 1993 amendments followed those adopted by the Fourteenth Party Congress in October 1992. Where these amendments sanction decisions already taken and reflect practices already in place, the experience of the crackdown suggests that the constitution is also available for manipulation by the party-state to legitimise its actions: in this case the declaration of martial law. However, the creation throughout China of institutes for the study of the constitution suggests that constitutional fickleness may be on the wane. In a third and perhaps more profound sense China's constitutional process is symptomatic of the tension between party rule and the personalisation of power on the one hand and the rule of law and institutionalisation on the other. This is a lesson of the crackdown with the intervention of Deng Xiaoping and the party elders and the allocation of responsibility for the disruption to public order and for prolonging the protest movement to the then Communist Party General Secretary, Zhao Ziyang.

The post-Maoist leadership faced a crisis of institutionalisation upon their assumption of power. Their own political experience had been influenced by a pre-eminent leader and the Maoist style of personalised politics. Yet in part they prolonged it through the manner of their own succession to Hua Guofeng. From the Cultural Revolution, however, they inherited institutional decay. The institutions set forth in the 1954 constitution had been replaced, although not constitutionally coded until 1975, or had been allowed to atrophy, while the failure, for example, to institutionalise participation, along with the discontinuities of mass mobilisation left a structural vacuum. China's reformers were determined to prevent a recurrence of the upheavals of the Cultural Revolution. Economic reforms were the centrepiece of a programme to establish their legitimacy, promote stability for development, as well as to revitalise and stimulate the economy. Concomitant with this were political reforms. In addition to reactivating the institutions that existed prior to the Cultural Revolution, notably the People's Congresses, the 1982 constitution tackled the question of elections to some leadership offices and of tenure in office. But effective implementation lagged behind the economic reforms. Elsewhere it is argued that whereas political scientists have claimed that Western political systems are adversely affected by overloading, China's political institutions suffer from under-loading (Benewick 1992).

At the same time political decisions of the highest order had been and were being taken by the state and party. The move to a market-based economy, the separation of management from the party in business enterprises, the opening to the international economy and world system and the decentralisation of economic and hence political power required considerable political bargaining and skill. The stakes were too high, however, to rely mainly on personalised power. Market reforms, the open policy and decentralisation created new interests with claims upon the state. If institutions could not accommodate, process and regulate them, more personalised means were available. This, in turn, led to allegations of corruption, favouritism and demands for reform. For Deng Xiaoping, however, corruption was a temporary phenomenon that had to be tolerated during the transition to market socialism.

When the economic reforms began to falter in the mid-1980s, having fostered a revolution of rising expectations, the basis for the leadership's legitimacy began to be called to account without the institutional means to rectify criticism. An absence of independent non-party intermediaries further encouraged the direct prosecution of claims and grievances. Zhao Ziyang confirmed the persisting primacy of personalisation of power over institutionalisation when he revealed to Gorbachev in 1989 that the party had agreed to refer all important decisions to Deng Xiaoping. In doing so Zhao revealed how the constitution had been undermined, foreshadowed his own demise and set the stage for the further intervention of the party elders leading to the crackdown.

To sharpen the argument, both the economic and political reforms and the personalisation and institutionalisation of power were out of synch. The first was a major cause of the urban protests and the second was a major cause of the crackdown.

The Tiananmen crackdown[1]

This section examines the events leading to the crackdown of 4 June 1989 in so far as they relate to the issue of institutionalisation. Tiananmen is the focus because of its symbolic importance and because of the large number of protesters involved. Many came from urban centres other than Beijing while a mobile population which may have swelled the numbers demonstrating and straining police resources, entered and left Beijing daily. The Mayor's description is revealing not only for what is said but, as with the constitution, for what is not said. This approach is possible because the events are well-known. Viewed from the perspective of the state, institutional weakness rather than the strength of demonstrations becomes crucial and this weakness *vis à vis* the personalisation of power is confirmed.

The Mayor's Report seeks to justify the violent suppression of the protest movement, maintaining that a tiny handful of people deliberately exploited student unrest to create a counter-revolutionary rebellion: 'Their purpose was to overthrow the leadership of the Chinese Communist Party and subvert the Socialist People's Republic of China.' Chen is also affirming an escalation of violence and, by placing responsibility on a small group, is employing a tactic familiar in the outbreaks of disorder where those in authority identify and isolate the leaders of the protest. This is further tempered by alleging involvement of outsiders, in this case 'foreign forces'. The main burden of responsibility, however, is attributed to Party General Secretary, Zhao Ziyang, thereby personalising responsibility and confirming a leadership struggle between reformers and hard-liners which has been widely credited as an explanation, at least in part, for the crackdown. In fact the split predates the urban protests and may even have prolonged Zhao's tenure in office. The official version also provides graphic accounts of the violent confrontations and killings that took place in the vicinity rather than in Tiananmen Square itself and maximises the PLA casualties.

The death of former Party General Secretary, Hu Yaobang, on 15 April 1989 was the flash-point for the urban protests. Flash-points, however, occur all the time but only a small number translate into behaviour and only a handful turn into adversarial confrontation. The particular context is a determinant. According to the Mayor's Report, a political situation was engineered by a small group – 'the rising wind forebodes a coming storm'. This was a reference to intellectuals articulating wider concerns of rising urban inflation, growing corruption, nepotism and advocating political democratisation.

A number of questionably illegal activities followed including demonstrations, occupation of the Square and putting up big character posters. Although Article 35 of the Constitution grants the freedom of speech, press, assembly, association, procession and demonstration, it is circumscribed by other articles of the Constitution, in particular Article 51 which declares that freedoms and rights may not infringe the interests of the state, society or the lawful freedom and rights of other citizens. The exercise of these rights for Beijing is controlled by the regulations of the Municipal

Government and as the Mayor's Report argues, the 'four big freedoms, i.e. speaking out freely, airing views fully, holding great debates and writing big-character posters', had been withdrawn from the Constitution.

The protesters' rights were accordingly subject to arbitrary interpretation at this early stage. This may have resulted in a degree of latitude and tolerance on the part of the party-state leaders which the protesters were reluctant to acknowledge, as well as the inability of the party-state to mount an effective response. Policing was at first within bounds of maintaining public order, perhaps reflecting the privileged status of students and that the mourning for Hu Yaobang was a defined period. A heavy-handed approach risked the protests spinning out of control, thereby recruiting other sections of the population. Unlike the response to the mourning demonstration for former Premier Zhou Enlai in 1976, party supporters were not enlisted to use violence to clear the Square. Alternatively, a failure of an authoritarian state to act decisively can be interpreted as a sign of weakness and an invitation to continue and escalate protest.

What is apparent is that protest was developing into a protest movement. Demands were being formulated, petitions drafted, classes boycotted, the number of protesters increasing, leaders emerging and, most threatening of all, an organisation founded, the Federation of Autonomous Student Unions. Of the options available to the party-state, negotiation was unacceptable. Dialogues were entered into but only on the condition that they did not constitute negotiations because:

1. to negotiate directly with the protesters would have been to afford them and their demands a legitimacy.
2. to negotiate with the Autonomous Students' Union would open the way for similar organisations as well as undermining official party organisations, the All-China Students' Federation and the Beijing Students' Federation. Institutionalising non-party organisations is an important step towards civil society (see Chapter 6).
3. as the protest movement gained momentum it attracted other interests, some of which also formed into organisations outside the party-state orbit, e.g. Beijing Autonomous Workers' Union and the Beijing Union of Intellectuals.
4. the movement's leadership was unstable and its demands were

in a constant state of flux so it was unclear who would command authority and on what conditions.

5.   there was no forum for negotiations or procedures empowering party-state officials to negotiate.

Interactive communication was effectively closed off, having been reduced to the non-binding dialogues or visits by party-state leaders to the Square or with the party-state Beijing Students' Federation. It is worth emphasising that similar considerations can apply in varying degrees to liberal democratic as well as authoritarian states.

With the protest movement outlasting the mourning period, the party-state leadership toughened its stance in the run-up period to the 70th anniversary of the May 4th Movement. The Party's Political Bureau established a group to deal with the protest and the Beijing Party was instructed to carry out propaganda work inside and outside the Party. A dialogue was conceded but the students were to be represented under the umbrella of the All-China Students' Federation and the Beijing Students' Federation. At this point Deng Xiaoping, whose only official position was Chair of the Party Military Commission, intervened to denounce the protests as political turmoil aimed at overthrowing the party and the socialist system. Deng's speech formed the basis of an editorial in the *People's Daily* on 26 April and, while the Mayor's Report describes this assertion of personal authority as having a salutary effect, the students remained defiant. This intervention, with the support of party elders, confirmed that early on in the chronology of the protests the leadership took them seriously enough to play the Deng card. Once on the table it was difficult to withdraw, which further weakened the Constitution and the existing institutions.

In the context of the Mayor's Report it is surprising that following Deng's intervention and the party-state's view of legality that demonstrations on 27 April and 4 May were allowed to take place. The party-state talked big but hesitated or was unable to convert words into action, for attempts by the police and apparently the PLA to halt the marchers proved futile. The Mayor's Report plays down the demonstrations and instead accuses Zhao Ziyang of escalating 'the turmoil' by his accommodating stance. The party-state's version is now highly personalised. Zhao's stance, the difficulties in agreeing the conditions for dialogues, and any perceived weakness of the state resulting from the demonstrations may well have contributed to the escalation in the form of the hunger strike that followed. More important, as the Mayor's Report admits, the students made use of Gorbachev's visit for the Sino-Soviet summit, to put pressure upon the party-state.

A watershed was reached once the hunger strike began. This would have been a highly-charged and delicate situation for any leadership:

1. the state conceded the need for educational reforms, yet the protest movement, impatient with the prevarication over talks, humiliated the party-state by preventing the state reception for Gorbachev taking place in the Square and forcing him to enter the Great Hall of the People though a side entrance.
2. the party-state was out-manoeuvred. The presence of the hunger-strikers made it difficult to clear the Square.
3. the combination of the hunger-strikers and the arrival of Gorbachev made for global media coverage.
4. it was a mobilising event. Messages of support were received, new 'autonomous' organisations appeared, and there were residents' demonstrations. The Mayor's Report admits to the involvement of several hundred thousand people, while other reports estimated one million.
5. it is even likely that Zhao Ziyang's conciliatory acts were counter-productive not only in terms of a factionalised leadership but in creating the appearance of factionalism on the one hand and exposing the institutional weaknesses on the other. Such a perception transforms a protest into an uprising.

The Mayor's Report accused Zhao Ziyang not only of failing to halt the hunger strike but, as already seen, encouraging it. This fudges the institutional responsibility between party and government and between the centre and the municipality. The hard-liners for their part, having failed to control the Square, allowed a non-violent protest to develop beyond the ordinary means of public order. Although the Mayor's Report outlines the steps taken to provide humanitarian relief to the hunger-strikers, it omits any reference to the acrimonious dialogue between Li Peng and representatives of the hunger-strikers which had been televised.

With one million people on the streets of Beijing and large-scale demonstrations in cities throughout China, the protest movement was labelled counter-revolutionary by Li Peng and martial law was declared (for demonstrations throughout China, see Unger 1991). If the state was under siege, a suspension of the Constitution could have been expected. Instead there were attempts to observe proprieties – of a kind. The Standing Committee of the NPC is invested with the power to invoke martial law which would have covered the Beijing Municipality (Constitution 1982: Article 67, Paragraph 20). This can be short-circuited, however, by the State Council which can declare martial law in selected areas and this provision was invoked (Constitution 1982: Article 89, Paragraph 16). Enforcement was more difficult and it stretches the imagination to assume that the choice was made out of regard for citizens' rights. More likely, in view of the attempts to bring forward the meeting of the Standing Committee of the NPC called for the end of June, it could not be relied upon to reach a united decision. According to the Mayor's Report, members of the Standing Committee of the Political Bureau had met to discuss the issue and the declaration was announced at a meeting attended by officials from the party, government and military. Since this was not a meeting of the State Council to endorse a decision taken elsewhere on its behalf, there is a question of constitutionality. This gives credence to the widely held view that the decision was Deng Xiaoping's. Either view demonstrates the low regard for institutionalised decision-making.

Once martial law was declared, an equitable solution was ruled out and the declaration confirmed that the hard-liners, backed by the party elders, were in command. President Yang Shangkun announced that the party elders were agreed 'that retreat was impossible since it would indicate the collapse of the government, and of the People's Republic of China'. Implementation is another matter. The Mayor's Report notes that implementation was the responsibility of the Beijing Municipal Government but also refers to the Party Central Committee's instructions to the troops.

World media attention remained focused on the Square despite the protest movement's loss of momentum; though after the hunger strike had ended at the end of May, it was somewhat revived by the construction of the 'goddess of democracy'. The goddess of democracy, breaking the north–south axis of the Square, standing between the portrait of Mao Zedong and the monument to the People's Heroes, and symbolising liberal democratic values, was a provocation adding to the humiliation of PLA troops being stalled *en route* by Beijing residents.

The Mayor's Report does not explain convincingly how the decision for the crackdown was made. An incident where three people were killed in a jeep on 2 June is cited as a flash-point but comes over more as an excuse. According to the Report the decision was taken by the Party Central Committee, the State Council and the Central Military Commission. This may provide institutional legitimacy but it sheds no light on how the decision was made and coordinated, especially as it implies a process too un-wieldy for a quick response. Once again, analysts are left to infer a personalised process focusing on Deng Xiaoping, advised by the party elders. Their intervention had occurred early on and there is no evidence that they had withdrawn from their involvement. The failure of the party-state leadership was in preventing protest turning into a movement and then preventing the protest move-ment from generating a popular uprising.

The future

The Chinese leadership employed massive and excessive force to protect the party-state and to ensure its own survival. The argu-ment presented here is that states are necessarily driven to behave accordingly and that in China's case the weak institutionalisation and the personalisation of political power was the driving force. In so far as the question of institutional failure has been addressed, following the Tiananmen crackdown, the emphasis has been on political stability to promote and further the market economy. This is a gamble, basing legitimacy on economic development and consumer consumption in recognition that when Deng Xiaoping dies China's leaders will no longer be able to rely on the legitimacy of the Long March and Liberation generations. The lessons of the Soviet Union are also ever-present in that political reforms pose their own threats.

China's approach, rather than synchronising political and econ-omic reforms, may widen the gap between the two. The pre-Tiananmen revolution of rising expectations has, if anything, ac-celerated, promoting interests with claims on, and needs from, the state, and furthering unequal and uneven development. Although the party-state may be able to ride out the trade repercussions of international pressures for improving their human rights record, the domestic market losers, currently the rural population, are a potential and historical threat to political stability. At present political stability is defined as improved public security.

One lesson is that although democracy may currently be beyond China's frame of reference, political power needs to be institutionalised rather than personalised. A second lesson is that the crackdown serves as a warning to would-be protesters and the world at large that China will bear the recriminations in order to defend the party-state and ensure the survival of the regime.

Note

1.   The crackdown extended beyond 4 June and refers to the continued use of force and the round-ups of protestors in Beijing and other urban centres.

2

The Decline of Ideocracy

Gordon White

'Pass off the fish eyes as pearls'

Ideology has played a crucially important role in the politics of state socialist or communist regimes. Such systems are 'ideocratic' – they rely on an explicit and codified system of political ideas derived from Marxism–Leninism which guides the actions of the political élite in the hegemonic communist Party, justifies the Party's monopoly on power and legitimises its proclaimed historical mission to 'build socialism'. In China the political role of ideology reached high points of intensity during the periods of Maoist mass mobilisation in the Great Leap Forward in 1958–59 and the Cultural Revolution decade from 1966–76.

In China ideological orthodoxy, or 'redness', is a particularly important attribute of the political élite – members and leaders of the communist party – creating and maintaining their identity and unity. But there are also attempts to spread the ideology to the whole population through the media and the education system. During the Maoist era, when ideological pressures on the population were at their height, government officials, professionals and intellectuals were expected to be 'red' as well as 'expert'. The Leninist logic of the 'vanguard party' presupposes that members of the Party are more ideologically 'advanced' than the general population and therefore politically qualified to rule. As the 'transition to socialism' proceeds, however, this distinction should disappear as the population is absorbed into the ideological world of the political élite. The hope in the meantime is that there will be a mutually beneficial political interaction between élite and mass. On the one side, the political élite is able to provide effective leadership because

21

the ideology gives them intellectual clarity and moral authority; on the other side, the 'masses' are willing to follow their leaders if the latter accept and live up to the values of the official ideology. There is an ideally virtuous cycle of élite–mass relations here but, if the relationship is upset through élite schisms, incompetence or venality on the one side and mass cynicism and discontent on the other, a vicious cycle is generated. According to the post-Mao Dengist leadership, the Cultural Revolution – and Maoist politics in general – had generated just such a vicious cycle. The party had been at war with itself and the official ideology – Marxism–Leninism–Mao-Zedong-Thought – came to function less as a unifying creed and more as a political weapon for competing leaders. The radical Maoist principle of 'politics in command' promoted political campaigns which disrupted lives and created mass resentment.

It was the task of the new leadership to reverse this vicious political cycle and to create a basis for their own legitimacy by redefining the official ideology and its role in Chinese society. A major shift in political ideas was also needed to legitimate the radically different economic system which was the objective of the reforms which began in 1978. Previously the official ideology had described and justified a system of centralised economic planning; now it had to legitimate the introduction of a 'socialist market economy'.

In so doing, party-state reformers sought three main objectives:

1. to repudiate the perceived ideological distortions and dogmatic excesses of the Maoist era;
2. to revive a perceived 'healthy' ideological heritage which had been established in the early years of the People's Republic;
3. to adapt the existing ideological framework to market socialism.

In tackling their first objective, the reformers succeeded in reducing the ideological influence of remnant Maoists, but also weakened the political credibility of ideological orthodoxy in general and their own version of Marxism–Leninism–Mao-Zedong-Thought in particular. To the extent that the second objective was achieved, it resurrected a traditional kind of Stalinist political thought which had less and less relevance to changing socioeconomic realities in China. The third objective led to a diffuse and diluted framework of political ideas which lacked cogency and vision. The net result was ideological decay, a loss of political faith and direction, not merely among the general population, but also among the political élite in the Communist Party.

Ideological demolition and the legacy of Mao

In the immediate aftermath of the death of Mao and the arrest of the radical Gang of Four in 1976, the emerging reform leadership under Deng Xiaoping pursued three main strands in their ideological critique of Maoism. First, the reform leaders wanted to desanctify and secularise the reigning ideology, a kind of Marxist superstition, which had an infallible source, the Supreme Leader, and brooked neither opposition nor qualification. This sacral ideological style was continued to some degree in the late 1970s by Mao's chosen successor, Hua Guofeng, and other Maoist leaders who were dubbed by their opponents as 'whateverists' who thought and did 'whatever Mao Zedong thought or did'. The reformers argued for an ideology based on the notions of 'practice as the sole criterion for testing truth' and 'seeking truth from facts'. These ideas became the watchwords of a more pragmatic approach, identified with and sponsored by the new paramount leader, Deng Xiaoping.

The second strand of ideological demolition was an attempt to limit the intrusion of the official ideology into the everyday lives of the population, through a process of depoliticisation or 'demobilisation'. During the Cultural Revolution decade, ideological instruction was achieved through pervasive 'ideological and political education', organised through small study-groups in workplaces and residential areas, or political study-classes in schools, and comprehensive political control over all means of mass communication. The aim of Deng and his reform allies was to reduce the range of politicisation, expand the space available for private life and allow greater autonomy for intellectuals and other professionals. In practice, this meant less attention to organised political education; less emphasis on political criteria in recruiting people for specialised training or professional jobs; less political interference in economic decision-making; a decline in the visible manifestations of political ideology (removal of posters and statues and reducing the political content of the mass media); and an effort to encourage greater intellectual and cultural freedom under the slogan of 'let a hundred flowers contend'. There was, however, considerable disagreement among the new leadership about how far this depoliticisation should be allowed to go.

Thirdly, the post-Mao leadership sought to repudiate or revise certain tenets of Maoism which they felt had pushed China in the wrong direction. Particularly important was the attack on the definition of socialist development as a continuation of 'class struggle' under 'the dictatorship of the proletariat'. In their view, this ideological notion had damaged the Party itself by organising vindictive and unjustifiable campaigns against key leaders (including Deng Xiaoping). It had also created a general atmosphere of antagonism directed, for example, at remnants of the former 'exploiting classes' and their families, or the intelligentsia which was labelled the 'stinking ninth category'. Moreover, the notions of 'class struggle as the key link' and 'politics in command' had, in their view, hampered economic development. The radical leftist 'Gang of Four' were criticised for allegedly maintaining that 'we would rather have a low socialist growth rate than a high capitalist one' and 'it is all right for production to go down so long as we do a good job in revolution'.

The reformers tried to reverse these themes, arguing that 'class struggle' had already lost most of its political importance in China's post-revolutionary society. The central strategic task for the future should be economic development, to be pursued through the 'four modernisations' and higher levels of efficiency achievable through structural reforms in the economy. The Maoist conception of economic development as a highly politicised process of mass mobilisation was repudiated. Models previously lauded as the embodiment of Maoist virtue in the economy, most notably the Daqing oilfield in industry and the Dazhai production brigade in agriculture were ignored or repudiated. Specialised expertise was given its full due as a central element in the modernisation process, which meant political rehabilitation for the cultural, scientific and technical intelligentsia who had been targets of the Maoist onslaught against potential 'new bourgeois elements'.

Maoist radical antipathy to the market was rejected, along with its opposition to policies seen as 'bourgeois', such as differential pricing, variable interest rates and wage incentives. Maoist notions of economic 'self-reliance' were attacked as economically unwise: at local levels because they fostered an introverted cellular economy within communes, counties or provinces, and at the national level because they denied China access to much-needed foreign technology and finance and to the potential benefits of foreign trade.

This process of ideological repudiation and revision was essential but costly. Members of the élite, particularly those socialised and recruited during the Cultural Revolution decade, were now being informed that most of what they had been told by the then Party leadership, including the formerly infallible Mao, and much of what many of them still believed, was at best wrong-headed and at worst heinous. At the same time ideas such as 'self-reliance' and 'egalitarianism' had set down broad roots among the population, so that efforts to discredit them were not greeted with general approval.

The post-Mao leadership tried to limit the potential political damage of their ideological *volte-face* by identifying scapegoats for the excesses of the Cultural Revolution, i.e. the 'Gang of Four' and Mao's alleged would-be assassin, Marshal Lin Biao. This enabled people who had been involved in these events to avoid personal responsibility. At the same time, this convenient demonology dramatised the ways in which official ideology had been used for over a decade as a tool for political deception and repression, by an allegedly correct leadership at the head of a proletarian party. Why should this not happen again in another form? In their efforts to reject the abnormalities of the past, the reformers revealed much of the normal substance of ideological and political control in a traditional state socialist system, thereby undermining themselves as well as their opponents.

The political contradictions posed by this attempt at ideological demolition were also evident in the problem of how to assess the role of Chairman Mao, the architect of the previous two 'disastrous' decades. After all, Mao was also the acknowledged leader of the communist revolution in China, hailed for so long as the person who had converted the foreign ideologies of Marx and Lenin into a powerful political creed for the salvation of China. How could the new leadership redefine Mao's heritage without undermining their own legitimacy and avoiding a repetition of Mao's mistakes, for example, by erecting a comparable leadership cult around Deng Xiaoping? They grasped this nettle at the Sixth Plenary session of the Eleventh CCP Central Committee in June 1981, which passed a 'Resolution on Certain Questions in the History of our Party since the Founding of the PRC'. This document criticised the later Mao, from the Great Leap Forward onwards, for his arbitrary leadership style, his ideological errors and, in particular, for his role in launching the Cultural Revolution which, the Resolution stated, conformed 'neither to Marxism–Leninism nor to Chinese realities'. Mao's mistakes were explained – and to some extent rationalised – by reference to China's historical tradition of 'feudal autocracy', the difficult domestic and international circumstances of the 1960s and the influence of scheming associates on an ageing leader. Unspoken was the commonly held belief that Mao's judgement had been seriously impaired by senility and disease in his later years, making him prey to delusions and subordinates.

However, 'Mao Zedong Thought' was still hailed as 'a valuable spiritual asset of our Party', as a successful expression of the integration of Marxist–Leninist theory with the realities of the Chinese Revolution. This attempt to bowdlerise Mao led to uncomfortable intellectual contortions; witness the following statement from a leading theorist of political reform, Su Shaozhi (Chang 1988: p 16):

> I think Mao Zedong Thought must be distinguished from the thought of Mao himself. Mao Zedong Thought is a theoretical system that is the crystallisation of the contributions of our entire party, not only Mao himself. Since Mao made such a big contribution, we call it Mao Zedong Thought. Mao Zedong Thought as a correct theoretical system can include only the correct thought. Some of Mao's own thought is correct and some in error, but the wrong part cannot be included in Mao Zedong Thought.

It was in this highly unconvincing, deodorised form that Mao's ideological heritage was confirmed as a central plank of the official ideology of the new era – Marxism–Leninism–Mao Zedong Thought.

The ambiguity of the Sixth Plenum document reflected the serious political dilemma facing the new leadership. They could not completely reject the heritage of Mao since to do so would be to reject much of the political rationale of the Chinese Revolution itself – its creation, the People's Republic of China, and its supreme institution, the Chinese Communist Party. Moreover, the Resolution's verdict on Mao reflected disagreements about his political merits within the leadership and the Party at large, disagreements which were mirrored among the general population where Mao's name was still respected, particularly among the peasantry, many of whom identified him with their liberation from the landlords. The Resolution thus represents a political compromise and, as such, its impact was blunted from the outset. But however malleable Mao might be, it was well-nigh impossible to portray him as a market-oriented economic reformer.

Ideological reconstruction and adaptation

The new leadership's strategy for remodelling the official ideology reflected a contradiction at the heart of the reform strategy, namely the desire to bring about swingeing changes in the economy while maintaining the political *status quo*. The political, as opposed to economic, content of the ideology differed considerably from its Maoist predecessor, but it was not new. Rather, it attempted to resurrect the political theory of the mid-1950s which derived from a Stalinist creed inherited from the Soviet Union. This political doctrine rested on the 'Four Basic Principles' enunciated by Deng Xiaoping as defining the core elements of a socialist polity: Marxism–Leninism and Mao Zedong Thought, the socialist road, the dictatorship of the proletariat and the leadership of the Communist Party. The first Principle asserted the necessity for a ruling ideological orthodoxy as the guiding principle of China's socialist state. Although Deng himself sanctioned certain political reforms in the early 1980s, they could not go beyond the limits imposed by the Four Basic Principles. When more radical reformers within the CCP leadership showed signs of being willing to go further, notably Hu Yaobang in 1986 and Zhao Ziyang in 1988–89, Deng and his conservative allies stepped in to bar the way.

However, while the central tenets of political theory remained, there was an attempt to bring the ideology's economic theory into line with the new era of market socialism. The most salient changes were:

1. the substitution of economic development for political 'class struggle' as the central strategic task of the CCP in accordance with the notion that 'what is good for the development of the productive forces is good for socialism';

2. ideological ratification of the positive economic role played by markets and material incentives;
3. a rethinking of the central issue of ownership which encouraged the emergence of a wide range of ownership forms, including private enterprise, outside the traditional 'state' and 'collective' sectors;
4. a greater willingness to open up the Chinese economy to a wide range of links with the international economy.

The results were often unrecognisable as anything that could be described as 'Marxism', let alone 'Marxism–Leninism' and still less 'Mao Zedong Thought', and could lay scant claim to 'scientific' rigour or plausibility within a Marxist framework. The intrusion of reality into theory diluted the latter into sometimes bizarre theoretical concoctions. For example, consider the attempt to change the official ideology to accommodate changes in policies concerning labour and employment. The economic reformers wished to raise labour productivity by moving towards a labour market. In order to justify this ideologically, however, they had to come to terms with the fact that, in the Marxist canon, acceptance of a 'market in labour power' requires a recognition that labour power is a commodity. Since this equation is a defining characteristic of a distinctively capitalist mode of production, it would seem incompatible with the role of labour in an avowedly socialist economy. Sensitive to possible charges of 'bourgeois' tendencies, reformers have had to decide how far to go in the process of theoretical revision: from the minimum, cosmetic tinkering through linguistic fudging, to an outright revision of fundamental principles. As the reform process deepened and the more radical reformers gained confidence in the mid-1980s the ideological frontiers were gradually pushed back and previously heretical ideas received a public airing.

But labour reform has been a contentious issue and disagreements over policy have been reflected in disagreements at the ideological level. The range of views reflected in the public debate has been remarkably wide. Answers to the crucial question 'Is labour power a commodity under socialist conditions?' have ranged from an emphatic 'no' to an equally emphatic 'yes', with a spectrum of shades of opinion in between. The traditional ideological position has support on the grounds, for example, that since enterprises are publicly owned and thus workers own the means of production themselves, it does not make sense to say they are selling labour power to themselves.

Some reform economists try to skirt the ideological problem by using more anodyne terms such as 'labour services market' or 'job market'. Others take the dilemma by the horns and change the theory to fit the new policies. They argue that it is the very purpose of the economic reforms to transform labour into a commodity by giving employers more power to hire and fire workers and workers more power to choose employers. This is but one inevitable consequence of the transition to a socialist market economy. Advocates of this view are vulnerable to charges from Party conservatives that they are advocating 'bourgeois restoration'. They are therefore at pains to point out that labour markets in the post-reform economy would have a different significance in a socialist market than a capitalist market economy since the relationship between employers and workers is not exploitative.

This debate gives some idea of the pervasive role of ideology in the process of reforming policy. The ideology is not inelastic; it contains potential for theoretical revision and provides a common language for debate between different viewpoints. Yet given its canonical status and its instrumental role to defend certain interests embedded in the political and economic *status quo*, it serves to constrain innovation. It also limits debate by its inherent tendency to polarise discussion into questions of unambiguous right and wrong, and convert the participants in the debate into believers and heretics. Intellectual argument becomes a potentially dangerous political game, which cannot but restrict the ability to think about and implement reforms.

To the extent that ideology acts to restrict adaptation to new realities, it undermines its own credibility and the authority of its exponents. Yet the reverse is also true. Ideology as afterthought or cosmetic rationalisation also loses force and credibility. Even if contending policy positions reach an agreement, the result, when converted into ideological pronouncements, is likely to be an implausible hotchpotch.

Thus, whether ideology impedes or adjusts, it decays either way. Nowhere was this more apparent than in the much-vaunted 'theory' of 'the initial stage of socialism' unveiled by Zhao Ziyang as the ideological explanation of the reform era at the Thirteenth Party Congress in October 1987. Zhao argued that traditional Marxist concepts about the transition to socialism should be abandoned. It should be recognised that China, as an under-developed country in which markets were weak, was in 'the initial stage of socialism' during which the sole priority in the economic sphere should be economic development. During this period, a range of institutions and policies were admissible as long as they fostered economic growth. While this document was clearly a serious attempt to harmonise ideology with the real world of policy, it failed on several counts: it did not succeed in its goal of being a 'blueprint' for a reformed future since its conception of the future was vague and contradictory; it was hardly a projection of any kind of 'socialist' future since the whole question of socialism in the economic sphere was postponed for a century; in the meantime, anything was possible so long as the leadership of the day thought it advisable and it could thus be dubbed 'socialist'. Not surprisingly, some Chinese called this theory a 'hundred-treasure bag' into which anything can be stuffed. It loses the predictive, inspirational and Utopian element of communist ideology and appears as merely a rationalisation of the current policies of the current Party leadership. In the political world of Chinese reformism, the officially proclaimed ideology of Marxism–Leninism–Mao Zedong Thought has increasingly become a residual.

To many of China's economic reformers, this is to be welcomed since they regard any notion of ideological orthodoxy as a fetter on creative thought and policy. In fact, one can see the very idea and process of market-oriented economic reform as a dagger aimed at the heart of communist ideocracy. Political conservatives have recognised this threat of ideological decay and have linked it to the decline in political and moral standards within the Party-state and the spread of 'unhealthy tendencies' and non/anti-socialist sentiments among the general population. They have been particularly sensitive to the 'unhealthy' effects of the open-door policy, highlighting instances of 'corrupt' or 'degenerate' practices imported from the West, such as rock music, immodest clothing, pornographic books and the like. Their response has been to mount periodic campaigns – negatively against 'bourgeois liberalisation' and 'spiritual pollution', and positively to strengthen a 'socialist spiritual civilisation'. These political movements, in ways characteristic of the Maoist period, raise the political 'temperature' of society by increasing 'ideological and political education' and saturating the media with ideological themes.

Though these campaigns recurred about every two years between 1980 and 1988, the largest conservative backlash came in
the aftermath of the Tiananmen crackdown of June 1989. The
ensuing onslaught against 'bourgeois liberalisation' intensified
ideological and political education; reiterated the need to inculcate
socialist morality and 'spiritual civilisation' and criticised ideological 'contamination' from abroad; advocated a return to previous
ideological themes, for example, the Maoist idea that 'class struggle
exists in the ideological sphere', and generally slowed the pace of
economic reform. And yet, in spite of the vehemence of this
ideological counter-offensive, it was commonly implemented in a
perfunctory fashion and was greeted widely by the population with
a mixture of cynicism, indifference and hidden hostility. This built
up an atmosphere of tension and repressed initiative which was not
lifted until early 1992 when Deng Xiaoping visited the Shenzhen
and Zhuhai Special Economic Zones, and issued a dramatic call
for bolder and faster economic reform. This ushered in a more
radical version of the economic reforms which undermined conservative ideological objections and political opposition and was
ratified at the Fourteenth Party Congress in October 1992. Once
again, ideology was subordinated to economic development.
The conservative counter-offensive had proved a resounding
failure.

Ideology in decay

The protest movements of 1989 and the Tiananmen crackdown
(see Chapter 1) dramatised the bankruptcy of the official ideology
as a force for maintaining political authority. Reformist calls for
people to 'liberate thought', particularly in the context of greater
openness to the outside world, led to greater popular awareness of
uncomfortable facts which clashed with ideological claims. For
example, information about the continued dynamism of advanced
capitalism and the impressive developmental performance of
Taiwan and South Korea made the ritual claim about the alleged
'superiority of socialism' ring hollow. Other systems of thought and
belief increasingly flooded in to fill the moral and political vacuum
created by the decline of ideology: notably Christianity in the
moral sphere and liberalism in the political sphere.

Thus by the early 1990s, China was a radically different place from that of a decade earlier. An ever-widening gap had opened up between state and society and the effort of conservative leaders to reimpose ideological conformity after the Tiananmen crackdown was not only doomed to fail but could only serve to widen the gap still further. The economic reforms not only challenged the old verities by introducing the new conceptual terrain of market economics, but also set in train profound changes in social structure and values which are increasingly at odds with ideological orthodoxy. Ideology has lost its claim to be the sole basis of authority in society.

In the early 1990s, there is evidence that, though the old categories of Marxism–Leninism–Mao Zedong Thought are still retained in official discourse, the real content of the ruling ideology has in fact been shifting. The ideology of 'late Dengism' has increasingly moved closer to the kind of authoritarian developmentalism characteristic of Taiwan, South Korea and Singapore. This rests on the two claims of nationalism and developmentalism: first, that the communist regime can unify the Chinese nation and represent its interests in the international arena; and second, that a strong authoritarian state under the leadership of the CCP can deliver rapid economic development and successful economic reform which will create a 'strong and rich' nation and realise the goals of Chinese modernisers since the late nineteenth century. Alarming political counterfactuals are cited to bolster this position: the danger of internal disunity and fragmentation which would weaken China internationally; and the threat of chaos resulting from any move towards rapid democratisation. The experience of the former Soviet Union provides powerful evidence for these kinds of scenarios.

While an ideological shift of this kind may prolong the life of the regime, it contains the seeds of its own destruction. An ideology which tries to legitimate authoritarian rule in terms of its superior capacity to promote economic progress will run into political trouble if the pace of economic growth falters. Moreover, even if economic success is maintained, the experience of other East Asian success stories suggests that resultant social changes increase the pressures for political liberalisation and eventual democratisation which will bring about the ultimate downfall of ideocracy and the authoritarian political system which it serves to legitimate.

Reference

Chang, Gordon H. (1988), 'A symposium on Marxism in China today: an interview with Su Shaozhi, with comments by American scholars and a response by Su Shaozhi', *Bulletin of Concerned Asian Scholars*, vol. 20, no. 1.

3

China's Political Structure

Tony Saich

'One log cannot prop up a tottering building'

Throughout the 1980s, while all different viewpoints within the Party agreed that some adjustment of administrative practices and the role of the Party was necessary to stop the economic reforms coming to a halt, a major overhaul of the system was resisted by orthodox Party officials.

Reform of the political structure for China in the 1990s will receive a comparatively low priority as the leadership concentrates on devising policies for rapid economic growth and transformation of the economic structure.

Leadership debates on structural reform

In the initial period after the arrest of the 'Gang of Four' (1976), little attention was paid to the politico-administrative system. Problems were put down to the excesses of the 'Gang', the bad working practices to which officials had grown accustomed during the Cultural Revolution (1966–76), and the remaining influences of a 'feudal' way of thinking. Increasingly, however, Deng Xiaoping and his supporters realised that many of the problems derived not from attitude but from China's political structure. The adoption of a market-orientated, decentralised economic strategy at the Third Plenum of the Eleventh Central Committee in December 1978 demanded officials who could give expert, technical advice and not people who felt at home hiding behind the rules and regulations of a rigid, overcentralised political system dominated by the Party.

Deng Xiaoping and his supporters decided that an 'administrative revolution' was needed to shake up the system. By 1980, there was a growing recognition that the demands of a modern economy required greater differentiation and clarification of roles for China's institutions. Institutionalisation and the 'rule of law' became key phrases of the reformers' vocabulary (see Chapter 1).

In August 1980, Deng Xiaoping highlighted the problems, such as bureaucratism, the excessive concentration of power, patriarchism, lifelong tenure in official posts and abuse of privilege, which were hampering China's development. These problems derived from faults in China's organisational system. Deng also argued that a high degree of democracy was important to make sure that the people genuinely had the power of supervision over the state in a variety of effective ways to supervise political power at the basic levels, as well as in all enterprises and undertakings.

During the early 1980s, a number of initiatives were undertaken to reform the political system, including the adoption of new Party and State Constitutions, measures to trim the bureaucracy, attempts to improve the quality of the cadre force, and steps to promote effective citizen participation. However, the question of the Party's dominant role was not tackled and many Party cadres balked at the idea of any curtailment in their power.

In 1986 more radical ideas about reform of the political system reappeared in the media. It seemed that significant elements in the Party leadership were willing to countenance a reduction in the Party's power. Deng's originally unpublished August 1980 speech formed the starting-point for discussions. The main reason for a renewed willingness to talk about reform was the fear among many that the economic reforms were in danger of reaching an impasse. The only political reforms seen as necessary were those that would oil the wheels of economic modernisation.

Throughout 1986, many of the Party's own intellectuals began to argue for radicalising the reforms beyond this parameter. To promote democratisation by strengthening the 'rule of law', intellectuals such as Cao Siyuan, Su Shaozhi and Yan Jiaqi proposed a strategy based on institutional reform. This would increase the parameters for democratic debate and was to be supported by the emergence of independent groupings in society that would gain in strength as the economic reforms progressed. By the end of the year, their ideas had been rejected and General Secretary, Hu Yaobang, who was thought to be sympathetic, was dismissed from his post.

The main reform proposals included improving the representativeness and independence of the people's congress system, granting delegates immunity during debates, and reducing party interference in government organisations and society at large. The process of institutional reform was to be accompanied by expanding the freedom of speech, assembly and the press. Finally, there was the Party itself. These reformers stressed the need to make the Party more accountable to outside organisations and to make it more democratic internally. Yan Jiaqi suggested that the formation of factions would provide the basis for the emergence of a multiparty system (author's interview with Yan Jiaqi, summer 1986). Su Shaozhi proposed that the Party limit its role by returning to a genuine vanguard role. If the Party was only composed of a small élite, this would make it impossible to interfere in too many aspects of political and social life. Further, he argued that intellectuals should have more influence in defining what the Party's leading role actually meant in practice (Saich 1986: p. 25).

These moderate pleas for 'reform from within' proved too much for many senior Party leaders. Opponents of more radical reform began to link them with 'bourgeois' contamination. To reinforce the view that the Party would remain firmly in command, Deng Xiaoping's March 1979 comments on the need to uphold the 'four basic principles' were widely publicised.

The student demonstrations of late 1986 confirmed the fears of the more orthodox Party members and provided them with the chance to launch a counter-attack and remove Party General Secretary, Hu Yaobang. Despite this opposition, Hu's successor, Zhao Ziyang, was able to steady the reform ship and introduce quite specific proposals for political reform at the Thirteenth Party Congress.

Zhao's proposals called for a redistribution of power both horizontally to state organs at the same level and vertically to Party and state organs lower down the administrative ladder. Zhao also acknowledged that under the leadership of the CCP there was room for limited political pluralism, as 'conditions vary in different localities, we should not require unanimity in everything'.

However, the concrete proposals put forward by Zhao had little time to be implemented before first economic austerity measures took priority over political reform and second the student-led protests of 1989 provoked a political crisis that led to his dismissal. The fact that a major overhaul of the political structure was so closely associated with Zhao made subsequent discussion very difficult. Other factors have also contributed to the downgrading of the importance of political reform. Veteran Party members could not comprehend the spontaneity of the 1989 protests and responded by denouncing the movement as 'counter-revolutionary. Second, the collapse of the East European Leninist regimes followed in 1991 by the Soviet Union itself shocked the Chinese leadership. This convinced them of the need for retaining tight political control and eschewing moves towards political pluralism. The need for tight political control is also supported by those who argue that the modernisation process requires a strong centralised political structure, especially in the early phase of takeoff, in order to prevent social divisions from undermining the drive for economic modernisation. They equate democratisation with chaos, and chaos with underdevelopment (Saich 1993: pp. 11–12).

Thus, it is not surprising that Party Secretary Jiang Zemin's 'Work Report' to the Fourteenth Party Congress (October 1992) adopts a much more cautious line on political reform. The only concrete commitments were to trim the size of China's bureaucracy and to clear up Party and government overlap, promises often made but rarely fulfilled. Party dominance at all levels is emphasised and the 'Work Report' proposes strengthening party cells in all organisations. Like Zhao, Jiang rejected the idea of a genuine multi-party system but whereas Zhao was ambivalent on the question of pluralism, Jiang ruled it out entirely.

In reality, the economic reforms are creating a much more diverse society, significant elements of which are no longer solely dependent on Party patronage for their well-being. The voice of radical reform has not been entirely silenced. For example, in January 1993, Hu Jiwei, the former editor of the *People's Daily*, took advantage of the more relaxed censorship provided by the local newspapers in China to relaunch calls for democratic reform in China. In particular, he called on wealthy entrepreneurs to mobilise for democratic change. He also repeated his 1988–89 calls for direct elections and the dismissal of leaders through a popular vote.

The role of the party

The political system centres on the role of the Party and its relationship to other organisations in society. Any fundamental reform must lead to a decrease in its power. The overconcentration of power within the Party has been ascribed by Chinese writers to historical factors such as the earlier need for a tight, highly disciplined, centralised Party during the long struggle for victory before 1949. The concentration of power in the hands of individuals is ascribed to the lingering influences of a 'feudal' political culture. Reform of power structures under these conditions will be much harder to achieve than economic reform because of the resistance of vested interests.

While Party hegemony has remained unchallenged, significant changes have, nevertheless taken place. The launch of the development strategy has created greater social differentiation and more interests to be brokered. It is apparent that new institutions must be devised to mediate between the Party and officially recognised sectors of society. The reform plan also acknowledges the need to loosen the Party's grip over other organisations in state and society. Still there remains plenty of ground for argument between agreeing that the Party cannot control everything and defining what its leading role means in practice.

When the political system came under stress during 1989, opinion on political reform among the top leadership crystallised into two main viewpoints: the pragmatic reforming and the traditional orthodox (Saich 1991: pp. 152–58). On occasion, Deng Xiaoping has seemed to move between the two viewpoints, giving the green light to far-reaching change, yet at crucial moments supporting the traditional viewpoint on political issues in order to preserve his economic reforms from attack.

The pragmatic view was presented by Zhao Ziyang at the Thirteenth Party Congress in 1987. Zhao contended that political reform was indispensable if economic reform was to continue. In linking the two processes, he stated '[t]he process of developing the socialist commodity economy should be a process of building socialist democratic politics'. As a result, the Central Committee had decided that 'it was high time to put political reform on the agenda for the whole Party'.

While neither Hu Yaobang in late-1986 nor Zhao Ziyang in early-1989 saw student protests as a major threat, the traditionalists in the Party regarded them as a challenge to the fundamental principles of Party rule. Crucially, Deng Xiaoping sided with the traditionalists. Whereas Zhao appeared willing to make concessions to the students' demands, his opponents felt that no retreat was possible as it would lead to a collapse of socialism. The Tiananmen crackdown highlights their fear of spontaneous political activity.

This group wants to run the Party and its relationship to society on orthodox Leninist lines. In particular, they are concerned about attempts to loosen Party control in the workplace. With the decentralisation of some of the decision-making powers to the workunits, they want the Party to retain a strong role in the enterprises to stop them deviating too much from Party policy.

This approach to managing the Party's role in the political system is clearly outdated in a modern society where economic reform and technological development are creating a more diversified and sophisticated society. Zhao's acknowledgement that a limited plurality is inevitable is rejected and the traditionalists prefer to think in terms of a single undifferentiated mass of people who work harmoniously for the creation of socialism. The Party's role, of course, is to tell the masses what their interests are as they strive to build socialism. These tensions have become increasingly apparent in the post-Tiananmen period and now that the Party leadership has decided to push ahead with policies for rapid economic growth they will inevitably be confronted by precisely the kinds of problems that they so manifestly refused to deal with in April–June 1989. Eventually, the Party will have to move back to the kind of relationship between Party and state and society that was envisaged by Zhao Ziyang and his supporters.

Party–State sector relations

In all state socialist societies Party and state are closely entwined, with a dominant role for the Party. In China, during the Cultural Revolution any pretence of a distinction between the two disappeared. Despite such measures as abolishing the revolutionary committees which were set up during the Cultural Revolution and which combined the functions of the pre-1966 Party and state organs in one body (Saich 1983), the state sector remains dominated by the Party.

The existence of groups of leading Party members in units of state administration ensure the structural dominance of the Party. They were established by the Party committee at the next highest level and were responsible to that committee. In 1987, Zhao Ziyang dramatically proposed the abolition of these groups. Prior to this announcement it had been normal practice for Party members who were leading members in state administrative units, enterprises or research establishments to hold caucus meetings to discuss policy within their organisation. These groups became increasingly powerful taking over more and more work of the organisation concerned (author's interview with members of the Institute of Politics and Law, Jiangsu Academy of Social Sciences, June 1988).

Zhao further proposed that Party committees at the various levels that paralleled a department in the state sector would no longer appoint a member of their Standing Committees to take charge of work in the state sector whether or not the person concerned held an official position in that sector. In the same spirit, all CCP work departments with functions that overlapped those of state departments were to be abolished. If such measures were implemented, the structural basis for Party dominance over the state sector would be significantly reduced.

At the basic levels throughout the second half of the 1980s attempts were made to loosen the Party's grip in order to improve economic efficiency. In the urban economic sector, more decision-making was placed in the hands of the enterprise manager, rather than the Party committee. While this did not change the Party Committee's primary responsibility, its powers were restricted to strengthening ideological and political work among Party members. In practice, this reduced the Party in the enterprise to a formal, ritualistic role. In rural areas the communes, where local Party officials too often reigned supreme, have been broken up and power redistributed.

These experiments met stubborn resistance from local officials. While those with technical skills pushed for greater autonomy, many Party officials fought to exert greater control over the enterprise's work in order to protect their own jobs.

With the removal of Zhao Ziyang as General Secretary and the campaign by the traditionalists to reassert Party dominance, it is unclear how strong the commitment is to the structural reforms announced at the Thirteenth Party Congress. At the Fourteenth Party Congress Party dominance at all levels was emphasised and Jiang's 'Work Report' contained no mention of the proposal to abolish Party cells in government organisations. On the contrary, Jiang called for Party organisations to form the 'political nucleus' of state-run enterprises. The separation of Party and state is now clearly of less importance for the current leadership. By comparison, Jiang stressed the need to separate government administration from enterprise management. This need is driven by the desire for efficient economic growth but leaves the question of the dominating role of the Party in the enterprises unresolved.

Party structure

Reforms have also brought a number of changes in the Party's organisational structure (see Figures 3.1 and 3.2). The principle of democratic centralism creates a hierarchical pattern of organisation in the shape of a pyramid. In theory, the top of this pyramid is the National Party Congress, or its Central Committee, which takes over the Congress's functions when not in session. In reality, power lies within the Political Bureau (Politburo), its Standing Committee, and, to a lesser extent with the Secretariat.

The post of General Secretary is now the most important position within the formal Party system. The Chairmanship system created by Mao Zedong has been abolished on the grounds that this abolition avoided the problem of functional duplication that would have otherwise arisen. A more important reason was the need to prevent too much power accruing to individuals in particular posts. The General Secretary only has the power to 'convene' meetings of the Politburo and its Standing Committee, and only presides over the work of the Secretariat. This 'prevents the recurrence of over-concentration of personal power and arbitrariness of a single person' (Hu Qiaomu 1982: p. 17).

The system of secretariats existed before the Cultural Revolution but was abolished during it. The Central Secretariat handles the day-to-day work of the Party while the Politburo and its Standing Committee concentrates on important national and international issues. Fears that the Secretariat might function as a

42

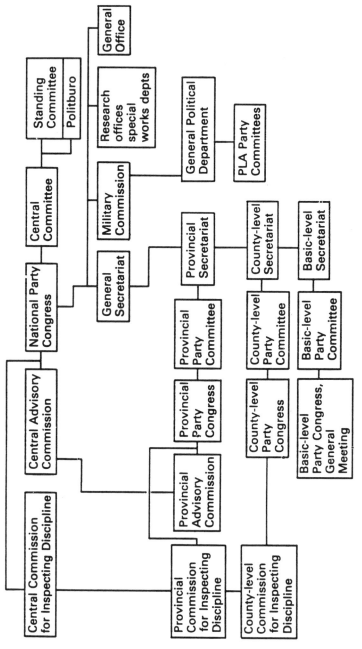

Figure 3.1   Organisation of the Chinese Communist Party

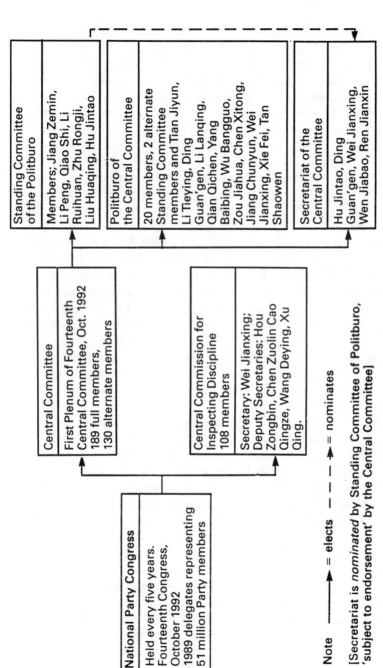

Figure 3.2 Central organisation of the CCP (simplified)

Standing Committee of the Politburo

Members; Jiang Zemin, Li Peng, Qiao Shi, Li Ruihuan, Zhu Rongji, Liu Huaqing, Hu Jintao

Politburo of the Central Committee

20 members, 2 alternate Standing Committee members and Tian Jiyun, Li Tieying, Ding Guan'gen, Li Lanqing, Qian Qichen, Yang Baibing, Wu Bangguo, Zou Jiahua, Chen Xitong, Jiang Chunyun, Wei Jianxing, Xie Fei, Tan Shaowen

Secretariat of the Central Committee

Hu Jintao, Ding Guan'gen, Wei Jianxing, Wen Jiabao, Ren Jianxin

Central Committee

First Plenum of Fourteenth Central Committee, Oct. 1992 189 full members, 130 alternate members

Central Commission for Inspecting Discipline

108 members

Secretary: Wei Jianxing; Deputy Secretaries: Hou Zongbin, Chen Zuolin Cao Qingze, Wang Deying, Xu Qing.

National Party Congress

Held every five years. Fourteenth Congress, October 1992 1989 delegates representing 51 million Party members

Note ⟶ = elects   - - - ⟶ = nominates

[Secretariat is *nominated* by **Standing Committee of Politburo**, 'subject to endorsement' by the **Central Committee**]

challenge to the Politburo because of its control over information
and the Party's agenda were addressed in amendments to the 1987
Party Constitution. It was reduced in size from ten to four members
(excluding the General Secretary) and one alternate and was made
the working office of the Politburo and its Standing Committee.
Instead   of   being   directly   elected   by   the   Central
Committee, its membership is now nominated by the Standing
Committee of the Politburo and approved by the Central Committee. A practical indication of the decline of power of the
Secretariat was the announcement that in future agendas raised by
the State Council for policy-making by the Politburo or its Stand-
ing Committee would no longer be 'filtered' by the Central
Secretariat.

The restoration of the pre-Cultural Revolution party structure
has led to the revival of the Commissions for Inspecting Discipline
and the Party schools. Both have been resurrected to overcome the
problems of bureaucratism, bad work-style, and opposition to
agreed Party policy. The schools are expected to educate Party
members in the way that they should behave and in the running of
the Party. The use of the commissions represents an important part
of the attempt to re-establish a system for dealing with discipline
and monitoring abuses within the Party. This system replaces what
the leadership saw as the arbitrariness and unpredictability of the
Cultural Revolution.

In 1982, the Twelfth Party Congress set up the Central Advisory
Commission, with subordinate commissions at the provincial level.
These commissions gave supposedly retired Party veterans the
opportunity to intervene directly in current affairs and the Central
Advisory Commission functioned as a focal point for opposition to
rapid change. Members of the Commission intervened decisively
to remove Hu Yaobang in January 1987 and took over affairs in the
crucial period of May–June 1989. It was important for reformers to
ensure that the Commissions did not become permanent features
of China's political landscape and they won a major victory when
the Fourteenth Party Congress (1992) decided to abolish them.
Their decision removes the formal regulation allowing elderly
Party members to attend Politburo or Central Committee meetings but it appears that Party organisations and various administrative organs have now adopted the practice of appointing them as
special advisors to help them in their work.

Reforms of the state sector

Post-Mao policy has led to a revitalisation of the state sector, with a renewed stress not only on the state's economic functions but also its legislative and representative functions (see Figures 3.3 and 3.4). The National People's Congress (NPC), constitutionally the highest organ of state power, has begun to meet annually and has produced a steady stream of legislation. There have been reports in the Chinese press about policy debates conducted during the sessions, and significant dissension from Party and government policy. In order to increase the effectiveness of the NPC its Standing Committee has been given legislative power and the power to supervise the enforcement of the Constitution. When the NPC is not in session, the Standing Committee can examine and approve partial adjustments to the State plan and budget. It is hoped that this will provide the state with flexibility and speed when reacting to problems in the economy.

The highest organ of state administration remains the State Council, which is the executive organ of the NPC. In theory, it is responsible and accountable to the NPC and its Standing Committee and is, in effect, the government of China. The work of the Council is presided over by an executive board composed of the Premier, Vice-Premiers, State Councillors, and the Secretary General.

Under the State Council are the various ministries, commissions and *ad hoc* organisations that administer China's economic and social life. The ministerial structure has been affected by the economic reforms and there has been a shift in power away from the organisations that ran the old command-economy to those that are to administer the market-influenced, foreign-trading economy. Thus, the State Planning Commission has seen its power eroded, while the influence of the Ministry of Finance and the People's Bank has increased.

The most recent example of this shift was the establishment of the Economic and Trade Office under the State Council in 1992 to replace the Production Office. It was upgraded to Commission level in 1993 and is set to become the most powerful organ overseeing economic work, with control over state enterprises, joint ventures and stock companies, and foreign trade.

Finally, involvement in the international economy and the increasing power of the provinces has led to a decrease in the power

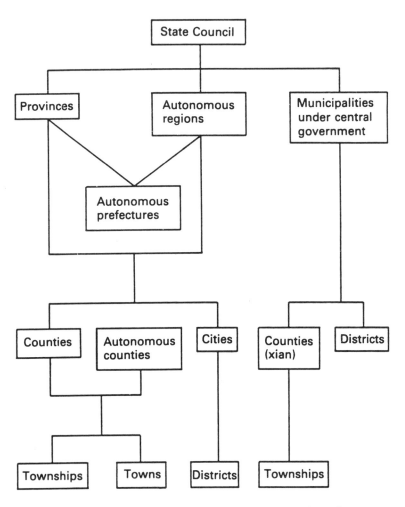

Figure 3.3   Levels of government under the State Council

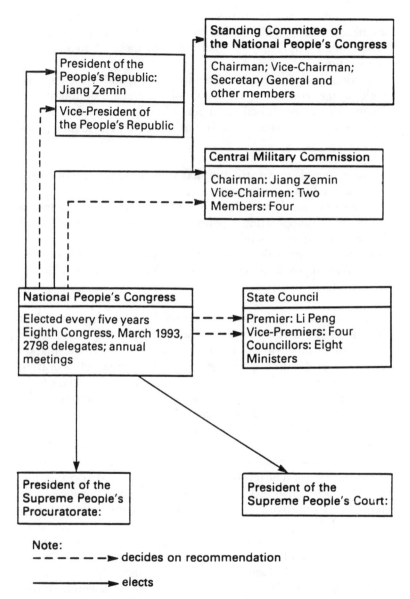

Figure 3.4 Central organisation of the Chinese government as at March 1993

of the national trade ministries and the rise in influence of organisations such as the China International Trust and Investment Corporation and the myriad of provincial bureaux and corporations.

During the reforms administration has expanded too rapidly, without the equivalent reduction of redundant organisations. There was a recognised need for administrative streamlining, outlined by Jiang Zemin as the key task for 1993. The main reasons are:

1. the administrative structure has to be brought into line with the needs of the economy;
2. the state needs to reduce its financial burden and administrative and operating expenses, accounting for 36 per cent of total financial expenditure in 1991;
3. with genuine political change ruled out, bureaucratic streamlining appears to offer quick results with no destabilising effects.

The streamlining is to be carried out by abolishing redundant organisations, merging those with similar functions, changing the functions of others that can operate successfully in the market economy, and reducing staffing levels. The number of ministries, commissions and other offices under the State Council was to be reduced from 86 to 59. Those organisations that can survive in the market economy will become economic entities. For example, the Ministry of Aerospace has been divided into two specialised corporations: a national aeronautics industrial corporation and a national aerospace industrial corporation. Numbers of Government employees at all levels are to be reduced by 25 per cent, while the 100 000+ personnel in State Council organisations are to be reduced by approximately one-third. It remains to be seen how successful this will be, since past experience does not augur well.

The revitalisation of the governmental sector has also breathed new life into the Chinese People's Political Consultative Conference (CPPCC). The Conference now meets annually, usually at the same time as the NPC. With the stress on social harmony rather than class conflict, the CPPCC provides the Party with an important link with members of other political parties, and also with key personnel who have no party affiliation. As the main forum for cooperation with non-Communist Party intellectuals, it provides the Party and the NPC with expertise that is necessary for economic modernisation. For its members, the CPPCC provides influence on policy-making over a range of economic, environmental and social questions. Evidence suggests that proposals from the CPPCC do have some impact, although they do not deal with fundamental questions of policy or principle.

Despite the stress on increasing the state's representative functions, it is clear that the people's congresses at all levels are not fulfilling this role. This has led to calls to make the system more democratic by increasing the powers of supervision and curtailing the power of local officials. A number of steps have been taken, such as ending the lifelong tenure system for officials, and extending the scope of competitive direct elections. The commitment to the election of officials was shown by the abolition of the appointed revolutionary committees and their replacement by the elected people's congresses. Despite this commitment, the process of county-level elections has not been a success and the Party has yet to structure genuinely representative institutions at the basic levels.

The non-central state apparatus has also undergone a number of changes in an attempt to improve its functioning. The powers of provincial-level people's congresses have been improved to allow them to adopt local regulations, and at and above the county level, standing committees were instituted to carry out the work of the congresses on a more permanent basis. Furthermore, neighbourhood and villagers' committees have been written into the new State Constitution as 'the mass organisations of self-management at the basic level'.

Yet the most important change is that the people's communes, set up as part of the Great Leap Forward (1958–60) no longer function as both a unit of economic and government administration. Now the township operates as a level of government and with the decollectivisation of economic life throughout the countryside, the commune has disappeared altogether as an organisation of substance (see Chapters 9 and 10).

Conclusions

Despite a considerable number of initiatives taken to try to reform China's politico-administrative system, major problems persist. Fundamentally, the crucial issue of the role of the Party has not been properly addressed by China's most senior leaders. The ingrained mentality of the superiority of the Party and the belief that the 'Party takes the lead in everything', combined with the resistance to change by those with vested interests in the *status quo*, form powerful obstacles to far-reaching reform of the political system. For many, reform is counterbalanced only in order to progress with economic development.

The process of institutionalisation has not progressed sufficiently despite the emphasis placed on it by Deng Xiaoping and his supporters. This was clearly revealed by the events of 1989, as was the decisive influence of powerful, veteran Party members (see Chapter 1). Individual prestige and length of service to the Party are far more important than any formal position one might hold. The real decision-maker has been Deng Xiaoping even though he holds no formal leadership position. The renewed drive for economic reform in the 1990s has been closely tied to Deng's name and prestige, and his capacity to prod other leaders to support his initiatives. This personalisation of the programme, while understandable over the short-term, reveals one of the enduring problems of the Chinese political structure: the incapacity to institutionalise policy-making and the consequent need to invoke the name of the 'supreme leader' to legitimise policy choice. In this respect, Deng chose, or was forced, to behave in precisely the same way as Mao Zedong. This opens up the prospect of a tenacious power struggle after Deng's death. Overreliance on the individual and the cavalier way in which the formal structures are treated mean that the main mechanism for leadership change and policy resolution remains the purge, making succession and policy management extremely unstable.

4

Leadership Politics since 1989

Simon Long

'Fighting over the Emperor's clothes'

Ever since Deng Xiaoping gained power in China in late 1978, at the age of 74, the issue of the succession has never been far from the surface in Chinese politics. Official Chinese historiography now describes the transition from rule by Mao Zedong up to his death in 1976 to rule by Deng as that from the 'first' to 'second' generation of revolutionary leaders. Similarly the transition to the post-Deng era is regarded as the handover to the 'third' generation. But this is a far more fundamental change. It is the transition from rule by peasant soldier to rule by urban bureaucrat. It is perhaps not surprising that it is fraught with problems.

In one sense, the Tiananmen crackdown of 1989 was an episode in the succession struggle, a factional battle among the leadership carried out, bloodily, on the streets of Beijing. But it was also a threat to the position of those leaders themselves. China was officially to characterise the 1989 protest movement as a 'student' wave, which very soon became 'turmoil' and on 2 and 3 June became a 'counter-revolutionary rebellion'. Chinese leaders described it as the worst crisis communist China had ever faced. They were probably correct in so far as the protests at one stage appeared to pose the most serious challenge yet to the rule of the Communist Party and its leaders. The challenge was successfully, almost dismissively, met, with the use of the army to suppress the protests in a matter of days. But, for leaders who claim to rule on behalf of the people, that is clearly not a sustainable option. The necessity to use force suggests a failure of leadership. This chapter will examine how the political leadership has responded to that failure. In trying to discern trends in leadership politics since 1989, it will identify five: a continuing mismatch between formal political rank and actual political power; the slow waning of the 'revolutionary' generation, accompanied by the quiet rise of their offspring; the rout of ideology as an important factor in leadership politics; the growing influence of provincial leaders; and the rise of the technocrats, including those in the military.

Nobody minding the shop . . .

It is necessary to sketch the starting-point – the nature of the senior leadership in June 1989. That is not as easy as might be supposed. One remarkable feature of the Tiananmen crackdown is that in its hour of greatest peril, the Chinese Communist Party did not even try to rule. Its then leader, Zhao Ziyang, made a tearful farewell appearance in Tiananmen Square on 19 May. Then he vanished, and there was no word of his fate until a month later, when his dismissal was reported. The world's largest communist party had no leader. There were no reported meetings of the politburo, or even of its (at the time) five-man standing committee, the group which, in theory runs the party and thus the country. Nor did the top organ of government, the State Council, meet, let alone the Standing Committee of the National People's Congress. It was by no means clear who was running the country. It still is not clear for, as Benewick notes (Chapter 1) there was a failure of institutionalisation.

When China's leaders emerged to face the television cameras on 9 June, to congratulate the martial law troops on a job well done, they appeared as a motley selection of senior politicians. Ten men were shown, and an eleventh, Chen Yun, was listed as sending his apologies. Of the eleven, only two held the most senior positions – Li Peng, the Prime Minister, and Yang Shangkun, the President, although the Presidency has been a largely ceremonial post in China. It was an informal coalition of party elders and political survivors from a younger generation. Still in charge was Deng Xiaoping, whose only formal posts at the time were the Chairmanships of both the Party's and the Government's Military Commissions. Deng confirmed this impression in remarks made in late

1989, but not published until the third volume of his collected writings and speeches appeared in November 1993. 'It was lucky I was there to handle the situation', he said, adding, self-depre-catingly, 'Of course, I was not the only one to play a role.' But, after expressing the hope that he would be able to retire 'once and for all', he said that 'in the event of chaos', he would 'take care of business again'. However, Deng's precise role after his 'retirement' in 1990 was a mystery.

One of the criticisms levelled at Zhao Ziyang was that he had 'revealed' state secrets to Mikhail Gorbachev, by informing him of the 1987 politburo resolution requiring Deng Xiaoping's endorse-ment of all important decisions. Remarkably, by late 1993, it was not known whether that resolution was still in force. In April 1991, Prime Minister Li Peng had implied, at least, that it had been rescinded. He said Deng was 'encouraging' him and his colleagues to be 'more independent and mature', but was still, like other octogenarian veterans, a source of advice.

Even authoritarian leaders rule at the head of an élite. So back in June 1989, Deng did not face responsibility alone after the crack-down. He was surrounded by his supporters and rivals. Chen Yun was Chairman of the Party's Advisory Commission. In addition to President Yang Shangkun, there was the hardline vice-president, the former general Wang Zhen, and three other octogenarian advisors who had been vociferous in condemning 'bourgeois liber-alisation', Peng Zhen, Bo Yibo and Li Xiannian. Of the 'younger' generation, apart from Li Peng, there were the two other surviving members of the Politburo Standing Committee – Yao Yilin, whose background is centralised economic planning, and Qiao Shi, who was in charge of the party's internal security apparatus. The eleventh member was the Chairman of the National People's Congress, Wan Li, the only one to have been previously identified with Zhao Ziyang's reformist wing – apart, that is, from Deng Xiaoping himself. Of the eleven men, seven were in their eighties, veterans of the 1934–35 'Long March'.

The continuing mismatch between rank and power

That political power resided with this ruling élite is an indictment of the party-state's failure to institutionalise the resolution of con-flicts, and the process of political succession. There has been little progress in this regard. After Mao Zedong's death in 1976, Deng Xiaoping was the only leader to achieve anything like the un-contested legitimacy that Mao at times enjoyed. But he did that without ever becoming head of Party, State or Government. There was thus a dichotomy between the constitutional sources of auth-ority and the reality of power. Nobody doubted that, for most of the 1980s at least, Deng was the 'senior leader'. This 'rule by man' becomes an acute problem when the 'man' approaches death. Deng had his 90th birthday in 1994, and was frequently rumoured to be in poor health. There was hence a battle for the political succession, fought out at two levels – among the men in their sixties and seventies, who held the formal offices of power, and among the octogenarians seeking to step into Deng's shoes as 'senior leader', and to place their protégés among the younger generation into the key jobs.

This tendency, evident throughout the post-Mao era has, if anything, intensified since 1989. The most senior positions in party and government have been held by men with serious political blemishes. Li Peng suffers from great unpopularity, and an identifi-cation with the Tiananmen crackdown decisions to declare martial law and use lethal force. Communist Party leader, Jiang Zemin, appointed in the reshuffle that immediately followed the crack-down and the removal from office of Zhao Ziyang, lacks credibility as a political heavyweight. Yet Jiang is repeatedly touted as 'the core' of the third generation leadership. He has accumulated the most impressive array of leadership titles ever enjoyed by a Chinese communist, with the sole exception of Hua Guofeng. In October 1989 Jiang took over Deng Xiaoping's chairmanship of the Com-munist Party's Military Commission; six months later he inherited the same post in the parallel State Commission; in April 1993 he became 'State Chairman', or President.

Yet few people regarded Jiang Zemin as a long-term successor. Rather, he seemed cast in a similar role to that of Hua Guofeng, who, after Mao's death was, for a period, Chairman of the Party and its Military Commission as well as Prime Minister, but was never more than a stopgap in the transition from Maoism to Dengism. Just how unstable is the succession process was suggested when Li Peng's position as Prime Minister was undermined in 1993 by the rise of Zhu Rongji. The latter 'helicoptered' up party and government ranks in the space of just three years to 'First Deputy

Prime Minister' but then helicoptered down as a result of his economic austerity programme.

The waning of the immortals and the rise of the 'princelings'

But an even more fundamental negation of constitutional government was the continued influence of the so-called 'immortals', the party elders in their eighties and even nineties, who continued to wield enormous influence despite the lack of any formal political rank. The period since 1989 has, however, been one of change in this respect at least. The influence of the 'immortals' is gradually waning. But the diminution of their power is less a function of political reform than of death, decrepitude and partial senility.

The period has seen the eight old men grouped together in the popular mind in 1989–90 as the immortals losing their formal positions of power. Most notably, President Yang Shangkun was replaced in 1993, and at the party's Fourteenth National Congress in 1992, the Advisory Commission was abolished, thereby depriving its chairman Chen Yun and his two deputies, Bo Yibo and Song Renqiong, of their jobs. Ironically, the Advisory Commission was created in 1982 to provide sinecures for party veterans as part of a Deng-sponsored programme of 'rejuvenation', intended to reduce their influence. But the stature of the commission's leaders gave it considerable influence.

Even after these changes, and the death of two of the immortals – Li Xiannian in 1992 and Wang Zhen the following year – the elders continued to exercise considerable influence. By far the most far-reaching policy changes since 1989 originated not from the formal leadership, but from Deng Xiaoping's 'Southern Tour' of 1992, when he launched a campaign for 'further, bolder reform'.

And it was not just Deng, who was in declining health and rarely appeared in public, who continued to exert his influence. His contemporary Chen Yun, who has also been rumoured to be in poor health since the mid-1980s, was reported to be politically active up to a point. So too, if Hong Kong magazines are to be believed, are the other octogenarians. One account of a 'meeting of veteran comrades' describes the old men 'calling each other names, flinging tea-cups, banging the table and even exposing one another's secrets' (Cheng Ming 1993).

The continuing role of the elders has tended to give a two-tiered character to the succession struggle. In the forefront was the tussle between the younger, 'third generation' politicians in their sixties and seventies. In the background was the question of who, if anyone, would take over Deng Xiaoping's informal role as 'senior leader', that is, as the arbiter of last resort, or 'in the event of chaos, who would take care of business?'

From 1989 until late 1992, it appeared that the then President, Yang Shangkun, was auditioning for that part. But his prospects diminished when he and his family lost ground in the army hierarchy. It began to look as if there was nobody left to succeed. In November, 1993, a usually reliable Hong Kong source quoted Deng, shortly after his official 'retirement' in 1990 that 'it is abnormal for the fate of a country to be dependent on one man.' 'That should be changed', according to Mr Deng, 'but it has to be a process' (*The Mirror* 1993).

Because of the near-legendary status of men like Deng Xiaoping and Chen Yun, the policy debate in the formal leadership, between 'reformists', led by Zhu Rongji, and 'conservatives' around Li Peng was often interpreted as a battle between the 'Deng' and 'Chen' factions. It may once have been true that the 'younger leaders' were puppets of the elders. But as old age takes its toll, the roles must gradually be reversed. More and more, it must be assumed, the elders are being manipulated by their juniors for their own political purposes.

Because access to the wise old men is severely curtailed, and because of the close-knit web of friendship and rivalry binding their generation, their loss of influence is accompanied by an enhancement of the role of their younger relatives – the so-called 'princelings', or 'princes' party'. Most, if not all, of the immortals have relatives who are prominent in central or provincial government or in business. Li Peng, for example, is the adoptive son of the late Prime Minister, Zhou Enlai, and Jiang Zemin found it necessary to deny reports that he was Li Xiannian's son-in-law. The Communist Party acknowledged in 1989 that protests about 'official corruption', including nepotism, were not unfounded. The Party is extremely sensitive on this point. Family ties are rarely publicised, and, at the Fourteenth Party Congress in 1992, the 'princes' party' was notable by its absence in the list of the newly promoted. While this may have helped the Party's image, it accentuated the divide between office and power.

The rout of ideology

Following the Tiananmen crackdown, 'Leftist' rhetoric reappeared, and Deng Xiaoping lamented the Party's failure in ideological education. Subsequently, there were campaigns against 'bourgeois liberalisation' and 'peaceful evolution', the internal and international aspects of an alleged conspiracy to subvert communism in China. But there was no return to the mass political campaigns of the past, and, in the politics of the leadership, ideology appeared to play a minimal role.

This is one of the fundamental legacies of Deng Xiaoping's years in power. Under Mao, power struggles were conducted under the banner of ideological purity. Leadership and policy decisions – whatever their cause – had to be justified in ideological terms. Under Deng, the reverse is true. Ideology has to be justified in pragmatic terms – whether or not it will make China richer and stronger.

Deng Xiaoping has never led a united leadership, and even since 1989, as in the period up to and immediately following his 1992 'Southern Tour', he has at times seemed at odds with government policy. But he has achieved a consensus about the terms of the debate. It is no longer acceptable to dismiss a policy – or a leader – as inherently wrong because it or he is 'rightist', and flirts with or embraces capitalism. Rather, 'leftists' have to justify their position in economic terms.

They are all 'pragmatists' now, even if the leaderships' public debates are still cloaked in the arcane rhetoric of Marxist dogma. This trend, evident throughout the 1980s, became even more pronounced after June 1989 and the subsequent collapse of communist rule in other countries. China's leaders decided their counterparts in other countries had lost power because they failed to achieve satisfactory levels of economic growth. At its Fourteenth Party Congress, the Chinese Communist Party wrote into its constitution the concept of a 'socialist market economy', an even more extreme version of the 'initial stage of socialism' adopted at the Thirteenth Congress in 1987. In essence, the concept gives blanket ideological authorisation for any form of economic management that appears to work.

This is not to say that there are no more 'leftists', or 'conservatives' in Chinese politics. On the contrary, many people have vested interests in the old system. But the political debate has moved decisively to the right, in the sense that at no point has there been a serious challenge to Deng's notion of 'taking economic development as the key link'.

The rise of provincial leaders

Under Deng Xiaoping central government revenue in China has dropped as a proportion of total national income from about 70 per cent to about 20 per cent. The history of economic policy since an austerity programme was introduced in the autumn of 1988 has been in part a battle for the recentralisation of economic decision-making, and a redistribution of government assets in Beijing's favour. A first attempt was aborted after Deng Xiaoping's inter-vention in the debate with his 'Southern Tour', tilting the balance in favour of the fast-growing southern provinces. In the nervous political consensus that followed the Tiananmen crackdown, the centre appeared to be winning. It regained control of the distri-bution of more commodities, reinforced restrictions on provincial government spending, and, through the People's Bank, used access to credit as a means of forcing provincial industry to slow down. These were relinquished again, until Zhu Rongji, in a more limited and sophisticated 'austerity programme' launched in July 1993, tried again to rein in provincial economic excesses. This attempt was halted by an intervention in the name of Deng Xiaoping. A difficulty for all reform measures, such as taxation, is their implementation.

However, the extent to which a number of provinces, especially on the south-eastern seaboard, shrugged off both 'austerity pro-grammes' to resume or continue very rapid rates of economic growth, suggested that the political consensus had been more crucial in the government's success in 1989–90 than its control of macroeconomic levers. In late 1990, Beijing failed to force the provinces into revenue-sharing arrangements more favourable to the central government, an issue Zhu Rongji took up again three years later. There are at present at least five different sorts of financial arrangement between Beijing and the provinces. The most important are the lump-sum contribution system employed – and jealously guarded – in Guangdong, which leaves the province the benefits of excess growth, and the proportional system used in, for example, Shanghai, which in the 1980s saw as much as 80 per cent of municipal revenues disappear to the capital.

Understandably in these circumstances, provincial leaders have considerable and growing power. Their governments are responsible for more than three-quarters of current civilian expenditure by the government. They also have the ability to bend official central policy to a wide variety of different applications. Thus the World Bank found that in 1990 prices on only six or seven basic goods were subject to official controls in some parts of southern China, while, at the same time, in Harbin in the Manchurian province of Heilongjiang, the prices of 383 consumer goods were tightly controlled. Provincial leaders are not just trying to get on with it without central interference. They are turning China into a patchwork of radically different, and in many cases competing economies.

This financial power naturally enhances the political influence provincial leaders enjoy through their membership of the Communist Party's Central Committee. As a body, they have votes enough to affect Party policy, and the Politburo cannot ride roughshod over their views. In the past, their loyalty to Beijing has been ensured through the Party's power of approval over appointments at provincial government level, and down to county level. However, more and more provincial leaders seem to be responding to local interests first and foremost. The Guangdong leadership is a case in point, where under the Governorship of Marshal Ye Xuanping (a senior 'princeling', in that his father, Marshal Ye Jianying was a key kingmaker in Deng Xiaoping's accession to power), the province became a bastion of market reform regardless of the political climate in Beijing. When Ye Xuanping was finally induced to leave his post in 1991, in exchange for a senior appointment on the Chinese People's Political Consultative Conference, it was only after he had ensured that his successor would be another 'local' man, Zhu Senlin. Short of another major political upset, the 'regionalisation' of political power is a trend that is likely to grow.

The rise of the technocrats

The discrepancy between formal rank and real power argues for caution in analysing the backgrounds of the Communist Party leadership as an indicator of trends. Nevertheless, China remains a country ruled by a communist party, and its top organs at the very least should demonstrate who is meant to be in power. The Fourteenth Congress in 1992 did install a new party leadership. What the official propaganda would have us believe is that this leadership is new, younger, more reform-minded and more technocratic. This is only partially true. It is certainly new – 47 per cent of the full Central Committee were new members, as opposed to 34 per cent in 1987 (though 63 per cent if you count a 'special' congress involving a reshuffle in 1985). It is more technocratic as measured by educational achievement – 84 per cent of Central Committee members have a college education, more than ten times the national average. But it is hardly younger. The new Central Committee was expanded from 175 full and 110 alternate members to 189 full members and 130 alternates. The average age was 56.3, younger than the outgoing Central Committee, but actually more than a year older than the average age of the Central Committee elected in 1987. The Politburo was younger – 62 as against 68. But its important Standing Committee, expanded to seven members from the six who had survived from 1987 or been appointed in June 1989 was on average the same age as the one elected in 1987 – 63. (And that was achieved partly by the election of a 'juvenile' – Hu Jintao, who at 49 was the youngest by ten years.)

There is more convincing evidence that the new leadership is reform-minded. A number of members identified as conservatives were removed from the Politburo, although some of the replacements are hardly stalwarts of reform. On the Central Committee, three ideologues believed to have played a key role in blocking the promulgation of Deng Xiaoping's appeals for reform in early 1992 lost their places.

Too little is known about the new Central Committee members to evaluate their politics, but some general points can be made. There is a slight reversal of the trend under Deng towards a reduced role for the military in the party leadership. Military members of the Central Committee now comprise 23 per cent of the total, up from 16 per cent elected in 1987. This reflects the role of the military in 1989, when it saved the party from ruin. Despite yawning budget deficits, the military's share of government expenditure has grown every year since 1989. Within the military leadership, too, the 'technocrats', in favour of modernisation as opposed to politicisation, seem to have won an internal battle in 1992–93. General Liu Huaqing, installed in the Politburo's

Standing Committee at the Fourteenth Congress is the most senior representative of this tendency. Similarly, but less openly, it can be assumed that those in senior positions in the state and party security apparatuses also wield considerable power. The most prominent example of this is Qiao Shi, head of the party's security branch. In March 1993, he became Chairman of the National People's Congress, and seemed to give the body new vigour. Along with Li Peng, Jiang Zemin, Zhu Rongji and Liu Huaqing, he is at the forefront of the 'third generation's power struggle'.

In the Politburo there was a strengthening of regional representation, with various provincial leaders promoted. There was an especially strong showing for Shanghai and Zhejiang province – with nine of the twenty politburo members. And many of the new leaders were trained in the Soviet Union or Eastern Europe – six in the Politburo, and three in the Standing Committee.

Conclusion

This suggests that the transition to the post-Deng era is a process whereby the assumption of power is by a group of predominantly Soviet-trained urban technocrats, whose careers and education have relied entirely on the patronage of the party or the People's Liberation Army. One tendency in leadership politics that has not been noticeable since 1989, except perhaps at the provincial level, is the separation of party and government, an aim much advertised in 1987. The top organs of state and party power still overlap so much in their membership as to be almost indistinguishable. Formal political power remains in the Party. But after its 'third' generation of leaders, there is a missing tier in the Party's family tree, of those who were educated – or not – during the Cultural Revolution. Real political change at the top of the Party may have to wait until the 'fifth' generation – of princelings and technocrats educated not in Stalin's or Khrushchev's Russia, but in the United States in the 1980s.

But the central Party leadership is gradually ceding power to lower levels of government. Paradoxically, this may promote a curious sort of stability in the post-Deng epoch. The vacuum that will be left by the absence of an 'emperor' who can resolve factional squabbles will almost certainly, as on Mao's death in 1976, open up a serious rift in the central leadership. But, with the memory of the

Tiananmen crackdown still fresh, all factions may feel that, as in 1976, they would be best advised not to wage their battles on the streets. Another surgical strike in the politburo would be safer. And, in the provinces, provided whatever new leadership to emerge did not seek to reverse the devolution of power, there would be no reason for the power struggle to result in nationwide turmoil. The provinces may see their best interests served by letting the Centre fight it out, while they pursue their own preoccupations. As one observer has put it, the centre will pretend to govern, and the provinces will pretend to be governed. In that sense, those scrambling for Deng Xiaoping's mantle may find that the emperor has no clothes.

5

Centre and Province in China

Shaun Breslin

'The mountains are high, and the Emperor is far away'

When the Chinese Communist Party came to power in 1949, it inherited a situation where effective control over the provinces had been absent for over half a century. The need to build a system of control throughout the country was immediate and obvious. For the Chinese Communist Party (CCP) the building of a new centralised state proved easier than maintaining effective authority in the longer run. It soon became clear that sustaining a highly centralised political–economic system in China was difficult. Given the physical size and administrative complexity of China, centralising political and economic functions in Beijing placed a massive burden on central planning organisations. In addition, the task of defining policies in Beijing that could be effectively implemented throughout China was daunting.

The alternative was to devolve a degree of power to lower-level authorities. But this policy was not without costs. If too much power was devolved, then the centre could not ensure the rational integration of economic activity. Furthermore, devolving power risked creating powerful local leaders who could initiate their own political strategies and even their own overseas trade links.

But the issue of decentralisation was not just about how much power the centre should give up but also to which administrative level power should be devolved. This problem meant that period 1949 to 1978 saw numerous oscillations in policy as the CCP attempted, with only partial success, to define a workable central–

63

local relationship. Such fluctuations in policy make it difficult to define the exact nature of central–provincial relations in China. Table 5.1 indicates some of the possible permutations.

In fact, when analysing central–provincial relations in China, whilst it may be possible to identify general patterns these generalisations can hide vast differences in the relationships of individual provinces with Beijing. Not all provinces have the same ability or desire to gain equal degrees of autonomy from the centre. Decentralisation policy is a significant factor in defining provincial relationships with the capital, but the specific nature of each province's position relative to Beijing is defined by the complex interaction of a number of factors.

For example, the level of development of a province's infrastructure is shaped by the legacy of pre-1949 policies, regional development, national defence considerations, the location of raw materials and so on. Change in any one of these variables has a profound impact on central–provincial relationships.

Table 5.1   Central–local relationships: possible permutations

Model	Description
Totalitarian	Power is highly centralised. Provinces carry out central policy to the letter. Decentralisation only takes place when the centre wants it to, and power can easily be recentralised if the need arises.
Centralist	Power is centralised, but there is a balance between political initiatives at the centre and those that originate in the provinces. General policy is formulated at the centre, but provinces are allowed flexibility in implementation. The centre can decentralise or recentralise as it sees fit.
Cellular	Balance of power between centre and provinces. Power is not equally distributed among the provinces, with stronger provinces (e.g. Shanghai) economically dominating neighbouring areas. Decentralisation was an inevitable process and not controlled by the centre.
Decentralist	Power is highly decentralised. The centre is nothing more than an amalgam of local representatives in competition, or an arbiter of competing local interests and claims. Decentralisation is the natural state that the centre cannot control.

Central–provincial relations in the post-Mao era

When the post-Mao leadership initiated the reform of the economic system in 1978, it also set in motion a process of political reform. Political reform here refers to the significant changes in the processes of political power within the existing framework of party rule. Arguably, these changes were more keenly felt in central–provincial relationships than in many other arenas.

The drive for economic growth impinged on virtually every aspect of central–provincial relations: the state-planning process was partially dismantled; the role and scope of market forces were increased; more central powers were devolved; and a new regional development strategy was adopted. In the old system political and economic channels of command were so inextricably linked, that economic reform could not take place without generating some changes in the political relationship between centre and province.

Although the old planned economy may not have been very efficient, participants in the decision-making process knew their roles and understood the rules of the game. With the weakening of this system and its gradual replacement with more market-orientated mechanisms, many of these certainties disappeared. Moreover, new economic and political relationships were continually being created. The pace and extent of economic reform created a dynamism and uncertainty in the political–economic system. Furthermore, the reforms were uncoordinated and frequently in conflict. Although such a lack of coordination is excusable given the extent of the changes that have taken place in post-Mao China, they nevertheless made a significant contribution to the emergence of new forms of central–provincial relations in recent years.

Economic transformation and central–provincial relations

The lack of coordination between reforms in different sectors of the economy was partly a consequence of political constraints. For example, it has been argued that in 1984, the time was ripe for a thorough reform of the centrally controlled pricing system. But reformers were aware that this would generate considerable opposition from those leaders who were sceptical of the way the reform process was proceeding. Unable or unwilling to push price reform through at this time, the reformers instead chose to devolve more power to the provinces. It was hoped that this action would expand the reform coalition into the provinces whilst simultaneously removing power from the conservative bastions of central planning and finance. Whilst this did indeed happen, the 1984 reforms also generated important dysfunctional consequences, the repercussions of which will continue to be felt for some time to come. Crucially, the regulatory mechanisms of state planning were reduced before effective and functioning market-regulatory mechanisms were introduced.

The process of economic reform also created a situation by the mid-1980s where economic activity was regulated neither by state-planning mechanisms, nor by an effective market system. In this situation, provincial authorities moved to maximise their local industrial base in order to raise local finances, irrespective of the impact on the national economy as a whole. This divergence of interests between local and national economic priorities is at the heart of a central–provincial conflict that has become a prominent feature of contemporary Chinese politics. Central leaders constantly complained that provincial economies were expanding at a rate and in a manner that conflicted with what the centre deemed best for the nation as a whole. But calls for unity fell on deaf ears when it came to a choice between national policy and the interests of the province. The most visible sign of this conflict was in capital construction investment. Despite continued calls for provincial authorities to obey, and the formal restoration of tight central controls in 1989, provincial spending continued to rise in a number of provinces.

Despite numerous attempts to rectify the situation, two main factors have obstructed the restoration of more effective control over errant provinces:

1.   The provincial authorities have seen themselves as acting rationally, given both the pervading economic climate and the obligations to raise capital that the centre itself had imposed on the provinces. The centre's economic goals placed a premium on maximising the local revenue base at a time when sources of investment capital not controlled from the centre were becoming increasingly available. Consequently, the centre helped to generate both the desire and the ability of some provinces to develop narrow, local, quasi-autonomous economic policies.

2. Although the introduction of market forces was meant to reduce administrative interference in economic affairs, attitudinal hangovers from the pre-reform era inhibited this process. Local leaders' concepts of what constituted legitimate interference in their economic affairs remains rooted in the past. They could see little harm in allocating scarce energy resources to local enterprises, leaning on banks to provide loans, or even erecting trade barriers against 'imports' from other provinces. For the Chinese economist, Chen Yize, this was a crucial factor in creating the conflict of interests between centre and province, and remains a fundamental obstacle to sustainable economic progress. He argues that such attitudes are reinforced by the structure of the political system, in so far as the provincial bureaucracies remain fundamentally unreformed. Where changes in the economy demand administrative reform, new structures are too often simply added to existing ones, rather than replacing them. With the instrumentalities of the old system still in place, they inevitably continue to be used to control economic activity. Furthermore, this pattern of behaviour is replicated at lower levels, where administrative control over local economic activity is, if anything, more of a problem given the more intimate relationship between party, state and enterprise.

Thus, what the central authorities need to do in order to rein in the excesses of provincial control is to promote the establishment of macroeconomic control mechanisms at a national level with a revamping of economic institutions and organisations at all local levels. However, such a move could challenge the power and influence of many local power-holders, who could prove an obstacle to future reforms perceived to run counter to provincial interests.

The tendency to place local interests first has contributed to the emergence of a pattern of economic activity that resembles the spatial pattern of production in the Cultural Revolution – a pattern that the post-Mao reforms were meant to replace. The regional development strategy of the Cultural Revolution encouraged localities to strive to become self-sufficient, which led to considerable waste of resources and duplication of production. The new strategy was one built around the exploitation of regional comparative advantage and economies of scale. However, although inter-provincial trade and other economic contacts have increased, formidable barriers to trade remain. By intervening to allocate raw materials to local producers and erecting barriers to imports from other provinces, the more efficient and competitive economy that market forces were expected to promote has been at least partially impeded. Indeed, in many respects, China has made a better job of opening up to the outside world than it has of opening up its own domestic market. Given this, are the impressive growth figures that China has recorded in the post-Mao era sustainable?

Rather than allow scarce resources to leave their local territory, local authorities have frequently stepped in to keep as much local wealth as possible within the province. It is not unknown for raw materials supposedly targeted for transportation to other provinces to be diverted for local use. Provincial authorities have also resorted to imposing tariffs and quotas on imports from other provinces to enhance the profitability of local enterprises artificially. As a result, more efficient producers in the coastal region were often starved of the supplies that the logic of market forces should have provided. In a now notorious case, trucks were sent from Guangdong to buy silkworm cocoons direct from their cultivators in Sichuan whilst the Sichuan authorities responded by setting up armed blockades to stop them leaving the province. Similar tensions between provinces also emerged over access to rice and wool.

Inter-provincial competition

Inter-provincial competition over the division of the national economic cake is nothing new, but this conflict seems to have been heightened by the post-Mao reforms. There are perhaps two key explanations here. First, the reconstruction of the economic system led to the emergence of new provincial winners and losers. For example, the concentration of heavy industrial complexes in the north-eastern provinces of Jilin and Heilongjiang, once the source of their wealth, has now became a millstone around their necks. Previously the major beneficiaries of central planning, state owner-ship and central investment, they now became the main losers of a strategy that favours small, non-state-sector light industrial enterprises.

Second, there is resistance in the interior and the west to the preferential treatment granted to provinces in the south and east. There were three main points to this argument:

1. low state-set prices for raw materials and semi-finished products were retained, whilst finished products increasingly fetched higher, market, prices. This irks many in the interior who produce raw materials.

2. many leaders in the interior are also disturbed by the special policies implemented in coastal provinces. Guangdong and Fujian have been the main targets of such criticism. Of all China's provinces, these two have the greatest freedom to retain locally generated income. They are also the site of three of China's four Special Economic Zones (SEZ). In the long run, it could be argued that the development of the coastal provinces should aid growth in the interior. Even in the short run, there is a convincing argument that the SEZs 'helped energise the country as a whole' (Crane 1990: p. 165). Nevertheless, the development of the SEZs to date has clearly aided the growth of Guangdong and Fujian much more than it has facilitated development in Gansu or other interior provinces.

   These feelings have been exacerbated because, although the SEZs were not intended to fall under the control of their provincial hosts, Shenzhen in particular has become an integral component of Guangdong's provincial economic strategy. Guangdong Governor Ye Xuanping's assertion that 'Shenzhen is a special zone of Guangdong' (Crane 1990: p. 139) expresses the position precisely.

3. leaders in the interior appear sceptical that the much-promised 'trickle-down' of wealth from the coast will in fact occur, and fear that an extension of market forces will instead lead to a polarisation of national wealth. These fears have reinforced the inclination to keep local resources within the province. Since this policy obstructs the expansion of inter-provincial trade, the suspicion that trickle-down will not occur may thus become a self-fulfilling prophecy.

   Conversely, leaders in coastal provinces counter the complaints from the interior by arguing that too much of their income is used by the state for investment in the interior. They suggest that if they are allowed fully to exploit their economic strengths, then this will indeed aid the interior through the process of 'trickle-down'. Furthermore, even within the coastal region itself, there is considerable inter-provincial conflict, particularly over the extent of Guangdong's privilege. Concern in Shanghai about its financial obligations to the government led to a successful challenge to Beijing. A draft report was submitted to the State Council in January 1987, and after visits by Party General Secretary, Zhao Ziyang, and Politburo member, Yao Yilin, new arrangements for Shanghai were finalised in February 1988.

This readjustment of Shanghai's financial arrangements highlights two important elements in the nature of contemporary centre-province relations in China. First, it demonstrates a new provincial confidence in dealing with the central authorities.

Second, it generated a wave of lobbying from other provinces with grievances about current policy. Immediately following Shanghai's successful approach to the centre, Inner Mongolia and Jilin formally asked (but without success) to be allowed to move to the Shanghai system. And Hunan and Jiangsu provincial officials similarly sought to be granted some of the preferential treatment afforded to Guangdong. We can only guess at the extent of the informal lobbying that also occurred.

Competition between regions for preferential central treatment has always occurred in China – indeed lobbying skills had been well honed by provincial leaders used to fighting for their share of resources under the old planning system. But the potentially higher gains made possible under the post-Mao economic reforms have enhanced this competition, and represent a heightened perception of provincial interest generated by the uneven central treatment of different provinces.

The centre's dilemma

The central authorities are thus faced with the almost impossible process of balancing varied and often conflicting provincial demands for action. If they listen to Shanghai and allow it to retain more of its locally generated income, then Beijing either has to take more money from other provinces, or reduce its investment and grants to less-well-off areas. And although all China's provinces are now better off than they were in 1976, the desire for a bigger provincial share of the national cake appears to be insatiable.

These conflicting pressures on the central government form part of a wider identity crisis of the Chinese state. There are, perhaps, two main components in this 'identity crisis'. First, in a relatively short period of time, many of the state's old mechanisms for controlling the provinces have been stripped away, leaving the central state unsure of what its role should be in the new system.

Second, and very closely related to the above, it is still far from clear what the new system in China will be. The state is torn between its desire to become an efficient economic power and its need to protect important groups from the negative impacts of market reforms. Of particular importance to centre–province relations are the massive subsidies paid to maintain production and employment in loss-making state-owned industries. Taken with compensatory payments paid to farmers and subsidies to maintain urban purchasing power, over a third of the national state budget is devoted to tempering the impact of competition, regional differences, and market forces. The interior has more than its fair share of outdated industrial capacity, and the highly uneven spatial distribution of economic activity in China ensures that solving this conundrum will have profound implications for future central–provincial relations.

Conclusions

There are two main issues then that characterise the issue of central–provincial relations in contemporary China. First, the growth of inter-provincial conflict and the centre's capacity to arbitrate between the many conflicting provincial demands that the reform process has generated. Second, the relative growth in provincial autonomy, and the centre's attempts to restore what it perceives to be the correct balance between provincial and central power. Perhaps the key factor here is the centre's over-reliance on old methods of control as opposed to the adoption of new regulatory mechanisms more in keeping with the requirements of the emerging economic system.

The decline in central control (and in particular the growth of Guangdong's economic autonomy) has prompted Western academics to question whether China may be in the process of disintegration. As the centre proves less able to control affairs, centrifugal tendencies may begin to take hold and the integrity of the Chinese state may be threatened. Proponents of the disintegration hypothesis suggest that the reintegration of Hong Kong into the mainland (a process which in economics is well under way) can only serve to reinforce the wealth and strength of Guangdong and the so-called 'Gold Coast'. This is a view of the future not without advocates in China itself.

The collapse of central control in the Soviet Union, Yugoslavia and Czechoslovakia has brought this question of disintegration more firmly into focus. But these were all federal states where unity under communist party rule masked considerable ethnic divergence. In China, while the situation in Xinjiang and Tibet is far from stable, ethnic tensions do not represent a fundamental problem. One should bear in mind that China's ethnic minorities in total comprise only six per cent of the population. But perhaps the best argument for the survival of the Chinese state is provided by asking who would gain from secession? The development of the southern coastal provinces in the 1980s was at least partly built around the supply of subsidised raw materials from the Chinese interior. Although the removal of price controls on basic raw materials will remove this hidden subsidy for the south's development, the best long-term prospects for the south will probably be through exploiting an economic system based on the complementarity of its light industrial production and the raw materials of the interior.

Indeed, rather than presaging the disintegration of China, the culmination of the 1980s reforms may be an enlarged Chinese economic entity. The reintegration of Hong Kong into China in 1997 is a question of the formal handover of political power and sovereignty, but the economies of southern China and Hong Kong are already so heavily intertwined that economic integration will be completed before 1997. And economic convergence between southern China and Taiwan is also accelerating.

An economic belt encompassing southern China, Hong Kong, Taiwan and possibly Singapore would be a dynamic force in the regional and global economy. Utilising the natural resources of the Chinese interior may provide China's motor for economic development in the Pacific economy of the twenty-first century.

6

Civil Society

Jude Howell

'Stones from other hills may serve to polish the jade of this one'

The introduction of market reforms since 1978 has brought about far-reaching changes not only in China's economy but also in the nature and structure of society. Decollectivisation, the Open Policy and the growth of a private economy have given birth to new socioeconomic groups such as rich farmers, private traders, private entrepreneurs and Chinese managers in foreign-invested enterprises. The structure of society in post-Mao China has become more stratified, differentiated and complex. The mechanisms and institutions of social control have become out-of-synch with these rapid social changes. The reforms have created a space for new institutional forms of association such as private entrepreneurs' associations, literary societies and professional associations and even stamp clubs. These 'social organisations' have mushroomed rapidly, particularly in the coastal provinces.

This process of institutional innovation reached a peak in the heady days of 1989 when new, autonomous, and politically motivated organisations such as the Autonomous Workers' Federation challenged the authority of the party-state. For Western analysts China seemed to be on the brink of a democratic revolution. With the crackdown on politically-oriented organisations after 4 June the pace of innovation slowed down.

The dramatic events of 1989 generated a spate of articles on the rise of 'civil society' in China. By civil society we understand a sphere of voluntary, autonomous activity located between the state and the family. In the eyes of Western scholars this proliferation of apparently voluntary and autonomous social organisations, some with a definite political purpose, provided the new institutional context for a challenge to state control and the potential for democratic change.

The focus on the concept 'civil society' has centred attention on these new institutional forms of voluntary association. However, the vagueness and imprecision of the concept, its multiple usages and interpretations have hampered investigation into the new social organisations, yielding only a partial analysis of their nature and functions. In particular, the civil society framework of analysis has underplayed the role of the state in the formation and existence of the new social organisations.

In this chapter the historical antecedents of civil society in China are explored and why this concept has become a catch-phrase in contemporary China studies is considered. This chapter looks at the nature and functions of the new social organisations and discusses their future role.

Historical antecedents

In the late Qing and Republican periods autonomous organis-ations such as guilds, clan associations, secret societies, temple societies, native-place associations flourished. From the early 1900s onwards the state promoted the formation of new professional associations such as chambers of commerce and lawyers' associ-ations in an attempt to gain control over local affairs. Although these professional associations were regulated by the state, they still enjoyed considerable room for manoeuvre. In many cities they proved to be the most powerful of all non-governmental associ-ations. Through these organisations local élites carried out official functions such as the provision of welfare, irrigation works and poverty relief schemes. For some China scholars the wealth of self-regulating and autonomous organisations was evidence that late Imperial China had 'a distinct premodern civil society'.

After 1949 the development of civil society suffered a severe setback. Through land reform, the abolition of private enterprise and collectivisation the Chinese Communist Party (CCP) under-mined the socioeconomic basis of autonomous organisations. The CCP orchestrated participation in public life through the trade unions, work units and mass campaigns. Most of the autonomous organisations which characterised late Qing and Republican life were banned. For example, severe restrictions were placed on the activities of Christians, Buddhist and Taoists. During the Cultural Revolution even party-state organisations such as the Women's Federation and Trade Union Federation were not permitted to function.

However, the post-Mao period has witnessed a rapid upsurge of autonomous organisations. Social organisations such as the Self-Employed Workers' Association, chess societies and democracy salons (at least up till 1989) have proliferated throughout China. Following the Tiananmen crackdown the party-state outlawed all political organisations which posed a threat to their authority and sought to bring all new social organisations under their control. Thus the Regulations on Social Organisations issued in 1989 required all social organisations to register with the Ministry of Civil Affairs.

Behind the euphoria for civil society

Some Western scholars have been eager to adopt the concept of civil society in their analyses of social change in China. Two considerations are relevant: first, the general intellectual climate of the late 1980s and early 1990s; and second, the particular features of the emerging social organisations.

The disintegration of Eastern Europe and the former Soviet Union in the late 1980s seemed to herald the triumph of the 'people' over an oppressive state. Grappling with these cataclysmic changes East European academics revived discussion of civil society. This spilled over into Western explanations of the demise of state socialism. Civil society provided a well-worn lens through which to focus on the dramatic events of 1989 in China and make comparative statements about Poland, Hungary and the former GDR. Civil society was seen as the indisputable alternative to state-led development in a global context of neo-liberalism.

However, it was not just that civil society was a fashionable concept that it was applied to China. The new social organisations in China seemed to display features associated with a civil society: initiated from below with a voluntary membership, autonomous from the state, occupying space outside the state and diametrically opposed to the state.

Multiple meanings of civil society

From the literature on civil society in China two uses of the term can be indentified. First, civil society has been used in the strong sense of an arena of political opposition to the state. The emergence of politically autonomous organisations such as the Capital Independent Workers' Union and the Autonomous Students' Union of Beijing Universities and Colleges (see Chapter 1), which confronted the power and authority of the party-state, provided evidence of civil society in this strong sense.

Second, it has been used in the weak sense of a sphere of voluntary, associational activity, situated between the state and the family. Although scholars disagree as to whether the events of 1989 heralded the rise of civil society in the strong sense, there is general consensus that associational life has flourished in the post-Mao period. Not only have informal connections (the ubiquitous *guanxi*) become increasingly important, but a plethora of associations permeate the social landscape.

The introduction of market reforms and in particular the growth of a private sector have fostered a sphere of autonomous economic activity which has given impetus to new institutional forms of association. At the same time the state has been in a process of transition, adapting existing institutions and rapidly creating new institutions. Within this context of new intermediate, participatory organisations linking the state with the economy and society have begun to proliferate. By mid-1991 there were already 1018 registered national-level social organisations. In reality, the number of social organisations is far greater as this figure does not include branch and local organisations. In Xiaoshan, a small prospering town in Zhejiang Province, for example, ninety-nine social organisations had registered in 1990.

Doubts about civil society

Both senses of civil society implicitly assume a state/civil-society dichotomy. In the first sense civil society stands in opposition to the state as a forum for setting limits to state power and checking excesses. In the second sense the associations are assumed to arise voluntarily outside the state and to operate autonomously from the state.

If we operate with this second sense of civil society as an autonomous sphere of voluntary associational activity situated between the state and the family, then to what extent do we find civil society to exist in China? Certainly there is ample evidence of new social organisations in post-Mao China. But to what extent are they autonomous from the state, voluntary or spontaneous?

In regard to the second sense of civil society four broad categories of social organisations can be identified along a continuum in terms of their autonomy, voluntariness and spontaneity. By *autonomy* we understand that a social organisation is able to set its own goals, determine its own structure and rely upon its own financial resources. A social organisation is *voluntary* if a potential member can elect to join the organisation providing certain criteria are met and that s/he may resign at any point. A social organisation is *spontaneous* if the members founded the organisations of their own accord. The four broad categories along this continuum are the old, *official organisations* such as the trade unions; the new *semi-official* social organisations such as the Private Entrepreneurs' Association; the new *popular social* organisations such as stamp clubs or Qigong societies; and the *illegal organisations* such as secret societies or underground political organisations.

Old, official social organisations

The old, official organisations such as the Women's Federation, the Federation of Trade Unions and the Communist Youth League stand near the pole of least autonomy, voluntariness and spontaneity. They are vertically integrated into the party-state, and have functioned as 'transmission belts' between the party-state and society, except during the Cultural Revolution when they were banned. Their staff are appointed and paid by the state. Although some leaders in the Trade Unions' and Women's Federation have sought greater autonomy from the state, these old organisations have basically served as implementers of party policy. In the wake of the current reforms they are desperately trying to adapt to the circumstances. The Trade Union Federation, for example, has set up enterprises to raise funds whilst the Women's Federation has encouraged women entrepreneurs to organise themselves.

New, semi-official social organisations

The new semi-official social organisations enjoy greater autonomy than the old social organisations but less than the popular or illegal ones. They warrant most attention because they fit less easily into the civil society framework.

They are semi-official because both members and the state are involved in their goal-setting, management and funding. Examples include the Private Entrepreneurs' Association, the Self-Employed Workers' Association and the Lawyers' Association. They are mainly formed around economic, technical and professional concerns and enjoy some degree of autonomy partly because it is in the interests of the state for them to do so. These organisations function both to the benefit of the state and their members. In the words of the economist, Xue Muqiao, they help to 'bridge the gap between the state and society'. The reform programmes of the 1980s have led to a weakening of state control over the economy and society. In this context these new intermediary organisations help to maintain the influence of the Party-state by providing a channel for communication and education. At the same time they enable members to promote their own interests *vis-à-vis* the state.

They also perform certain economic functions through providing a mechanism for linking isolated economic actors and various ministries and agencies. This enables the state to manage sectoral policy and the private economy more effectively. It also enables the members to exchange information and develop bonds of common sectoral interest. Through these new organisations officials and individuals are able to extend their network of contacts (*guanxi wang*), which is important for promoting both collective and particularistic interests.

From the point of view of the state the semi-official organisations assist in regulating the market and maintaining legal and social order. Through these organisations the state can ensure safety and hygiene standards, improve tax collection and gather information about the market. At the same time members can utilise these organisations to protect their interests in the market-place, guarantee the supplies of raw materials and influence price-setting. They also provide a channel for obtaining authority, prestige and resources from the state.

It is not surprising that these organisations have to varying degrees received funding from the state. In Xiaoshan, for example, the Association of Self-Employed Workers and the Association of Private Entrepreneurs had nearly all their expenditures covered by the Industrial and Commercial Bureau. Other associations rely more on their own sources of income. For example, the Poultry Breeding Association in the same town received 80 per cent of its income from technical service fees. There has been growing pressure from these new semi-official organisations to be allowed to set up their own companies as a way to increase their revenue and autonomy.

The hybrid character of semi-official organisations is also reflected in the involvement of state cadres in the day-to-day running and management of these organisations. Leaders and working staff are drawn both from related government departments and members. In some cases officials from affiliated government organisations occupy top posts. For example, leaders from the Industrial and Commercial Bureau occupied top positions in the Association of Self-Employed Workers and the Association of Private Entrepreneurs in Xiaoshan. Members also participated in the high-level committees of these organisations. In the permanent council of the Private Entrepreneurs' Association, for example, seven of the fifteen council members came from private enterprises.

Membership of the semi-official organisations is complicated. In some organisations membership is compulsory, in others voluntary. Private entrepreneurs and self-employed households automatically become members of their respective organisations upon registering their businesses. The cement enterprises in a small town in Zhejiang Province felt obliged to join their provincial association as this had the authority to grade enterprises, which was important for their reputation. However, only 57 per cent of respective enterprises had joined the Association of Producers of Dried and Preserved Vegetables, partly because it was not seen to be successful.

The origins of semi-official organisations are also relatively complex. The Poultry Breeding Association and Dried Turnip Association have been created by their members. The Self-Employed Workers' Association as well as the Private Entrepreneurs' Association were formed in response to pressure from below as well as calls from the State Council to organise themselves. Local officials concerned about the uncoordinated growth of cement factories played a key role in the setting-up of the Cement Industry

Association. So the semi-official organisations arose as a result of pressure from below and encouragement from above.

New, popular social organisations

The new popular social organisations, such as chess clubs and *qigong* societies, stand more towards the pole of greater autonomy, voluntariness and spontaneity. They enjoy a greater degree of autonomy than the semi-official organisations, relying on their own fund-raising efforts, setting their own goals and managing their organisations with their own voluntary labour. They are not totally autonomous, however, as they are required to register with the state. As long as they operate within the confines of the law and do not pose a threat to the state, they have considerable leeway in their activities. Although the popular organisations have in general been founded by their members, their creation has been conditional upon party-state tolerance for such organisations.

Illegal social organisations

Illegal social organisations are the most autonomous, voluntary and spontaneous of all four types, precisely because they are not permitted. Examples include the secret societies, ethnic associations and underground democratic political groups. These again set their own goals, raise their own funds and manage themselves. However, this is not to say that individual officials or indeed local departments may not be involved in their activities. Over the last few years the Hong Kong media have revealed state collusion in organised crime and especially in the smuggling of luxury goods into China.

From this discussion of the four broad categories of social organisation it is evident that associational life in China is far more heterogenous than the concept 'civil society' suggests. Social organisations differ in the extent to which they might be called voluntary, autonomous and spontaneous. Semi-official organisations in particular have an ambiguous character for on close inspection they reveal varying degrees of state involvement in their activities, funding and staff. In many respects they reflect the tension between dependence and autonomy that characterised the professional associations of the early Republican period. Can we then justifiably call this realm of association a 'civil society'?

Beyond civil society

It is apparent that the term 'civil society' fails to capture the diversity of organisations that have emerged in China since reform. The assumption of unity and independence from the state masks the variety of organisations, their forms and relationships with the state. The civil-society/state dichotomy forces the student to place associational activity into the camp of either civil society or the state. An analysis which privileges civil society over the state leads to explanations which are limited in three ways:

1. they focus attention on the autonomous, voluntary and spontaneous characteristics of these organisations at the expense of their relationship with the state;
2. they implicitly assume an oppositional and conflictual relation with the state, neglecting the cooperative dimensions;
3. they assume a one-way impetus to the formation of these organisations, that is from below.

This echoes the Hegelian and Marxian interpretation of civil society which links the rise of these autonomous organisations with the emergence of a new sphere of autonomous economic activity. This approach soon leads to problems. Where for example do you place the semi-official social organisations? Do they belong in the sphere of the state or of civil society?

The concept civil society has a particular history in Western political thought, but this creates its own set of specific problems for studying China. First, not all social organisations have as their purpose the determination of the limits of state power. Stamp clubs, poetry societies, chess clubs exist to bring together people sharing similar cultural interests. This is not to say that they may not at some point be involved in addressing the limits of state power but this is not their *raison d'être*.

Second, with the introduction of market reforms in China it is tempting to interpret these changes in organisational life as the rise of civil society, in line with the historic development of Western Europe. However, to expect these organisations to assume a historic role in the emergence of a democratic China not only assumes that history repeats itself regardless of different times and political cultures, but also imposes a set of political and moral values. The danger is a blurring of vision, with its potential for misjudgement.

Finally, given that civil society has been linked to the rise of capitalism, it is again tempting to assume that the proliferation of these new social organisations in the post-Mao period is causally related to the introduction of the market. The semi-official organisations are, however, as much a product of fundamental changes in the nature of the state itself and its relations to society and the economy as they are of the market. This should not be surprising given the dominant role of the state in the economy and society since Liberation.

Despite its value-laden, ambiguous features 'civil society' has focused attention on the rapid changes in associational life and the socio-economy in China. However, it has clearly outlived its usefulness and is unable to generate questions which further understanding of this thriving associational realm.

What then are the prospects for China's social organisations? In their present Janus-face form the semi-official social organisations are transitional structures appropriate to an economy that is semi-planned and semi-market and a society that is becoming increasingly complex and stratified. As the semi-official organisations accumulate more of their own funds and rely less on the state for financial support, there will be growing pressure within these organisations for a looser relationship with the state. As the state too is keen to shed some of its economic and welfare commitments and to relegate a larger role to the private sector, it can be expected that these semi-official organisations will become more rather than less autonomous over the decade. Popular organisations will continue to flourish. It is unlikely that the underground political organisations, which have weak bases of support, will be able in the near future to shed their illegal status. The Tiananmen events were a salutary warning to the party-state about the dangers of losing social control. Perhaps the greatest threat to the party-state and to this associational realm would be the development of a coherent consciousness by these disparate associations which might be translated into the political sphere. In that case a civil society could truly be described in the strong sense.

7

Justice and the Legal System in China

Donald C. Clarke

'Of the ten reasons by which a magistrate may decide a case, nine are unknown to the public'

The best way to understand justice and the legal system in China today is to begin with the understanding that traditional Chinese thought never intimately connected the two. If by 'justice' we mean simply a state of affairs where people get what they deserve – and what they deserve is defined ultimately by cultural norms – then this is not to say that Chinese culture cared less about justice than other cultures; it is simply that the Chinese by and large did not look to a system of laws to get it. Nor is it to say that the two have no connection in Chinese culture today; the 'culture' of over one billion people is neither monolithic nor static. But to connect justice and legality today is to do something relatively new in the history of Chinese thought. Understanding why this is so will tell us much about where China has been and where it is heading.

Traditional China

Thomas Stephens (1992: p. 4) has succinctly summed up the differences between traditional Chinese and Western thinking about dispute resolution and the maintenance of social order:

> In Western thought, the antithesis of chaos is order, and order is conceived of ... as an artificial objective deliberately brought

about, managed, and controlled ... according to the conscious will of a transcendent power external to the flux, by the enforcement of codes of rigid, universal, specific, imperatives constraining conduct.

In Chinese thought ... the antithesis of chaos is harmony, which is thought of simply as a natural characteristic of a state of affairs that arises and persists automatically in a hierarchical universe so long as all the individual parts of that universe ... perform their duties and offices faithfully ... in whatever station or function of life they find themselves born to or assigned to by superior authority.

A number of consequences follow from these differing notions of order and harmony. The notion of order is inseparable from the notion of rules, for it is rules that distinguish the orderly from the disorderly. The provision of just rules and their impartial enforcement were always among the chief duties and sources of legitimacy of the European ruler from the Middle Ages onward.

In China, by contrast, disputes were resolved and harmony restored by an authority superior in rank to both parties. Obedience to superiors in a hierarchy of authority, not rights, is the heart of this system. Where European monarchs viewed the settlement of disputes as an important foundation of their claim to rule, traditional Chinese thought viewed the very existence of disputes as a sign of moral failure – either on the part of the litigants or on the part of government.

We might sum up the differences between Western and Chinese thinking by contrasting the concept of *order* maintained through a system of *rules* with the concept of *harmony* maintained through a system of *roles*. A fundamental concept of Confucian thought often translated as 'propriety', is essentially the set of precepts governing proper conduct in relationships between individuals in their proper social roles (Schwartz 1957: p. 63). But, like any other set of rules, these precepts were not intended to be strictly followed regardless of their consequences. What, then, was the Chinese attitude toward systems of rules? The history of government and society in China provides no shortage of often quite elaborate sets of rules. Guilds and clans had their own sets of formal rules, and the state bureaucracy was governed by detailed codes. But these rules were never more than guidelines. It was never supposed that justice would follow more or less automatically from the application of the rules, or that the strict application of the rules had any value independent of the outcome of that application. 'Let justice be done, though the heavens fall' is a concept alien to traditional Chinese thought.

One of the major historical differences between the systems of rules promulgated by the Chinese state and laws promulgated by Western legislatures is that the Chinese rules did not, and were not intended to, grant rights. The rules of the traditional Chinese state are best understood as directives to officials or as the internal operating procedures of a bureaucracy.

Thus, the Chinese word often translated as 'law', *fa*, historically had a connotation of 'model' or 'method'. Where it meant an imperative rule, it was the command of a superior. Thus it is tempting but ultimately misleading to apply the terms of modern Western law to the traditional Chinese system of dispute resolution and maintenance of order. The imperial official in charge of a district is often called the 'magistrate', but in fact settling disputes was a minor part of his functions, and deciding conflicting claims of right would have been unthinkable.

In a system like that of traditional China, rules and directives are used for convenience and uniformity, and never bind the issuing authority. That authority might choose to follow the rules for the sake of consistency and stability, but a rule can be violated 'whenever the considerations of administrative efficiency that led to its adoption point the other way'. (Unger 1976: p. 67) There is no way for inferiors to compel superiors to follow a rule, nor any notion that such an act would be possible or desirable (Stephens 1992: p. 29).

Modern China

Before the era of extensive contact with the West, China had a set of institutions and practices – and an appropriate language to describe them – for dealing with many of the problems dealt with by law in Western societies. What has happened to these practices and this language in twentieth-century China, and particularly since the founding of the People's Republic in 1949? It would be remarkable if, in a society that has undergone such momentous changes, thinking about social order and the resolution of disputes were to remain somehow immune. It is clear, however, that there *are* remarkable continuities between traditional and modern views. What makes the current era so interesting is that despite a *practice* that remains substantially indebted to traditional thinking, the language used to describe the institutions of the modern Chinese 'disciplinary' system has become more and more associated with a substantially different set of expectations: the expectations of Western jurisprudence. Take, for example, the official document entitled *xianfa* and usually labelled in English as China's constitution. Is this translation justified? The answer is: it depends on what you mean by 'constitution'.

China has had several *xianfa*: in 1954, in 1975, in 1978, and in 1982. All have been described as 'constitutions' in the government's English language publications. All were said to be the basic and most fundamental law of the land. All described, in greater or lesser detail, the institutions and structure of a system of government.

Black's Law Dictionary (1979: p. 282) describes a 'constitution' as:

> The organic and fundamental law of a nation or state, which may be written or unwritten, establishing the character and conception of its government, laying the basic principles to which its internal life is to be conformed, organizing the government, and regulating, distributing, and limiting the functions of its different departments, and prescribing the extent and manner of the exercise of sovereign powers.

Yet, as more than one observer has noted, 'The constitution seems to bear no relation to the actual government of China' (Jones 1985: p. 710). The government has never been obliged to follow its precepts, and there is no mechanism for making it do so. A well-known case is that of Premier Liu Shaoqi, deposed during the Cultural Revolution without any regard for the procedures prescribed in the 1954 *xianfa* and imprisoned until his death without regard for any rules about the circumstances under which citizens are deprived of their freedom.

Does it make sense to condemn this and other acts, as many have done, as 'unconstitutional'? It is true that such acts go against what is called for in the *xianfa*, but the *xianfa* is simply not a document of legal significance. The 'rights' it provides are more akin to the right to the pursuit of happiness proclaimed in the American Declaration of Independence. The *xianfa* might thus more appropriately be viewed as a kind of National Declaration. Each *xianfa* has marked the ascendancy of a particular leading group and policy orientation. Each has contained a clear indication of the policy directions the government at the time intended to take. Thus, they have been far from insignificant. But they have not been binding law and no Chinese government has ever treated them as such. On the contrary, changes to the *xianfa* are often quite explicitly intended to be the final stamp of legitimation on already existing and approved practices. Land leasing, for example, was carried out experimentally, and with central government approval, at the local level *before* the prohibition on it was written out of the *xianfa*.

That the *xianfa* is not in fact binding law does not mean it is insignificant. Ever since the fall of the Qing dynasty and the end of Imperial China in 1911, Chinese governments have viewed a Western-style constitution proclaiming popular sovereignty as a necessary hallmark of legitimacy, something that would never have occurred to a Chinese government before contact with the West. In proclaiming the *xianfa* to be that constitution, a government in effect legitimises the treatment of the *xianfa* as a constitution. Although the government is not in fact bound by the *xianfa*, it cannot admit it.

The practical importance of this change in rhetoric should not be overestimated. There is no neutral judge to impose sanctions on the side that loses the argument. A claim by a Chinese citizen that the 1989 declaration of martial law in Beijing was invalid because it was not made according to the procedures outlined in the *xianfa* would similarly get nowhere in court. But the *xianfa* is, by the government's own admission, *supposed* to bind it. There is thus a constant pressure, imposed by the government's own decision to proclaim the *xianfa* a 'constitution', to act according to its provisions. The revisions leading to the 1982 *xianfa*, in fact, show evidence of this pressure. Although the government has never in practice allowed strikes, the right to strike was put in both the 1975 and the 1978 constitutions as appropriate to a workers' state. By 1982, the government had not changed its mind about the right to strike, but it had changed its mind about how far the *xianfa* should reflect reality: the provision was removed.

A similar process can be traced in criminal law. The Chinese government has promulgated documents conventionally translated as the Criminal Law and the Criminal Procedure Law, as well as other documents describing the substance and process of state-imposed punishments. If one assumes that the Criminal Law and the Criminal Procedure Law are indeed Western-style 'laws' – in other words, that they constitute or should constitute a known and written standard that determines impersonally whether and how a person shall receive punishment – they are bound to be found wanting. Consider, for example, the provision for analogy in the Criminal Law: a 'crime' not stipulated in the Criminal Law, or elsewhere, may be punished according to the most nearly applicable article. This shows that the determination of whether a particular act constitutes a crime is something that must take place *outside* the Criminal Law. The Criminal Law is simply a standard or method for punishments. In this respect, the Criminal Law resembles the rules for punishment of Imperial China, which stipulated any number of punishable acts in great detail, but also contained provisions allowing for analogy and punishing 'doing what ought not to be done'.

The rules of the Criminal Procedure Law, which purport to govern the process under which punishments are imposed, are similarly unsatisfactory if viewed as part of a Western-type legal system. Observance of the rules by police, prosecutors, and courts is essentially voluntary. This is just not true in practice, as the extended pre-trial detention of many defendants following the Tiananmen crackdown in 1989 showed. The coercive institutional structure of which they form a part makes them optional in theory as well. The structure and fully intended consequence of the system of order is clear: if the police want to detain a citizen for questioning for any reason for an extended period of time, they may do so without needing permission from any other body.

As with the *xianfa*, however, there is a source of instability built into the present system as it affects the imposition of punishments on citizens: the system is described with terms such as 'law', 'statute', and 'legislature' to which many Chinese have come to attach the expectations that Westerners attach. No educated Chinese two hundred years ago would have said, 'China has no law.' The Qing Codes were there for anyone to see. But this is precisely the complaint of many educated Chinese today, despite the explosive growth of legislation and associated institutions since 1979. What they mean is something very specific: the government is not restrained by its own rules, *and it should be*.

More and more articles in newspapers and legal journals decry the cavalier attitude of government bodies to the rules under which they are supposed to operate. And a government body accused of acting unlawfully will never say publicly that it simply is not bound by legal rules; it will instead insist that it acted according to relevant law even while refusing to specify what that law is. China is not a state where government acts need to be authorised by law to be valid. A government act is valid if it can actually be done.

Legal advisors

So far only the rules have been discussed. But what of the institutions designed to administer the rules and their personnel?

The notion of the private citizen with expertise in the law has been as unwelcome under the Communist Party as it was in traditional China. In Imperial China, those who assisted litigants in framing complaints to bring before government officials could be labelled 'litigation tricksters' and punished. In one reported case from 1820, an elderly man was sentenced to three years of penal servitude for having drafted five litigation documents. This was a *lenient* sentence because there was no evidence that he had conspired with government clerks, tricked the ignorant, or engaged in intimidation or fraud. In post-1949 China, 'lawyers' have similarly been suspect. The government has encouraged the spread of knowledge about laws, but only on its own terms: the publication of statutory compilations without official authorisation is illegal.

The regulations governing the work of legal advisors specify that they are 'state legal workers' and must be 'loyal to socialism'. In general, legal advisors cannot work as individuals or be paid directly by clients. They must work in and be paid through a law office, and that office operates under the jurisdiction of the Ministry of Justice and its equivalents at the local level.

Although they are deemed to be employed by the state, legal advisors may be asked, particularly in criminal cases, to oppose state bodies. They are supposed to protect the interests of their clients and to keep their secrets, creating the potential for a clash between conflicting obligations.

In the government's view, legal advisors are and should be subject to state direction. This is particularly obvious in politically sensitive criminal cases. For example, legal advisors defending persons charged with crimes related to the Tiananmen protests of 1989 were instructed to 'do a good job of ideological work on the defendant and his family members, encouraging them to admit the crime and submit to the law.' (*Human Rights in China* 1993: p. 8) As another circular pointed out in the same context:

> Defense is not a matter of victory or defeat, and the legal advisor is not competing with the procuratorial and court personnel to see who comes out on top; it is a propaganda effort, directed at the citizens, to condemn vice and praise justice. (*Human Rights in China* 1993: p. 19)

Legal advisors are often required to report to and probably secure the approval of local government justice agencies before entering a plea of innocent (Gelatt 1991: p. 12, n. 56; *Human Rights in China* 1993: p. 8).

The financial wall between advisor and client in the traditional model is quite openly designed to prevent excessive loyalty by the legal advisor to the wishes of the client and insufficient loyalty to 'socialism' as defined by the authorities. Clients who wish the advisor to give their case special attention must make a further secret payment in addition to the often nominal fee paid to the law office. The extra payment is characterised as a bribe if discovered.

Although little has changed in official attitudes since the promulgation of the governing regulations over a decade ago, the logic of post-Mao economic reform has brought the possibility, and in some cases the reality, of change in the way legal advisors work. For the growing numbers, the term 'lawyer' may not be too misleading.

Most importantly, economic reform has seen the transfer of a number of government functions to the market. Legal services are part of this trend. The mid-1980s saw the growth of incentive systems in law offices, and the late 1980s the establishment of 'cooperative' law offices which, while still subject to the administrative control of the justice departments of local government, were financially self-supporting. The government has been clear that even legal advisors working in cooperatives are expected to support the socialist system and are never to act as 'independent professionals'. Regardless of official pronouncements, however, when there is competition and livelihood is not guaranteed by the state, it is natural to expect a greater degree of zeal on behalf of the paying client.

A sense among legal advisors of how things ought to be also drives the continued change in their role. Foreign firms tend to steer clear of Chinese legal advisors as much as possible in part because of concerns over their ultimate loyalty, and Chinese legal journals contain open complaints about government and Communist Party interference in the work of legal advisors. Chinese legal advisors, at least in the cities, are well aware of the social status and high incomes of lawyers in Western countries, and it seems obvious to them that their work is essentially the same. They argue, they should have the same sort of financial and administrative independence that Western lawyers do. For its part, the government, while continuing to maintain publicly that legal advisors must be loyal to socialism and not simply try to get the best deal for their clients, feels constrained to hide and deny all cases of specific, concrete intervention in the work of legal advisors. The documents cited above instructing legal advisors how to handle cases related to the Tiananmen protests of 1989 were secret.

The courts

Finally, it is important to understand the limited role played by hearing officers (judges) and the courts. Systems of rules in China are typically assigned to a bureaucracy for enforcement. The prospects for successful enforcement depend on the bureaucracy that 'owns' the law. Thus, public security regulations can be enforced effectively, while environmental protection and land-use regulations are often ignored.

Courts in China are just one bureaucracy among many. Their competence is limited to matters of 'law', narrowly defined as a particular subset of the normative documents promulgated by governmental bodies at various levels. Neither in theory nor in practice are they permitted to pass judgement on the validity of all government acts or failures to act.

This limited competence follows quite naturally from the traditional view of the relationship between the government and its systems of rules. There is no single person or group of persons able to conduct the entire volume of government business, so certain tasks are delegated to specialised bodies. One of these tasks is the application of rules to concrete disputes. But the rules themselves are no more than guidelines for administrative convenience, and a body with the authority to administer one set of rules certainly has no authority to administer a different set, or to decide on its own how far its authority extends.

If a court were to go against the government's expressed will the matter would be treated as would any case of insubordination within a government bureaucracy. The court's rulings would be ignored and its hearing officers replaced.

Although courts and their officers have what to Western eyes is a low status in the Chinese political system, *in theory* they are not just another bureaucracy. Although they are subject to Party control, their jurisdiction is supposed to cross bureaucratic and administrative boundaries. Thus, a court in County *A* in Province *X* theoretically has the authority, in a proper case, to order someone in County *B* in Province *Y* to do something. This stems from a conception of law as a universally binding norm that supersedes all other norms. Needless to say, the local government of County *A* has no such authority, and the local court, in practice an arm of local government, will find it very difficult to exercise such authority if the government of County *B* opposes it. Nevertheless, the theoretical foundation for that authority now exists, ready to be used in the service of any political force that finds it advantageous.

Conclusion

The very act of discussing the Chinese legal system is risky because it assumes *a priori* that China has a set of institutions that constitute a system that can usefully be called legal. China does have a set of institutions for the preservation of social order and governmental authority, but these institutions operate on very different principles from institutions usually called 'legal'. The governing principles of China's order system are those of discipline.

The notions of both Chinese and Western, while sometimes useful, grossly oversimplify, as do the terms 'legal system' and 'disciplinary system'. The richness of a particular society's order system can only be appreciated through a full description. One should not assume that all controversies in the West are decided by judges impersonally applying law, nor that the law as we think of it is a useless notion in understanding China. But although no pure system exists, and contradictory elements can coexist, nevertheless there *are* substantial differences and these differences outweigh the similarities.

A fascinating and important aspect of the Chinese order system is precisely the existence of contradictory strains of theory and practice within it. While the institutions as they actually operate are more or less internally consistent within a traditional Chinese conception of the relationship between government and systems of rules, they are studied and described with a theory and a vocabulary whose connotations are further and further removed from reality. The result is sometimes simply academic irrelevance, but it can also be an adjustment of reality to fit the theory better, as when the government decides to act according to law in order to bolster its claim – deemed essential – to be acting according to law.

What does this mean for the future? That the government of China feels obliged to justify its actions in the language of legality is certainly new. The old categories are breaking down; they are not so overpowering as once they were. Yet we cannot confidently predict a triumphant progress from the old disciplinary system to the modern legal system as if the latter were the necessary destination of historical change. We must just learn to live with the simultaneous existence of the different and sometimes contradictory ways of thinking about social order in the Chinese polity.

8

Young Offenders and Juvenile Justice

Nicola Macbean

'Scratching an itch from outside one's boot'

In the upheavals of twentieth-century China young people have become an important social and political force. As key participants in the Movement of 4 May, the Cultural Revolution and the demonstrations of 1989 China's youth have rocked the ruling élite. Rapid economic growth and China's Open Door policy over the past decade, have provided a further challenge to traditional values and contributed to the emergence of a youth culture with its own music, fashions and art. The opportunities afforded by economic development and the changing values of a modern society have helped to give rise to the concept of youth as a transitional stage between the dependency of childhood and the responsibilities of the adult world. Unlike earlier generations, young people in China today have no experience of war or famine, neither do they share the optimism and commitment to socialism that characterised the youth of the 1950s and 1960s. The Chinese Communist Party of the 1990s looks back on that early period with nostalgia as it struggles to develop an appropriate policy response to the challenge which young people pose to its authority. Nowhere do we see these problems more clearly than in the authorities' reaction to growing juvenile crime.

In comparison with crime statistics for Europe the reported incidence rate for youth crime in China is still remarkably low. The upward trend – despite considerable fluctuation – is, however, unmistakable. Chinese statistics show a crime rate in 1991 which,

Table 8.1 Crime rates in the People's Republic of China 1950–91

Criminal cases per 100 000 population			
1950: 93	**1960**: 33	**1978**: 55.30	**1985**: 52.06
1952: 42	**1961**: 61	**1979**: 64.80	**1986**: 51.91
1955: 37	**1962**: 62	**1980**: 76.30	**1987**: 54.12
1956: 23	**1964**: 35	**1981**: 89.37	**1988**: 77.41
1957: 58	**1965**: 33	**1982**: 74.02	**1989**: 181.49
1958: 120	**1966–75**: 40–60	**1983**: 59.81	**1990**: 200.90
1959: 35	**1976–77**: 53	**1984**: 49.91	**1991**: 209.44

Source: Bakken 1993.

at 209.44 cases per 100 000 of population, was 2.7 times the 1980 figure (Table 8.1). 75 per cent of crime is attributed to young people. As young people in China reach physical maturity earlier the average age of the young offender is declining and the profile of crime increasingly violent. Public opinion surveys in China reveal a widespread fear of crime and of juvenile crime in particular prompting debate amongst criminologists, and in the media, on its causes and on the need for the government to respond.

Profile of youth crime in China

International comparison of crime statistics is always problematic because of different reporting practices, laws and definitions of crime; Chinese statistics, however, present a particular problem. Access to sensitive data is restricted, especially for foreign researchers. Published statistics on crime are likely to understate the scope of the problem. It is also unclear to what extent the widespread use of administrative sanctions in China, which do not lead to a criminal record, is reflected in the official statistics.

Chinese literature typically refers to all crime committed by those under 25 as youth crime. Article 14 of the 1979 Criminal Law, however, calls for more lenient treatment of offenders under 18 years of age and sets the minimum age of criminal responsibility at 14 for anyone 'who commits the crimes of killing another, serious injury, robbery, arson, habitual theft, or other crimes seriously undermining social order'. This lack of clarity may cause confusion in reconciling standards of criminal procedure with traditional values. Still Chinese statistics on crime are very low. A UN survey suggests that China's crime rate in 1981 was just 6.8 per cent of the world average. In contrast, the ratio of juvenile crime (14 to 18-year-olds) to total crime in China is two to three times as high as the international average of 7.7 per cent (Bakken 1993).

Young people in China are said to be responsible for a disproportionate amount of property-related crime, sexual offences and hooliganism. Although most countries share a common understanding of serious offences, such as murder and robbery with violence, minor offences are, to an extent, culturally constructed. Sexual offences in China are widely assumed to include any promiscuous activity and the high proportion of female offenders in this category suggests that women may be more likely to be accused of certain offences. The wide-ranging definition of crimes of counter-revolution as 'All acts endangering the People's Republic of China committed with the goal of overthrowing the political power of the dictatorship of the proletariat and the socialist system' ensures that any form of political protest can be defined as criminal. Crime statistics from 1989 reveal a sharp rise in youth crime following the nationwide student demonstrations that year. For example, the number of reported youth cases in Chengdu, Sichuan province jumped from 8200 in 1988 to 13 091 in 1989.

The coastal cities and the Special Economic Zones (SEZ) experience significantly more crime than the rural inland areas. Much of this increase is attributed to the floating population drawn to the cities by the prospect of employment. Beijing and Shanghai have over one million unregistered migrants looking for employment in factories or on construction sites or peddling goods on the streets. The majority are young, single and male. Data from Tianjin suggests that the crime rate amongst the migrant population is 9330 per 100 000 compared with a rate of 360 per 100 000 for the resident population. Traditional methods of social control which rely on household registration and community surveillance are deemed inadequate in these circumstances, heightening public concern and increasing demands for tough government measures.

Explaining juvenile crime

The sharp rise in juvenile crime in the early 1980s was initially attributed to the destructive effect of the Cultural Revolution. During those chaotic years schools were suspended, production in factories disrupted and traditional family values came under stress. Children were encouraged to denounce their parents as counter-revolutionaries leaving many to fend for themselves while their parents were detained for re-education. Teachers were criticised and abused while diligent students were accused of 'lacking revolutionary spirit'. As urban youths, sent down to the countryside, returned to the cities there was little prospect, for many, of either employment or education. It is not difficult to understand why this 'lost generation' might resort to crime.

As youth crime, however, continued its upward trend criminologists could no longer attribute it entirely to the effect of the Cultural Revolution. The increase in youth crime with the Open Policy prompted many Chinese commentators to blame delinquency on the influence of the West. Foreign pornography, for example, is condemned as 'spiritual narcotics' which 'corrode the youngsters physically and mentally and lead them into illegal activities'. Opposition to the counter-culture of the 'hooligan' illustrates the hardline attitude of the authorities to anti-social behaviour. Although originally a term used to describe the petty criminals of pre-war Shanghai it now has a wider meaning: 'Rapist, whore, black-marketeer, unemployed youth, alienated intellectual, frustrated artist or poet ... It is an embryonic alternative culture' (Minford 1985: p. 30). Chinese authorities are less sympathetic; to them the 'hooligan' element is symptomatic of ideological breakdown and moral crisis.

Sociology and psychology have been reinstated as academic disciplines and give authority to explanations for juvenile delinquency that draw on problems within the family and society. Psychologists argue that the single-child policy is creating a nation of spoilt children whose family aspirations place them under great pressure to succeed. Some parents are accused of abusing academically unsuccessful children while others encourage them to work rather than stay on at school.

Unsurprisingly surveys have shown that juvenile offenders are more likely to be unskilled and less-well-educated. A nine-year compulsory-education law was introduced in 1986, but the cost of sending children to school in regard to fees and lost income is an obstacle for many, mainly rural, families with the result that a large number of children under 16 are not in school. In Tianjin, school dropouts are said to represent about 50 per cent of inmates in the juvenile prison. Secondary education in China is highly selective and oriented towards the college entrance examinations. Attempts to complement the academic system nationwide with vocational schools for the less-gifted have been frustrated by the shortage of funds.

Juvenile justice

Traditional mechanisms of social control are rooted in the Chinese system of household registration. This system established the importance of the family in maintaining social order and emphasised mediation, hierarchical relations and social harmony. Maoist criminology reinforced this traditional policing with an emphasis on the role of the community and the concept of the mass line. The modernisation of the legal system in the post-Mao era has emphasised the importance of criminal procedure and strengthened, in principle, the role of the lawyer and the courts (see Chapter 7). Legislation has been published which indicates the new priority of law over traditional policing methods.

China has ratified the 1989 UN Convention on the Rights of the Child and in 1991 introduced its own legislation for protection of minors under 18. The Chinese legislation attempts to criminalise 'feudal practices' such as drowning or abandoning infants, employing child labour and arranging marriage contracts for children. It also obliges parents to 'use healthy thoughts, good conduct and proper methods to educate minors ... prevent and stop minors from smoking, indulging in alcoholic drinking, roaming about, gambling, taking drugs, and prostitution'. A number of institutions, including the Communist Youth League, the Women's Federation, the trade unions and the Young Pioneers, are listed in Article 6 with the requirement that they should help to protect minors. Their specific duties and responsibilities, however, are not described.

Efforts to modernise the legal system and apply the rule of law have not supplanted the informal disciplinary system that characterised the Maoist era. Although legitimate rights have been introduced there is little guidance for implementation. The Ministry of Public Security, the police, plays a critical role in the extra-legal processes of administrative detention. Although it was originally envisaged that these informal measures would be temporary their continued use today suggests that they fulfil a specific purpose in the government's criminal justice policy. As a signatory to the UN Standard Minimum Rules for the Administration of Juvenile Justice, the 'Beijing Rules', China is committed to the principle of diverting young people from the courts and the criminal justice system. The underlying purpose of Article 11 is to avoid the damaging effect of labelling youngsters as criminals and sending them to prison. As a result young people in China are more likely to be subject to administrative sanctions than sent to the courts.

Police in China were unprepared for the rise in crime during the 1980s. As traditional forms of social control were being undermined by a more mobile population travelling in search of trade and employment opportunities, the Ministry of Public Security was under pressure to bring crime under control. Its response was to expand and develop a campaign style of policing with the key features being the identification of target areas, offenders and crimes. Police effort was concentrated in the urban, coastal regions. Certain categories of suspects were targeted including those already sentenced to public surveillance, those suspected of hooliganism and other public order offences and those who had been released from penal institutions. Individual movement was restricted, surveillance increased and secret files maintained.

In August 1983 the Ministry of Public Security launched a high-profile anti-crime campaign largely targeted at youth crime. During the first, most violent, phase of the campaign many young people found late at night on the streets, in the parks or in restaurants were detained as the police responded zealously to local quotas. Estimates of the total number arrested during the six-months campaign vary from 80 000 to 965 000 (Rocca 1984). Public sentencing and executions were a prominent feature aimed to reinforce the power of the state and act as a deterrent. Statistics for youth crime in 1984 show a marked decline, but the campaign's 'success' was shortlived; by 1985 crime rates had risen again. Subsequent, though less violent, campaigns were launched in 1986 and 1989.

Government propaganda has been widely employed to reinforce the message of anti-crime campaigns. The 1983 drive coincided with a campaign against spiritual pollution which highlighted the negative influence of Western culture. Regulations were published setting standards of behaviour for middle-school students. Hung prominently in every classroom the regulations prohibited long hair for boys, and girls were told not to curl their hair, use make-up or wear high-heeled shoes. Moreover, 'students are not allowed to use dirty words, to go to commercial dance halls or bars, to gamble, to take part in superstitious activities, to read books about sex or violence' (Thøgersen 1990). There has been some concession to sex education in schools following surveys suggesting that about 90 per cent of 'sex criminals' are under 20 years of age. Crime prevention strategies on the whole, however, indicate little practical effort to approach underlying problems such as high youth unemployment and family breakdown.

Juvenile delinquency is brought to the attention of the local police and the neighbourhood committee at an early stage. Public security organs can detain anyone 'if his identity is unclear and there is strong suspicion that he is a person who goes from place to place committing crimes; or if he is carrying on "beating, smashing and looting" and gravely undermining work, production or social order' (Criminal Procedure Law: Article 41). Suspects can be detained for up to ten days before a decision to arrest them formally is taken. Once arrested a suspect's family should be notified within 24 hours of the reasons for detention and the place of custody. In practice this system is widely abused and there are reports of suspects being held for over a year without charge and without notice being given to their family. There is no evidence to suggest that procedural abuses are limited to the adult system.

Interrogation of the suspect by the courts or the police should also take place within 24 hours of arrest and juvenile suspects under 18 are normally entitled to have a legal representative present. According to Article 14 of the 1991 Law for Protection of Minors, and in accordance with international standards, juveniles should be held in separate custody from adults. It is, however, acknowledged privately that because of a shortage of facilities this is not always possible.

While policing measures may have changed little in style and substance since 1949 efforts have been made to modernise the court system. In 1984 the first youth court was set up. Procedures in the youth court are designed less to intimidate and more to 'cultivate an atmosphere in which the two sides can communicate with each other' (*Beijing Review* 1990: pp. 6–7). Judges are given the task of 'investigating the background, motives and character of the delinquents'. They are also entrusted with the responsibility of visiting young offenders in prison and to assist in his or her rehabilitation.

China acknowledges both penal and welfare criteria in its treatment of young offenders as the principle of two-way protection; protecting the interests of both society and the juvenile. Society's interests are to be protected by punishing the juvenile offender, but because of their lack of maturity young people should also be treated leniently. Article 38 of the 1991 Law for Protection of Minors states that in dealing with young offenders the emphasis must be on 'education, persuasion and redemption'; punishment should be secondary. This is in accord with the ideology of Chinese penal policy which emphasises the need to reform and re-educate the criminal. Re-education in practice, however, relies almost exclusively on institutional treatment.

The most widely documented measure for dealing with young offenders is the work-study school. These were first set up in the 1950s to provide a middle-school education for children who had committed minor offences. The work-study school was suspended during the Cultural Revolution, but re-established in the post-Mao era in response to rising juvenile crime.

These schools are under the authority of the State Education Commission, but the school staff usually includes public security officials. Juveniles are referred to these schools by the neighbourhood committee who act on the recommendation of the local police, the child's regular school or even the parents. The authorities emphasise that these students are not seen as criminals and, therefore, avoid the stigma of being given a criminal record, improving their chance of reform. The primary objective is the re-education and rehabilitation of the young offender. Typically, the work-study school provides a strict regime of political and moral education, productive work and general academic studies. Students are normally weekly boarders and may be required to attend for two years. In 1991 the State Education Commission reported that there were 97 such schools catering for just 5600 students. The total number of juvenile offenders aged between 14 and 19 years dealt with by the courts in 1991 is reported to be 32 723 (Lin 1992).

Many of the female students in work-study schools have been accused of 'sex offences'. In a country where contraceptives are not widely available to the unmarried, pregnancy is a common outcome of premarital sex. Discovery is likely to result in abortion and a period in reform school. In China's coastal cities prostitution has once again become a serious problem. Measures to control prostitution include rounding-up both prostitutes and their clients for 'education'. The Ministry of Public Security has been given responsibility under new compulsory administrative measures to take in prostitutes for periods between six months and two years for 'legal and ethical education' and to take part in 'productive labour and to study production techniques to enhance their awareness of labour'. Those 'excused' re-education include girls under 14, pregnant and nursing women and women forced into prostitution.

In addition to the work-study school, several cities have also set up work-study factories to accommodate older youth. The work-study factory class at Fangcun, Guangzhou (Epstein 1986) caters for young people from 15 to 25 years old and the average stay is six months. Like the work-study school, ideological and political education are an important part of the regime. About four hours a week are devoted to general education and a further four to vocational study, but the majority of the day is spent in unskilled manual labour. Participants may often be required to participate in construction work demonstrating publicly evidence of their reform and rehabilitation. An alternative short-term option also administered by the police is shelter and education through which youngsters may be detained for several months for re-education.

Two other measures for dealing with young offenders exist and these mirror the adult system of re-education through labour, and reform through labour, more closely. Young offenders can be given a period of re-education which, like the work-study school, is a form of administrative detention that does not result in a criminal record. It is widely used for petty offenders in situations where work-study schools have not been established or have failed to deal successfully with persistent offenders. The cases of young offenders sentenced to re-education are not considered by the youth courts, but by a committee established by the public security bureau. They do not, therefore, have the benefit of legal representation or independent review.

Under the 1991 legislation offenders under the age of 18 are required to be detained in separate institutions from those holding adult offenders. Juvenile reformatories usually include young offenders sent for re-education as well as young criminals sentenced to prison. There are also reports of juvenile offenders being held in adult institutions. Chinese observers accept that this is far from ideal, but argue that it is a necessary short-term measure due to the shortage of separate institutions. Wu (1992) suggests that the total juvenile prison population is approximately 200 000 to 300 000 held in some 50–80 juvenile offender camps.

The Law for Protection of Minors contains no clear guidance on sentencing policy apart from a general requirement that young offenders should be treated with a degree of leniency. No special provisions for probation are made, but prisoners sentenced to three years or less and who have shown repentance are eligible. Under Chinese law the death sentence cannot be carried out on persons under 18 years of age. A death sentence suspended for two years to allow criminals 'to truly repent' can, however, be given to 16- and 17-year-old offenders convicted of serious crimes such as murder.

Chinese penal theory argues that labour plays a critical role in reforming the offender and work is, therefore, central to the penal regime. It aims to meet three objectives: the moral transformation of the offender through participating in productive labour, reintegration into society through learning vocational skills and a financial contribution to prison costs through the sale of prison products. The ideological commitment to the value of work in reforming criminals is publicly validated by the published rates for recidivism which are very low. Privately, however, Chinese observers concede that the unbelievably low recidivism rates of approximately 5 per cent are not true. The value of the vocational skills is also questioned. Epstein (1986) argues that they are generally low level-skills offering poor preparation for later employment. Unemployment levels among graduates of work-study classes are reportedly high.

China has been criticised internationally for its widespread use of prison labour and its export of prison products. Productive labour in Chinese prisons is not new, but evidence suggests that the use of forced labour to produce goods for export in both adult and juvenile correctional institutions has become *de facto* government policy (Epstein 1993).

Officially the state acknowledges its responsibility to help offenders to find employment on release from prison. In practice, however, it is readily admitted that ex-offenders experience discrimination. Files are maintained on all individuals in China and forwarded to future employers: loyalty to the Party as well as any criminal records are noted. Reports that students imprisoned after the democracy protests in 1989 are still experiencing difficulty in finding employment are common. A large number of adult prisoners are not released on completion of their sentences, but required to work for a further period under forced job placements. It is not clear whether these arrangements may also apply to juvenile offenders who complete their sentences in an adult prison.

Conclusion

In the past decade China has made efforts to establish juvenile justice on a more substantial legal footing with its ratification of international conventions and its introduction of domestic legislation. In practice, it is penal policy that dominates the Chinese juvenile justice system; social welfare concerns and the rights of the child are secondary. Article 19 of the Beijing Rules states that 'the placement of a juvenile in an institution should always be a disposition of the last resort and for the minimum necessary period'. The evidence suggests that custodial treatment is the standard response to juvenile offending. Furthermore, the extensive use of administrative sanctions by the Public Security Bureau raises a number of questions about police accountability.

Juvenile crime in China is unlikely to decline to pre-Cultural Revolution levels without a radical decriminalisation of many activities. Meanwhile the protection of children's rights in the criminal justice system will depend on more than just legislation.

9

Collectivism, Contractualism and Crisis in the Chinese Countryside[1]

Marc Blecher

'When you drink from the well, you should thank those who sank the shaft'

In its heyday, from the mid-1950s through to the late 1970s, collective agriculture was widely regarded as one of China's success stories. A growing population was being fed, a great deal of infrastructure was built to combat the effects of flood and drought that have historically plagued the country, and breakthroughs were being made in rural industrialisation and the mechanisation and modernisation of agriculture. In social terms, large gains were made in increasing the equality of income distribution, and the communes had a major role in broadening health care and education. Politically, the countryside was freed from the corruption and suffering of imperial and republican days, and new institutions were built that involved a modicum of popular participation and a degree of political stability great enough to avoid the worst depredations wrought by the Cultural Revolution in the cities.

It is therefore puzzling that the post-Mao reforms began in the countryside, and that they have achieved their greatest and most lasting effects there. While reforms of state-run industry and commerce and of the political system were slow to start and were in many ways still stalled even fifteen years into the post-Mao period, rural decollectivisation was complete within four years, and the 'rural responsibility system' of household farming that replaced it became firmly entrenched. The stability of the post-collectivist mode of production is all the more enigmatic in light of the palpable, even profound, problems of stagnant agricultural production: enduring poverty, underemployment and unemployment, crumbling infrastructure, and rising rural discontent and protest.

It is commonplace that the future of China's economy depends crucially on the countryside, encompassing both agriculture and rural industry, whose fastest growing sector is 'rural collective enterprises'. What is less commonly recognised is that the rural areas will also play an increasingly important and active role in shaping China's changing politics. In the maelstrom of 1989, when so many Chinese eyes, and almost all Western ones, were fixed on the cities, Deng Xiaoping suppressed the protests with the passive support of most of China's villagers and the active support of its heavily rural-based armed forces. The need to keep the Chinese countryside content, productive, and politically quiescent has been a central goal of the reformers, but also a principal worry and point of attack of Chinese critics of reform. Yet China's villagers have responded to the growing financial, distribution and political crises engendered by the reforms by moving from acquiescence to noncompliance and even to resistance, some of it armed. They have increasingly become active and censorious participants in the new politics of the post-Mao period.

Collective agriculture and its legacy

The collectivisation of Chinese agriculture proceeded gradually through the early 1950s, and then took a radical and disastrous turn at the end of the decade with the infamous Great Leap Forward. Institutional and policy changes after the Great Leap created a collective agriculture in China which settled down in a fairly standard pattern for the next fifteen years. Within the three-tiered commune, the lowest level, called the production team, was a small group averaging between 20 and 40 households – roughly 100 to 200 people. It owned the land and most of the basic productive resources. The team was the unit of income-sharing among team members; that is, each farmer's income was a share of the net distributed income of the team. The size of shares was determined in relation to work done, which in turn was set, often in quite a participatory way, using time- and piece-rates. But teams, brigades and communes also provided many public goods, such as housing, education and health care. At a higher level, major economic decisions – about cropping and investment – were heavily circumscribed by state plans implemented by brigade and commune authorities. The key institution was the Communist Party, whose commune and brigade committees supervised local governments.

Nevertheless, rural China was not a totalitarian system in a strict sense. Team leaders and brigade officials, whether or not they were Party members, frequently acted to protect their villages from state interventions that they regarded as harmful. Team leaders were often elected democratically, and it was not uncommon for villages to ignore the wishes of state officials in making their choices. These participatory habits, along with grassroots leaders' capacity to protect their localities, were in many ways products of the way the Communist Party had led the revolution and organised post-revolutionary rural institutions. But over time that same Party gradually restricted the scope of local politics and the latitude available to local leaders, even while continuing to encourage and often even demand popular participation. This obvious contradiction fuelled increasing political disillusionment in the villages, and helped to pave the way for the collapse of collective farming.

By the time this occurred, though, China's great experiment with collective agriculture could point to several solid achievements. Grain production managed to stay slightly ahead of population growth, rising from an annual 288 kg per capita in 1952 to 319 kg in 1978. *Per capita* production of meat and fish rose at considerably faster rates. Life expectancy at birth, the best all-round indicator of health, which in 1953 was in the low 60s for urban China (and therefore surely lower in the countryside), reached 68 in the countryside by 1978.

Yet all was not rosy. Restrictions on rural markets and on trade among production units made it difficult for farmers and collectives to obtain what they needed. These constraints also blocked the entrepreneurial potential of individuals and collectives, as do controls on the development of rural collective enterprises. Slack supervision by the state, with an emphasis on rapid, labour-intensive construction by rural collectives of infrastructural projects such as dams, canals and reservoirs led to considerable wasted time, effort and money.

This is reflective of a much wider motif which economists would term low labour productivity, and which farmers experienced as backbreaking work year after year for incommensurably low returns. The argument that Chinese agricultural collectives did not provide labour incentives is dubious both in theory and in practice. An economic model of rational behaviour under uncertainty can suggest, on the contrary, that the payment structure of Chinese collectives gave farmers incentives to apply super-optimal quantities of labour. That is, since they did not know in advance how much their work points would be worth, farmers worked harder and longer than made sense from the point of view of labour efficiency. With growth rates slow or stagnant, China's farmers were running at top speed just to stay in the same place.

The post-Mao period

The political dynamics of rural decollectivisation were complex and varied from place to place. Beginning in 1979, farmers in some places, particularly those in poor villages and areas, began spontaneously to dismantle their production teams and brigades. In other places, farmers and local officials experimented with contractual relationships known as 'responsibility systems'. Some of these involved work points given out by the team (thereby maintaining collective mediation of income) and some only a simple cash nexus; some were based on work groups and some on households. Meanwhile, official policy began to emphasise the need to break down production teams into work groups or even households as base units for production and reward. This 'policy' was little more than a game of catch-up in which the state was putting its *imprimatur* on each successive step toward decollectivisation taken by farmers and local leaders.

Yet elsewhere, particularly in places where rural collectives had been relatively successful, there was little palpable enthusiasm for decollectivisation. This may have had to do with the opposition of grassroots leaders, for whom decollectivisation would mean the loss of their institutional base. But many villagers too supported collective agriculture which, after all, provided economic security, social services, and a sense of community. In these places, decollectivisation was forced upon the countryside by the state in 1982 and 1983 in ways not too dissimilar from those used to promote rapid collectivisation in 1956.

By the mid-1980s, then, the vast majority of villages had adopted the most extreme form of responsibility system known as 'household production contracting' (*bao chan dao hu*). It was still in place in 1994, with no major change in sight. Under this system, individual households contract for the use of a plot of land, a piece of machinery, or even a workshop or enterprise, and they assume full financial responsibility for operating it. Land contracts specify a quota of crops to be grown on the land, which must be turned over to the collective partly as taxes and partly as a fee for use of the land; contracts to run workshops or machinery specify a cash fee. The contracting villagers keep all profits, but must also bear any losses.

In order to encourage the most productive use of these resources most restrictions on private commerce have been lifted: private markets have re-emerged. Further incentives have been provided to farmers by periodic increases in the state procurement prices of grain. And to help to ensure that that would be implemented and that farmers would utilise the responsibility systems to the fullest, free of fears of political criticism, the state undertook a general depoliticisation of the rural economy. All class labels ('poor peasant', 'middle peasant', 'rich peasant', 'landlord') were abolished. Economic and political administration were separated: communes were first stripped of their political control over agricultural production, and by the middle of the decade they were abolished altogether, replaced by new township governments. These were to have far more modest roles in economic life than the communes, although in fact they have remained very important in enforcing state cropping policy and developing and managing rural industrial enterprises. The state has also maintained its control over local affairs through the Communist Party, whose rural work departments maintain considerable power over finance, land allocation and reallocation, leadership recruitment and evaluation, technical and industrial development, and political reform (author's interview, Shulu County (Hebei) Communist Party Rural Work Department, 11 July 1990).

As a mode of agricultural production, household contracting is arguably not fully 'capitalist'. No land markets exist. Rather, the charges farmers pay to use the land, and most of the crops they plant on it, are set by the state. Farmers quickly discovered that they could exchange their contracted land for cash payment. Some of these exchanges amount to something closely approximating rent, except that the 'market' is very underdeveloped: the parties are generally brought together through existing social (often kinship) networks rather than markets, and the financial terms are not set by strict market forces. This has led some to view these land exchanges not so much as re-emergent tenancy but as a more benign form of social adaptation that benefits all parties.

If the responsibility system is being drawn into a form that may resemble exploitation, other forces pull it in the opposite direction. Sometimes this occurs through the same social forces leading toward land exchange: in many places, farmers are banding together, often with relatives, to pool land or engage in other forms of economic cooperation. But the state too is a force which promotes more collective relations within the household responsibility system. It is commonplace for farmers to purchase inputs and farm services from agricultural service stations operated by village governments. The maintenance and operation of water conservancy works also remains an area requiring cooperation. And particularly in the ideological backlash following the 1989 crackdown, there were significant moves toward recollectivisation of agriculture. These soon fizzled out. But the fact that they occurred at all suggests underlying tensions, at least in the political élite, beneath the apparent consensus on the responsibility system.

If household contracting is the reformers' approach to rural production, the renewal of markets is the approach to exchange. 1985 saw the publication by the state of 'Document No. 1' – on the first day of the year to highlight its importance! It announced the abolition of the state grain procurement system. It was to be replaced by a contract between the state and farmers for part of the harvest, with free markets taking the rest. This followed an unexpectedly large harvest in 1984 which had overwhelmed the state's procurement system. Thus, farmers did not necessarily experience 'Document No. 1' as a liberation. In practice, marketisation has moved haltingly and unevenly. By 1992 state regulation of grain prices on the free market had been removed, but mandatory cropping quotas for grain and cotton were back in many other places.

In sum, the institutions which have emerged in the Chinese

countryside since 1978 are a complex and novel mixture of state control, individual autonomy, and local organisations and practices.

State–society relations and local politics

State–society relations in post-Mao China involve intricate and reciprocal interactions. The complex shifting game of cat-and-mouse which has ensued over cropping reflects as much. Farmers seek to plant what is profitable and are pitted against the state's interest in assuring adequate harvests of key but less lucrative crops such as food-grain and cotton. In 1985 the state decided to do away with mandatory grain procurement precisely at a moment most disadvantageous to farmers, who were then facing plummeting market prices. The farmers responded by cutting back on grain in subsequent years. In fact, they resisted in several ways. Often they have simply ignored the quotas. They have also commonly purchased grain on the free market, reselling it to the state to meet their quotas. Sometimes they have lied to procurement officials, saying that their best efforts to meet their quotas were frustrated by drought, flood or blight. The state became so frustrated with these tactics that by 1990 procurement policy began to switch from output to area quotas, backed up with inspections of fields to make sure the farmers had actually put into the ground the crops that the state demanded. But the farmers were not beaten yet – some responded by refusing to tend those crops assiduously, diverting their energy and investment to other, more profitable pursuits. In this game, intermediate and grassroots officials often work for the benefit of their localities, even when this means undercutting the plans assigned to them by central and provincial governments (Blecher and Wang 1994).

Even the Communist Party in China is enmeshed in complex relations with society. In Shulu County (Hebei), for example, the Party Rural Work Department responded to farmers' protestations that lucrative orchard contracts had gone to only a few households. It undertook the complex but popular process of completely recontracting the orchards in several townships (Blecher and Shue). However, there is also some anxiety about the strength of the Party in the countryside. A front-page story in the flagship *People's Daily*, published in 1991 on the Party's Seventieth Anniversary, reported that as a result of decollectivisation, many farmers believe that 'there is no more need for the party cell'. The Party was so concerned about its deteriorating relations with villagers that, in a move reminiscent of Maoist days, it dispatched one million members to the countryside during the two years after the Tiananmen crackdown. In other instances, grassroots Party organs tried to repair their relations with society, and to meet their responsibilities to the higher levels, by working through social institutions which the Party has traditionally held in contempt. Party officials in Ningjin County, Hebei, have relied on a Catholic priest to persuade farmers to meet their grain sales obligations. And in many villages the Chinese Communist Party is in danger of becoming the captive of emergent social and economic élites.

The lively, often obstreperous participatory politics of Mao-period villages has mostly vanished. This is partly a result of the disillusionment with the ways in which participation was simultaneously encouraged but also emptied of meaningful content during the late 1960s and the 1970s. The decline of participation also flows from the fact that the household responsibility system takes production out of the public sphere. And, finally, as politics now competes with ever-more lucrative economic pursuits, influence and power in post-Mao Chinese villages are sought not, as in the past, through political participation, but through clientelism, horizontal social networks and increasingly through economic exchange.

Economic outcomes of rural reform

Under the rural reforms, the Chinese agricultural economy achieved very strong economic results through 1984, and then stagnated (see Table 9.1). While analyses of the increases in crop production often seek to attribute this to decollectivisation, it is in fact difficult to do so. For at the same time that the collectives were being broken up, procurement prices were being raised, markets were being opened, and the amount of chemical fertiliser applied to the land roughly doubled. Whatever the causes of the spurt of agricultural and industrial production may have been, it combined with continued growth in rural industry to cause rural incomes to skyrocket.[2]

Table 9.1 Basic economic indicators 1965–92

Average annual growth in:	*1965–78* %	*1979–84* %	*1985–92* %
Per capita grain production	1.2	3.7	0.6
Cotton production	−1.9	18	−0.3
Oil-bearing crops	0.6	13.3	−1.0
Collective industry output value[1]	7.6	7.5	21.3
Net rural income per capita		17.7[2]	10.2
(current yuan/ constant yuan)		10.3	0.4
Rural consumption per capita[3]	2.2	11.8	

[1] In current *yuan*
[2] 1978–84
[3] In constant *yuan*
Sources: State Statistical Bureau, *China Statistical Yearbook 1989* (Beijing: China Statistical Information and Consultancy Service Centre, 1989); *Beijing Review* 26 February–4 March 1990; 11–17 March 1991; 23–29 March 1992; 8–14 March 1993.

But after 1984, rural production and income stagnated, for several reasons. With each passing year it becomes harder to raise farm yields. In many of China's most fertile areas, yields are already reaching and sometimes over-reaching the capacity of the land even with modern inputs in use. Elsewhere, yields could be increased, but only at costs which are beyond the reach of the farmers who now make decisions about investment and production. In many places, farming is being neglected as rural industry attracts the lion's share of investment and labour. Irrationalities in land contracting and state cropping policy even result in farmland being left idle by those who have contracted for it, a remarkable development given that it is one of China's most precious resources.

The reforms have revealed the enormity of China's rural underemployment and unemployment problem, and begun to address it. Under collective agriculture, farmers' incomes were regarded as the objective of production: they were calculated not as a cost but rather as a residual after meeting costs. Thus, there was little incentive to economise on labour or to use it efficiently. While this had the advantage of providing work and income for many, it also meant a great deal of underemployment and hidden unemployment. With the onset of the reforms, farmers began to experience underemployment or unemployment directly, as a cost which they would have to bear themselves. Estimates of rural underemployment and unemployment run as high as 28 per cent – 120 million out of 420 million villagers of employment age.

However the reforms can be credited with revealing the problem, they have also gone some way toward ameliorating it. Rural industry, a Maoist innovation which has experienced tremendous growth in the post-Mao period, now employs 100 million villagers. Without it, rural unemployment would be more like 48 per cent (*China News Digest* 1993). In view of these enormous numbers, migration of rural people to urban areas in search of employment has been relatively low so far. Part of the credit for this goes to the continuing state administrative controls on residence and movement. But the sheer size of China's unemployment problem, along with the declining regulatory capacity of the state, threatens to breach the dikes. In August 1993 the Ministry of Agriculture announced plans to permit 50 million farmers to migrate to cities.

Increased economic inequality was nothing less than an explicit objective of the rural reforms. Criticising collective agriculture for damaging incentives by being excessively egalitarian, reform leaders began very early in the process to speak of 'allowing some farmers to get rich first'. The beneficiaries have included people in wealthier villages, households with more or better-skilled labour power, and those able to contract for the best land or other assets. Among the latter is a disproportionate number of local officials, who were in a position to manage the contracting. The new rich also included a disproportionate number of former rich peasants. This was partly so because in many villages land contracts were drawn up to replicate pre-collectivisation holdings, despite a quarter of a century having elapsed. In other cases, pre-existing socio-commercial networks, in which traders, money-lenders, and rich peasants were well situated, were revived. In addition, the re-emergence of former village social and economic élites is eloquent testimony to the tenacity of entrepreneurial inclinations and skills passed down through families.

The reforms also initially reduced the inequality between China's rural and urban areas, as the rural changes produced far better economic results than those in urban industry and commerce. In 1992, average farm incomes rose by 10.6 per cent, while urban incomes increased by 18.2 per cent. This is partly to do with farmers facing rising input prices and declining output prices.

Another factor depressing rural incomes was the increasing number of exactions by local governments.

Rural problems under the reforms

The problem, known in Chinese as the 'farmers' burdens', has attracted a great deal of attention, particularly since 1989, when the state became obsessed with stability, and was increasingly aware of the need to keep the farmers satisfied in order to ensure it. In 1990, for example, the official paper, *Farmers' Daily* ran an investigative report detailing the 67 levies and fees charged to farmers in several Hunan villages – including such arcane items as a tree-seedling deposit and a rodent control fee.

The problem was regarded as so serious that in late 1991 detailed regulations running to forty-one articles were issued. But in June 1993, farmers were still expected to contribute to scores of preposterous funds such as 'subsidies for lost working time of students of agricultural radio schools' and, more puzzling, 'administrative expenses for ... individually-owned mining concerns' (*Summary of World Broadcasts* 1993). The state responded by passing still more regulations – in May 1993 it banned forty-three funds for which local governments were collecting money from farmers, and in July announced new statutes. But if laws and regulations failed to work in 1991, there was little reason for farmers to trust them in 1993. Some were resorting to class action lawsuits against local officials, and others to a more traditional approach.

The deterioration of China's rural infrastructure is another growing problem. Shortages of funding and administrative support for water conservancy contributed to the seriousness of the effects of massive flooding in 1991 (Ash 1992: p. 546). While some in the leadership blamed the farmers for neglecting water conservancy, Chen Yun, China's leading Maoist economic planner, and still a pre-eminent Party patriarch, pinned the responsibility clearly on the reforms. Responding to growing concerns about agricultural stagnation, widening urban–rural inequality, and rural uprisings, the State Planning Commission announced a 32 per cent increase in state investment in agriculture for 1993.

Part of the explanation for the decline of rural infrastructure is a financial crisis which besets many village governments, which are responsible for collecting funds and organising construction and maintenance work at the grassroots (see Chapter 10). While some village governments are accused of accumulating large financial caches at farmers' expense, others are literally bankrupt. One survey in five Hubei counties found a full one-third of village governments 'have suffered severe economic losses, reducing their collective economies to mere skeletons'. The reasons were losses by collective enterprises, financial mismanagement, and lack of managerial talent as specialists leave local government service for more lucrative pursuits.

The collapse of village governments is a serious obstacle to maintaining or raising agricultural productivity. Many farm tasks, in both production and distribution, are most efficiently and profitably performed by farm collectives or village governments (Ash 1992: p. 554). This is especially so given China's underdeveloped marketing structure and trade barriers erected by local and provincial governments to protect their economies. Some leaders have tended to reproach China's farmers for these economic problems, accusing them of being apathetic and unwilling to take risks. But the problem lies much more with local and national government policies and practices that have undermined rural collective institutions, and with the effects of reform in corrupting local governments or enticing them away from some of their basic economic responsibilities.

A final major headache for the state has been agricultural procurement. Despite some feints in the direction of reducing its control over the harvest, the state has been unwilling to do so. It is also increasingly unable to marshal the physical and financial resources needed to maintain the control it would like to have. Decentralising reforms in industry, finance and commerce have caused significant central government deficits, leaving procurement agencies without the cash they need to pay farmers for the quota sales they have imposed. In the Autumn of 1992, those agencies had less than 2 billion of the 11 billion yuan they needed to purchase the grain for which they had contracted. As early as the 1984 bumper harvest, farmers found themselves being paid with IOUs. The state has repeatedly issued assurances that this would not recur. But these have been in vain. Issuance of IOUs recurred early in 1993. On 15 April the *People's Daily* proudly announced that 'the practice of issuing IOUs is no longer allowed'. But the ink had hardly dried before it became clear, this time in statements emanating from a conference convened by Vice-Premier Zhu

Rongji, China's top economic leader at the time, that once again IOUs would have to be issued.

China's farmers have responded to these problems with growing unrest, including violence. In one example reported in the Chinese press, in June 1993 spontaneous protests by farmers in Renshou County, Sichuan, against road construction levies led to 'beating , smashing and looting ... [in which] some people ... stormed the district and township governments and schools, beat up cadres and teachers, smashed public and private property, and illegally detained grass-roots cadres and public security personnel'. When police responded with tear gas, some were taken hostage by the angry crowd, and police cars were set on fire. But farmers are not the only perpetrators of rural violence. In Anhui, a villager who had the temerity to complain about 'unreasonable retention of funds' was beaten to death by several village cadres in April 1991. In a Hunan village, a farmer too poor to pay more than 220 of a 319 yuan levy was hounded daily by local cadres until he committed suicide. A riot ensued when his body was pulled from the pond in which he had drowned himself.

Rural violence has broken out over a range of issues besides local government levies. Farmers were enraged by what they perceived to be insufficient state attention to water conservancy work and mismanagement of relief efforts. This provoked over 100 incidents of mass rallies, looting of state warehouses, armed clashes, and even efforts to set prisoners free in four provinces. In Guizhou alone thirty people were reported killed.

Violence is spreading in other forms, for other reasons and with other targets. Even routine work by local officials, in land reallocation, population control, dispute mediation and public welfare work, is often met with reprisals from farmers. Battles have broken out between villages over property rights and access to water. Secret societies are making a strong comeback, which ought to frighten the leadership most of all because they hold the possibility of more organised protest.

The crisis of rural reform and the future of Chinese politics[3]

As these problems develop, the Chinese countryside is increasingly restive. In 1989, Deng Xiaoping could count on the support or acquiescence of China's hundreds of millions of villagers. But with rural violence growing, this cannot be counted on the next time the cities rise up. For the moment there appears little possibility of an organised rural popular movement against the state. Even less likely is an alliance of urban and rural popular protest, such as the one that contributed to the success of the Chinese Revolution. The gap between town and country in China remains far too great for that. But even unorganised rural revolt, triggered by an urban uprising but separate from it in form and content, directed against very different targets, and oriented to very different goals, can nonetheless contribute to threatening the structure of a state.

This is heady stuff. Yet increasingly, observers of contemporary China sense that a change of some kind is in the making. China may not go the way of the Soviet Union and Eastern Europe, but it will have a difficult time staying where it is or has been in the 1980s. Plausible scenarios include a transition to Western-style parliamentary politics; a transformation of the Communist Party into a more limited and self-restraining political force which could preside over a benign process of economic development; and the break-up of the country into competing or even conflicting provinces.

In all this, China's farmers have already shown their capacity to play an increasingly active role. The more they do so, the less likely is the parliamentary scenario. For China's farmers will be an unruly force for urban, parliamentary politicians. They may be susceptible to political manipulation by emergent local élites of various political stripes, including anti-Western nationalists of the left or right, or even the Communist Party or any successor to it. China's farmers are, we have seen, prone to violent outbursts, which do not provide a sustaining culture for representative politics.

As for the possibility of a single-party authoritarian state under a reformed Communist Party, in Taiwan this was accomplished because the ruling Guomindang founded its legitimacy on ardent anti-communism and its role as a catalyst for rapid economic growth and prosperity. The Chinese Communist Party lacks a clear ideological source of legitimacy among villagers, unless it becomes stridently anti-foreign. That is unlikely because xenophobia would torpedo the economic 'opening' which remains a major engine of economic growth.

Most dangerous of all there is the possibility that China's villagers could provide a social basis for the centrifugal forces of regionalism and localism that already threaten to split the country. Here they could become active allies of local neo-warlords. Or simply through their continuing spontaneous outbursts, they could provide emergent local satraps with political and military opportunities to grasp and hold power.

It is these fears, in the context of post-Tiananmen China, which are prompting the leadership's renewed concern about the countryside. Their state is, after all, the product of a rural movement. During the Chinese Revolution, their task was to organise and articulate rural discontent. This time they face the much harder task of fostering rural contentment. The question is whether they have the wisdom and resources that they need to do so. Only if rural–urban inequalities can be limited, and if rural industry continues to grow, will the state get the breathing room it needs in the countryside.

Notes

1. Thanks to Gordon White for opening his copious clippings files to me during the research for this chapter. I also share with many other colleagues a profound debt to the many hardworking people who have selflessly developed and maintained the *China News Digest*.

2. The statistics in the fourth line of Table 9.1 refer to all collective industry, most but not all of which is owned by rural governments. They also exclude individually-owned industrial enterprises in the countryside, which proliferated particularly after 1985. Thus these data should be treated only as a rough approximation of rural industrial growth.

3. Space does not permit exploration of rural education and health. But there are worrisome trends, including declining rural educational attainment and literacy, especially for girls, and difficulties in assuring broad health-care delivery, which had been a hallmark of the Maoist period.

10

Village Politics[1]

John Dearlove

'Sheep's wool comes off the sheep's back'

Reorganising agricultural production

The quest for prosperity

During the 1970s, there was a growing conviction that 'too large a dose of socialism had been imposed upon too backward a country-side' (Chan, Madsen and Unger 1992: p. 270) and that rational, self-interested, farmers could do a great deal better for themselves and the food supply if they were left to their own devices. Communes were abolished; agriculture was decollectivised; and the egalitarian but incentive-sapping system of work-points and the collective distribution of income was replaced by the near-universal adoption of the 'household responsibility system'.

Under this system the right to use land was given to peasants who were then free to work as self-employed 'farmers', making their own decisions about production and sales so that they could benefit directly from their own labours within the constraints of meeting a state-imposed grain quota and paying such other taxes as were exacted by local governments.

The demise of collective agriculture involved the distribution of land and of other collective assets. This facilitated the development of China's township (xiang), village, and private enterprise (TVP) sector. This sector has the greatest independence from state control; is most responsive to market forces; and is especially well-developed in the richer eastern coastal provinces. In 1971, the TVP sector was responsible for only 3 per cent of total industrial output but by 1990 it rose to 32.5 per cent, a rise mirroring the declining share of the state sector from more than 80 per cent in 1975 to just 56 per cent in 1989.

Rural industry mushroomed for a number of reasons. First, the household responsibility system stimulated agricultural productivity. This created a surplus that was available for investment at the same time as underemployed farm labourers were forced to work in non-agricultural enterprises. By 1986, 20 per cent of the rural labour force was employed outside agriculture. Second, years of state neglect of light industry created openings for small firms, openings that could be exploited because the state was prepared to relax restrictions on the large-scale expansion of non-agricultural activities by rural communities. And, third, township governments (created at the level of the former commune) and village governments ('non-governmental institutions' outside the state structure) had every incentive to encourage rural industrialisation.

The household responsibility system and the development of the TVP sector have transformed China's rural economy in terms of growth, incomes, and forms of ownership. There are also various 'joint ventures' as foreign capital moves into China. Moreover, there are the collective enterprises owned by basic-level governments, some of which are run directly by the governments whereas others are managed from within the enterprises.

Reorganising rural politics

The quest for stability

Economic reform boosted rural output and income through much of the 1980s – but at a cost. Change has had a profound effect on income stratification and on the cleavages – and conflicts – between peasants. A landless and footloose rural worker has interests very different from those of an ordinary peasant farmer, and different again from those who 'got rich first' in the specialised households engaging in business.

Naturally enough, party and state have wanted to manage the adverse implications of the commercialisation of the countryside because it threatens their hegemony but they have had to do so in a situation in which that very commercialisation has altered the power relations between state and locality, party and peasantry. During the commune period the peasants were bound to the collective for their livelihoods. Political and economic power were fused; politics was authoritarian and top-down; and peasant interests were subordinated. State-inspired economic change has reduced the power of the party at the local level at the same time as it has reduced the capacity of the central state to control and direct events from Beijing. Many economic decisions that had been the preserve of the collective came to be located in the hands of peasants operating in the market.

In 1982, the state recognised this emerging rural reality and hurried it along, stripping the communes and brigades of their economic powers and concentrating political and administrative power in new township governments and villagers' committees. A range of economic decisions was separated out from politics in order to encourage rural enterprise even though this cost party and state their capacity to exert as much control over the rural economy.

Not surprisingly, there was initial local leadership opposition to rural reforms, partly because of ideological objections to reforms that looked anything but socialist, but also because the new system threatened to destroy the bases of their power. For example, power to direct production and divide up the harvest was now given over to peasants and so production team leaders were left without a role. They were forced to leave the historical stage – or find a new power base for themselves outside agriculture in the emerging rural enterprise sector. Many leaders under the old system have learned to work the new system to their advantage. It is difficult for the state to secure effective rural leadership when it is now possible for potential officials to engage in more rewarding entrepreneurial activities.

Party and state were delighted to see rural economic growth but they were less happy to lose officials and to lose control of the countryside. By the mid-1980s there was concern about the breakdown of party institutions and party life consequent upon the loss of monopolistic economic control; and anxiety that village political institutions were in disarray after the dismantling of the old production brigades. It was also apparent that increasing numbers of peasants, now less dependent on collective provision, were coming to see grassroots party leaders as unnecessary and even parasitic. Party and state were concerned to stabilise the countryside; to streamline rural administration; to secure the services of younger, better educated, leaders; and somehow to train peasants in civic spirit. There was no consensus on how to secure these ends.

Traditional leftists advocated an ideological approach based on a socialist education campaign to eliminate 'bourgeois tendencies', mobilise the masses, and strengthen the party at the grass roots. More modern and pragmatic reformers viewed these methods as no longer workable in the changing countryside and so they pressed for

> developing autonomous organs of decision-making within the village, making village life more democratic by holding elections for village officials, creating mechanisms for holding cadres accountable to villagers, and encouraging greater peasant participation in decision-making processes within the village (White 1992: p. 2).

In requiring peasants to elect their own village officials and

> by making local cadres more responsive to local opinion, central authorities hoped to undermine opposition to their new agricultural policies. Officials linked the right of peasants to elect their own leaders with the introduction of the responsibility system in agriculture

and they also hoped that 'elections would stabilise village leadership groups' (Burns 1988: pp. 89–90).

Villagers' committees

Over the period 1982–87 some villagers' committees were established spontaneously in response to the need for local government. However, the passing of the Organic Law of Villagers' Committees in 1987 gave a major fillip to rural political reform. In the first two years after the Law came into force pilot projects were launched in selected villages in 1093 counties in fourteen provinces and in 1990 policy-makers decided to establish 'demonstration villages' that would introduce the new system and provide models for others to emulate. By mid-1992, eighteen provincial people's congresses had enacted implementing regulations and 80 per cent of China's villages had completed at least two rounds of elections. It is true that 'villagers' committees lie dormant in many villages and are dominated by township governments or party branches in many others', but O'Brien (1990: pp. 1,9) recognises that 'early accounts report discernible progress popularising the reforms, especially in relatively well-off areas with a history of good leadership' where notions of representative and responsible government were beginning to bite, with unpopular leaders removed from office and the township appointment of village leaders resisted.

Decentralisation and villagers' committee autonomy

China has a unitary system of government. There is no clear division of responsibilities between various levels of government from provinces down through counties and cities to districts, townships and villages but, in practice, levels do tend to have different responsibilities. The central government has primary responsibility for capital spending and defence, while local governments undertake most of the current civilian expenditure and subsidies.

The Chinese budget is consolidated and includes the budgets of all administrative levels. The budgetary process remained quite centralised throughout the Maoist period but after 1980 fiscal reforms reassigned to local governments most of the surplus generated by local industry. Virtually all taxes have been assessed and collected by local governments before being 'shared upward' on the basis of a negotiated contract between each province and the centre. Consequently, provinces have been able to bargain down the centre, retain more revenue, and enhance their own autonomy. This autonomy has been reinforced consequent upon the ability of local governments to raise increasing amounts of extra-budgetary funds outside the framework of central controls. The budgetary system is now in the process of a major overhaul. One of the major goals is to readjust the proportion of national revenue allocated to the central fiscal authorities to the 60 per cent level of the early 1980s.

The official position with respect to village autonomy is somewhat confused. Villagers' committees are outside the state system and are classified as 'non-governmental institutions'. On the one hand, they are defined as 'the primary mass organisation of self-government, in which villagers educate themselves and manage their own affairs'. On the other hand, they are supposed to assist township governments. The township is able to 'give guidance, support and help to the villagers' committees'; and 'the villagers' committee must stand for the leadership of the Party' (Organic Law, Articles 3,2, Fujian briefing, 1992). The matter has not been resolved one way or another and there is much nuancing with respect to the distinction between 'leadership' and 'guidance'. Those asserting the power of township and party emphasise leadership, whilst those making the case for village autonomy argue that a weaker guidance relationship is the new order of the day.

Given perceptions of China as a totalitarian polity it is inevitable that Western comment has tended to dwell on the extent to which villagers' committees do not enjoy real autonomy from either the township or the local party branch. Potter and Potter (1990: pp. 280, 271), on the basis of fieldwork in Zengbu village in Guangdong province near Hong Kong, note that although villagers' committees 'have some autonomy in managing their village's affairs ... [t]hey are still under the authority of the Zengbu xiang Party Committee and the *xiang* government, which ensure that they follow general party policy'; they further note that candidates for the villagers' committees 'had to be chosen from a slate approved by the party'; and so they conclude that 'all general policies of import to the countryside are made by members of higher party levels, or the centre, and then transmitted to the local levels of the society, to be implemented by the rural cadres'. In Chen village, also near to Hong Kong, Chan, Madsen and Unger (1992: p. 318) report that 'ostensibly there were village-wide elections to select the committee, but there were no nominations and the slate of five members was determined beforehand; only those five stood. Afterwards, the five formally decided among themselves how to divide up the posts, similarly to the procedure of previous decades.' And, writing more generally, Kelliher (1991: p. 333) argues that 'China's shift toward privatisation leaves much of the former relationship between state and countryside intact ... Villagers' committees enforce state policies on family planning, health, and education.'

This nothing-has-really-changed picture of village politics is reinforced if one looks at, firstly, the overlap between the village party branch and the membership of the new villagers' committees and, secondly, the extent of township control. There is a superficial cogency to these assertions, but they are open to challenge.

'Overlap' does not prove the simple 'party in control' thesis since in a situation in which one party has dominated politics it would be surprising if most potential villagers' committee members were not also members of that party. Moreover, in Fujian, Ministry of Civil

Affairs figures show that (only) 68 per cent of villagers' committee directors elected in 1991 were party members and nationally it has been estimated that (only) about 75 per cent of the members of villagers' committees are party members. Just how these figures are interpreted depends on the expectations brought to them, but given that the party once monopolised all leading village positions they could be seen as embodying a loosening of party control. What, then, of township constraints on village autonomy?

The notion of village autonomy is troublesome to many county and township leaders who fear they will 'lose their legs' if they cannot rely on villagers to carry out their orders in the same way that production brigades followed commune instructions in the past. Meanwhile, village leaders continue to be caught between township above and peasantry below, but in a situation where the balance of influence has tilted towards the peasantry and where the forces of localism have been strengthened. Not surprisingly, village leaders are reluctant to implement unpopular directives, a reluctance reinforced by the fact that they are not part of the state apparatus but local people with local connections, reliant on local revenue for their incomes.

Focusing on China it is easy to forget that all ambitious central states seek to restrict the autonomy of their local governments. In all cases, however, the reach of central states is limited; all local governments attempt to avoid central control; and it is always difficult to establish what constitutes evidence of 'real' local autonomy. Having said that, however, if villagers' committees are not entirely dependent on other levels of government for their revenue then they are more likely to be able to go their own way, and also, diversity with respect to villagers' committee performance in terms of taxing and spending can be construed as evidence suggestive of autonomy.

Villagers' committees depend heavily on extra-budgetary revenues from village and private enterprises, revenues that they are increasingly free to keep for their own uses. In economically advanced Fujian province in south-east China, one villagers' committee operating in a favourable market situation in a 'special economic zone' and with a number of collective and contracted private enterprises under its wing was able to raise an amount equivalent to 44 per cent of total *per capita* village income for public expenditure. On the other hand, a poor and remote rural village in the same province was less able to develop rural enterprise, and was heavily dependent on agricultural production, so the villagers' committee could only raise an amount equivalent to 3 per cent of total *per capita* income. Agricultural villages have no choice but to raise the bulk of village revenue through either a *per capita* tax; a tax on the amount of land occupied (with those unable to pay donating up to twenty days of labour to collective endeavours); or user-charges for services provided. In contrast, industrially developed villages need to impose neither direct taxation on the peasantry nor user-charges, because villagers' committees are able to secure substantial income direct from rural enterprises.

In Fujian, diversity with respect to the amount and sources of villagers' committee income was matched by diversity with respect to patterns of villagers' committee expenditure. Certain poor villagers' committees chose to spend the bulk of their meagre public income on limited social service and welfare provision, whereas richer committees were geared to the expenditure of large sums of public monies on roads and bridgebuilding, running water and electricity, and other items that help to facilitate the economic and industrial development of the village.

Diversity does not prove autonomy but it is suggestive. Moreover, although the privatisation of agricultural production has robbed the commune and the team of power over agricultural production, the data from Fujian and elsewhere indicate that villagers' committees are an important focus for collective activity even though the functions of village government have changed in China's new, market-oriented, environment.

Villagers' committee functions

The Organic Law gives villagers' committees responsibility to 'manage the public affairs and public welfare services of the village, mediate disputes among the villagers, [and] help [to] maintain public order'; to 'support and organise the villagers in cooperative economic undertakings'; to 'administer affairs concerning the land and other property owned collectively by the villagers'; and to draw up 'rules and regulations for a village' covering all aspects of village life (Organic Law, Articles 2,3,16).

Privatising agricultural production has not so much eliminated the role of village government as refocused it. Villagers' committees still wrestle with state directives and targets, mediate disputes, maintain public order and provide welfare services, but economic reform has meant that these committees have come to involve themselves in a range of new and demanding economic tasks.

Villagers' committees act as general contractors. Some villagers' committees have set up land-contracting companies to take over farmland returned to the collective by peasants who do not wish to cultivate it, contracting it out to third party 'expert cultivators'. Many committees have also been involved in allocating what were once collectively-run enterprises to individuals, and in these cases the committees have had to decide the terms and conditions of the contract and the extent to which the public purse should gain from the provision of an opportunity for private profit.

Where a villagers' committee decides not to contract out the running of collective enterprises, then it will have a more direct responsibility for organising production. That responsibility may be discharged by a subcommittee or some kind of 'economic development corporation' which could itself be largely composed of members of the villagers' committee or it may be given more directly to enterprise managers who are likely to be paid by results.

The increasing importance of factory jobs and the absence of a truly open labour market means that villagers' committees play a major role in allocating jobs in the collective and state sectors at the same time as they are able to exert 'influence' with respect to jobs in the developing private sector.

The village is also responsible for distribution – most importantly, agricultural inputs such as fertiliser and diesel fuel, but leaders also have influence over access to draft animals and tractors. Connections (*guanxi*) are important in securing all these things.

In a situation in which the market has been opened up to peasants who have had little or no experience of market relations, who are anxious about uncertainty and who lack basic information, local leaders and villagers' committees act as brokers, middlemen, and general 'fixers' of some power and importance.

Villagers' committees are able, and increasingly willing, to incur expenditure on capital projects that they hope will foster the economic and industrial development of their village. Villagers' committees that are able to develop the village economy are able to add to their own power and capacity.

Of course, not all villagers' committees are engaged in performing all the above functions or with the same degree of intensity, since power and capacity are critically dependent on the extent to which a committee is able to raise revenue. Villages that are wholly dependent on agriculture can only tax the peasantry and extract modest user-charges for services provided, but villages close to markets are able to run successful collective enterprises and at the same time raise revenue from those enterprises contracted out to specialised households. And when those villages are situated in 'special economic zones' they are well-placed to set up joint enterprises with foreign capital in order to provide still more money for committee coffers and well-paid jobs for villagers.

Problems and prospects for village self-government

Arguments about the power of party and state have tended to encourage a perspective on village politics that is insensitive to the possibility of autonomy and democracy. These arguments are not unimportant but they tend to ignore the burgeoning forces of localism; the realities of rural economic change; and the implications of these changes for village politics as new classes and old identities challenge for supremacy. Official enthusiasm for rural entrepreneurship may have nurtured a new type of person for party and state to promote as village leaders but in a context in which today's villagers are enabled to have a say through elections even though their choice may be restricted as local bosses make a comeback.

The commercialisation of the countryside, whilst giving a little to those with 'small peasant mentalities', has given a lot to those with entrepreneurial skills and contacts. In a situation in which those with skills and contacts are likely to have had leadership positions in the party, it is not surprising to find that a large percentage of those who have prospered are themselves leaders or former leaders. There is some evidence of villagers' committees seeking to restrain rural entrepreneurs and regulations of the Fujian Provincial People's Government require that village leaders 'don't contract for the village-run enterprise'. But for all the good intent, the benefits that village leaders and entrepreneurs can secure from working together suggest that we are likely to see leader–entrepreneur alliances effecting an informal fusion of political and economic power. In effect, village democratic institutions tend to be 'captured' by the rural rich so that rural community power structures are geared to using villagers' committees to advance élite interests. Villagers' committees have complex and often conflicting roles and responsibilities. They provide public and social services but they are also property holders and profit-oriented economic entities. They have an interest in favouring those groups that can best quench their thirst for revenue. So they may be reluctant to act as good employers or assume a regulatory role with respect to those enterprises that are polluting or failing to observe safety standards if that cuts into their own prospects for revenue.

It is just possible that democratic politics could come to act as a check on leader–entrepreneur alliances and on rampant corruption. The halting development of civil society (see Chapter 6); the emergence of distinct social and economic interests; and the need for a more 'open' politics to promote economic growth and change, could all serve to facilitate a truly viable and competitive electoral politics within a village. Members of villagers' committees would then come to be held to popular account, not just through the vehicle of three-yearly elections for office, but through the gradual development of a more democratic and participatory culture centring on the importance of citizenship and popular control. We should not forget that ordinary peasants, unlike their urban counterparts working through weaker Residents' Committees, have become property-holders and taxpayers with a real stake in the way that village government is conducted – and in whose interest.

It is hard to predict how villagers will use their right to vote or how far they will be truly 'free' to use their vote if leader–entrepreneur alliances hold sway. The Organic Law has created many possibilities and expectations, even though in practice poor villages may lack the capacity to do much at all. Moreover, if poor villagers' committees are pressured by the democratic process to seek more resources then they may engage in 'fiscal predation'; they may (over)tax enterprises in order to provide popular public services even though this would hit at the growth prospects of those enterprises so that the whole village economy stagnates further (Byrd and Lin 1990: p. 341).

Party and state have been keen to see rural economic development and they have accepted that this needs to be managed through a new kind of local politics that is somewhat beyond their control. Although the governing élite has long been hostile to anything akin to Western-style democracy, it is probable that the development of community power structures dominated by rural entrepreneurs is not viewed with much alarm. However, if these local power structures – still more a viable village democracy – come to work against central intent then party and state might well want to reassert their power over village affairs. But in having opted for a particular model of economic development they have opened up a local political dynamic that they cannot easily control or reverse. It would be hard to put the genie of 'localism' and democracy back into the bottle – the more so given the exhaustion of the Chinese party-state, its crumbling legitimacy, and the problem in reaching down to the countryside.

Note

1. My understanding of village politics has been facilitated as a result of research in three county towns and eight Fujian villages in July 1992, and attendance at a conference convened by the Ministry of Civil Affairs that brought together Chinese officials and foreign scholars with an interest in the implementation of the Organic Law of Villagers' Committees. I should like to thank the Ministry and the Ford Foundation for enabling me to take part in this research, and I acknowledge the help I received from Wang Zhenyao, Bai Guangzhao, Jonathan Hecht, Tyrene White, and Kevin O'Brien.

11

New Economic Élites[1]

David S. G. Goodman

'Prosperity and a magnanimous spirit walk hand in hand'

During the first few months of 1993 the considerable speculation in the Chinese press on the number of millionaires to be found in China drew attention not only to the extent of economic change but also to the emergence of new economic élites. The rapid growth of China's economy during the 1980s – and an average rate in excess of approximately 9 per cent per annum – has created new categories of those who either control or own substantial wealth and thereby have the ability significantly to affect the lives of others. Given the pace of economic modernisation the emergence of new economic élites is probably only to be expected, and has significant potential consequences, particularly for China's social and political system.

By world standards a million dollars in Chinese yuan may not seem very much money, except when we notice that GNP per capita in 1991 remained under 1800 yuan. In any case, there would appear to be a substantial number of US dollar millionaires.

The most publicised of these new economic élites are often originally small-scale private-sector owner-operators whose businesses have expanded rapidly. However, they also include entrepreneurial financiers and managers in the state and collective sectors; as well as managers and developers of rural and suburban enterprises, and enterprises derived from local government activities and 'all-people's' enterprises.

To regard China's economic development since 1978 and the start of the reform programme as modernisation is accurate but misleading. The economy had also achieved a high growth rate from 1952 to 1978 – an average of 6 per cent per annum – despite year-on-year fluctuations, some of which (such as the worst excesses of the Great Leap Forward) were severe. Well before 1978 China had already achieved some of the milestones usually associated with the process of modernisation: the creation of a modernising state system and bureaucracy, a higher percentage of GNP derived from industrial rather than agricultural production, and the growth of a substantial service sector of the economy.

In fact, for China's economy in the late 1970s the major problems were not those associated with low levels of growth, but the inefficiencies of a Soviet-style economy, albeit one adapted to China's conditions. A wholesale economic restructuring was required to redistribute resources into more productive channels with greater potential for long-term sustained economic growth, and particularly to transfer resources from heavy to consumer industrial production.

The distinction between modernisation and economic restructuring is important in understanding the genesis, location and aspirations of the new economic élites of the 1990s. A modernising élite based on state bureaucrats, managers of state enterprises and technocrats already existed in China before 1978. The new economic élites, however, are inherently more entrepreneurial: specifically those able to take advantage of the changed policies of the reform era. These include the introduction of market economics into an economy that was previously command-oriented; the changing role of the state from direct economic management to indirect market supervision; and the opening of the domestic economy not only to international trade but also to foreign investment.

Interestingly, the new economic élites have concentrated on the search for wealth and status rather than political power, not least because of the entrenched political position of the established economic élites. This is not to suggest that there is a clear differentiation between political and economic élites. Some of the post-1978 new economic élites have been drawn from the ranks of the pre-1978 economic élites, and in any case the continuing power relations have required the new economic élites to compromise, and often placed them in supplicant as well as subordinate positions. Almost without exception, the successful new economic élites require good and close relations with the party-state system. Nonetheless, so far few of the new economic élites appear to have become centrally involved in politics or to regard the pursuit of political power as a suitable goal.

Necessarily, given the complex processes of economic growth and development, the new economic élites of the 1990s do not form a cohesive group. Unfortunately, official statistics and categorisations of social stratification, enterprise structure and ownership systems do not aid understanding. The categories used in official statistics were inherited from the Soviet Union and their meaning has become extremely attenuated. Thus, although all enterprises are regarded as being exclusively in one of the state, collective, private, or foreign-invested sectors such distinctions are no longer readily maintained. Almost all successful private entrepreneurs own businesses officially registered as a form of collective enterprise. Managers of state-sector enterprises have established subsidiary collective-sector companies. Nonetheless, it is possible to identify several different broad categories of the new economic élites according to the bases of their wealth and influence, and the nature of their activities.

Owner-operators

The most visible of the new economic élites are the owner-operators, private entrepreneurs who have developed their own businesses. These owner-operators have been a new and key feature of the reform era. Originally they were regarded by the Chinese Communist Party [CCP] as small-scale entrepreneurs who could be mobilised to meet demands not easily met by the planned economy. Thus, the retail sector rapidly came to be dominated by owner-operators. As the state withdrew from direct economic management of enterprises and market reforms were introduced, owner-operators developed larger enterprises in a wider range of activities, notably light industry. Similarly, whereas the first owner-operators had been regarded as having 'unsatisfactory political backgrounds', and thus had other channels of advance blocked to them, economic expansion and the changed political environment of the 1990s meant that owner-operators have since been drawn from a wide range of society.

One reason for the high profile of owner-operators is their conspicuous wealth. In a society where in the recent past any consumption was regarded as conspicuous and where with few exceptions private entrepreneurship was discouraged, its sudden re-emergence is likely to be equated in the popular mind with untold wealth. However, it is clear that not all owner-operators' businesses can become large-scale, nor all owner-operators necessarily wealthy. The vast majority are business people on a very small scale. They are street traders, hairdressers, or shop-owners; they run local repair shops or small eating-places, and often earn less than they did before striking out on their own. One reason for becoming or staying an owner-operator is often the non-economic reason of wanting to work for oneself.

The fabulously wealthy among owner-operators are the exception, but they exist throughout China. At 1993 prices it would seem that in East China a steady annual income of about 20 000 yuan, and personal assets of roughly 250 000 yuan is regarded as 'comfortably well-off', though necessarily there are likely to be regional variations. Yet there is a wide range of wealth. There are those with annual incomes of 10 million yuan and assets in excess of 100 million yuan. One such is Chen Jinyi, an industrialist and property developer in the Shanghai–Hangzhou region, who emerged spectacularly into the public limelight with his 'fire-sale' purchase of six bankrupt state-sector factories in Shanghai in October 1992. Chen, who was only born in 1960, started off by raising bees and making honey, managing to save about 10 000 yuan in three years, and diversifying into textiles, and later soft drinks. He now heads a large corporation employing 2000 people. This has been entirely developed from his personal assets but, he is now considering going public on the Shanghai Exchange.

A more typical example of the owner-operator among the new economic élites is You Lianshan. You was born in the 1940s and had been politically and socially handicapped as a child because his father, who had long since died, was said to have been a member of the Nationalist Party. Under such a burden You and his family remained in poverty until the late 1970s. With the advent of the reform era You started raising quails for the local restaurant market and by the mid-1980s had amassed a working capital of some 20 000 yuan which he then invested in the development of a workshop producing a simple food-mixer and employing a handful of people. The enterprise was so successful that You was soon looking for additional space and labour to develop new product lines.

Until this time, You's company had been registered formally as a private enterprise but, for both political and economic reasons, if he wanted to continue to expand it was necessary to become part of the official collective sector. The political reasons were a form of insurance policy against any future change of heart by the CCP. In addition, the tax environment for the collective sector is better than that for private sector enterprises, and land and labour can be provided in cooperation with local government. You therefore turned his company into a collective and in the process appeared to have surrendered his personal assets, though paradoxically both he and the local authorities still regarded it as 'his' company. For a number of years, in the absence of any regulative framework, You formally only received a salary as manager, though in effect he had access to all the collective's assets. This unsatisfactory state of affairs was clarified with the establishment of a limited-liability share-based company in which You is not only the manager and chief executive, but also the major shareholder.

Suburban executives

The development of rural (or town and village) industry has been only slightly less publicised than the private sector. However, as one would expect, most of this rural industrial development has been a function of urban development, located in the suburbs in what are only technically regarded as rural areas. Some 84 per cent of the industrial output by value (GNP) of 'rural' industry is based in these areas, specifically the rural districts of administratively higher-order cities and urban areas.

The explanation for this phenomenon is the formality of the PRC's policy on urban and rural designations. The boundaries between rural and urban areas were fixed in the 1950s, as were different regulatory regimes for housing, work and economic management. Suburban villages had always benefited from the availability of both technical inputs to their production and urban markets for their output. They were consequently well-placed to take advantage of decollectivisation and economic reforms in the early 1980s that were first implemented in rural areas. This comparative advantage was further increased when economic reforms were extended to urban areas after October 1984. In many cases, after a decade of economic growth, the physical difference between rural and urban areas is indistinguishable, but there remain significant differences in land usage and the regulation of economic management on either side of the road.

The economic wealth of these suburban villages is not personal but is wielded collectively on behalf of villages and townships by executives who form an important part of the new economic élite. Though the personal wealth of these new suburban executives is not negligible – they will earn roughly 20 000 yuan a year in salaries and bonuses or contract earnings – their real importance is the economic wealth they control. Village enterprises often expand and develop subsidiaries in a largely unregulated way, so that they come to act as conglomerates owned nominally by the village. It is interesting that these new suburban executives, and the new conglomerates they preside over, have for the most part emerged from the previously collectivised economy. The former agricultural-machinery-repair workshops have been transformed into light industrial enterprises; village construction departments have moved into property development, and the hotel and hospitality industries; and local marketing and supply cooperatives have taken advantage of market reforms and become more specialised as well as more efficient.

For the most part, those who were the village-level cadres and administrators of the former activities have become the managers and executives of the new enterprises. A case in point is Li Hongfu, born in 1950 in a suburban village to the north of Hangzhou. Although his education was interrupted by the Cultural Revolution he was able to teach himself accounting practices and business management during the 1970s, and by 1980 had become an official in a commercial department of the rural district government. Seeing Hangzhou's potential for tourism during the early 1980s he suggested that the village should build a hotel on unproductive land which it had been forced to acquire several years before, and which lay inside Hangzhou's urban district boundaries. Local government was eventually persuaded and Li was placed in charge of the hotel development with an initial capital of 1.5 million yuan. The project was so successful that the village has now used the profits and developed a further two hotels under his leadership.

Another instance is Yang Jianhua, who is in his mid-fifties and looks and talks like a CCP cadre but has never been a party member. He runs a suburban village conglomerate of six different factories, with a range of product lines including stationery, wire goods and plastic moulding, with fixed assets in excess of 21 million yuan, all of which, under his guidance, grew out of one commune's production brigade machinery repair workshop. Although a native of the suburban village where he now lives, Yang left home in the early 1950s when he joined the People's Liberation Army and was posted to north-west China. On demobilisation he entered university to study mechanical engineering, but ran into the political uncertainties caused by the 'Hundred Flowers Movement' of 1957 and the Great Leap Forward, and found himself back in north-west China. At the start of the Cultural Revolution, he volunteered to 'go down to the countryside' so that he could be posted back to his native village, where he proceeded to work as a tractor and machinery repairer until the mid-1970s. At that time he persuaded the village to let him turn the workshop into a factory, but received little support until the early 1980s. For local decision-makers the key economic factor that led them to support Yang was the promise of foreign markets and investment. Despite a total lack of foreign experience Yang negotiated contracts in both Japan and Hong Kong, and has used his contacts to expand the village's industrial operation.

State capitalists and model managers

Managers of state and collective sector enterprises cannot be considered part of the new economic élites, particularly where their specific enterprises existed before the start of the reform era. However, some have taken advantage of the market reforms to alter their own enterprise structure radically, or to become distinguished formally as 'model managers'. In the state sector, and even in nationally prestigious heavy industrial concerns, some managers have transformed themselves into a kind of 'state capitalist' by decentralising their corporations and establishing conglomerates. Managers of 'all-people's' enterprises – owned in principle by the state – and those in the collective sector, have frequently been awarded 'model' status for the achievement of financial independence.

As with the suburban executives, personal wealth is less important than the control of economic wealth. The new breed of state capitalist, like their predecessors in the state sector, is ultimately responsible for considerable investments of state capital and the employment of large numbers of people. Model managers are also influential in that they are held up for emulation by the party-state system.

The director of a chemical processing plant in north China is a good example of the new kind of state-sector managerial capitalist. In his early fifties and educated in chemical engineering at Qinghua University in Beijing, where he joined the CCP, he served in Shenyang and Wuhan before joining his current company as deputy director in the early 1980s. He was part of the management team that helped to reorganise the company so that each section and workshop became a separate economic entity producing for the wider market as well as for the parent company. Thus, the transport pool established a trucking company; the glass products workshop became a company producing glass receptacles for other industrial concerns, and has been so successful it is no longer organisationally related to its parent plant. As in the private and collective sectors of the economy, the state sector is bedevilled by questions of ownership.

Zong Qinhou, the General Manager of the Wahaha Corporation, is an excellent example of a model manager. The Wahaha Corporation originated as an 'all-people's' enterprise, an economic enterprise attached to a primary school in Hangzhou. Such enterprises had been created during the Cultural Revolution, and in this case the primary school had established a factory making paper and stationery. Zong, who was born in 1945, was originally a teacher and succeeded to his mother's teaching post at Youdian Road Primary School when she retired in 1978. In the mid-1980s three of the staff came together under Zong's leadership to see if they might not develop a more profitable enterprise. Wahaha, which is a soft drink specifically targeted at children was the result. (Wahaha was somebody's brother's childhood nickname and like the shape of the bottle and much else besides about the exercise was deliberately chosen as a marketing ploy after considerable research.) From an initial capital of 140 000 yuan the original company has now become a conglomerate with several associated companies whose total assets are worth more than 400 million yuan, employing several thousand workers, and now about to become a traded enterprise on the Shanghai Exchange. Having conquered the domestic market, where its advertisements are as familiar as the drink is popular with children, Wahaha is now turning its attention to Taiwan and the Chinese communities of South-east Asia. For his efforts with Wahaha, Zong has been designated a 'model worker'. Though his managerial salary is only 400 yuan a month he earns considerably more in bonuses, from the contract negotiated with the Hangzhou Department of Education who are nominally responsible for Wahaha, and also from the state for being a model worker.

Wheelers and dealers

Economic development during the 1980s and into the 1990s has occurred with a weak if not non-existent financial infrastructure. The need for credit facilities, the provision of ready investment, and the facilitation of both has created considerable space for middlemen and brokers. It has also meant that individuals with relatively liquid funds of their own or with access to such funds have been much in demand as potential investors. Both middlemen and investors are an essential part of the new economic environment, and in some cases considerable personal wealth has been amassed.

One problem in analysing such activities is that they exist on the boundaries of the permissible and the questionable. Certainly not all such behaviour can be described as either illegal or impermissible. The legal framework is ambiguous, as with the division of the economy into state, collective, private and foreign-invested sectors; and there is a general imperative for unused or under-utilised resources to be used efficiently and productively. At the same time, it is certain that specific aspects of the current economic system may be exploited for all they are worth. Particularly where cadres become entrepreneurial both within and outside public service, there is not only cause for concern but also the possibility of judging cadre behaviour as either criminal or unacceptable when it may be neither.

The most obvious examples of the middlemen role are found in the share-trading houses that have been established in the wake of the fast-growing open stock exchanges of Shanghai and Shenzhen. Most cities now have fairly large trading houses in their central business districts. Each carries share listings and other indicators in its window and during trading hours a large crowd will gather. However, the major trading, especially in the money markets, all takes place well off the streets and out of public sight.

The less-obvious wheelers and dealers are to be found in the private deals that depend on personalist ties and access to the party-state system. A particularly illustrative example concerns a one-time academic who by 1993 had managed to build a personal wealth of more than 6 million yuan and was about to develop a major entertainment centre. The academic was originally a teacher of foreign languages who had savings of about 20 000 yuan from translation fees by the mid-1980s. Looking for an investment, his wife put him in touch with the Director of the Personal Department of the state sector enterprise in which she worked. Together with another cadre who had contacts in the local food supply system they went into business and established a restaurant, supported by a number of other investors. The contribution of the Director of the Personal Department was that he put the new business in touch with the local retired cadres' association. In return for a fixed annual payment to the retired cadres' association – a fee fixed by a contract for three years at a time – the restaurant operated as a tax-exempt charity in the name of the association. At the same time costs were further reduced because the restaurant was located in a previously unused area of a public building, with only a relatively low rent being paid to the municipality. Immediately the area had been converted to restaurant usage the investors were offered five times their original investment for the business even before trading had started. By 1992 the restaurant was clearing 1.2 million yuan a year and the academic, building on his contacts, had been able to diversify his interests. He is now engaged in various enterprises including foreign joint ventures with partners from Taiwan and Hong Kong.

Trendsetters

A final grouping in the new economic élites has influence rather than access to absolute wealth, though most are also by no means poor. They are the trendsetters that others follow. Because of their intense concentration on the search for wealth and status the new economic élites are very fashion-conscious – meaning more than just clothes and personal appearance. Though they undoubtedly set the trends for the new middle classes, the patterns of conformity for the new economic élites are to be found in the newly emergent 'star culture' created around sports stars, pop music idols, and television personalities; the activities of the 'princelings' (the children and grandchildren of high-ranking cadres); and at the more local level, the world of the private restaurateur.

Some of the conformities which have emerged are universal functions of economic growth and copy new rich behaviour elsewhere. One of the first investments made as personal wealth increases is to buy a house. Cars, and especially the most obvious luxury cars, also have an immediate appeal, though in most cases they are technically bought by the enterprise rather than the individual. Both Rolls-Royce and Cadillac did excellent business in China during 1992 and 1993 (Xiao Xie, 1993). China's new economic élites also attempt to provide their children with a good education.

Some of the trends set by and for the new economic élites are more specific to the time and place. The most obvious example is the mobile phone, costing about 30 000 yuan to buy and the same amount again to run for a year, which has become a potent status symbol, and is carried accordingly. With the increase in mobile phone provision – there were scheduled to be 200 000 in Guangdong alone by the end of 1993 – mobile phone numbers thought to bring good fortune have become all the rage and are auctioned by the telecommunications authorities for prices up to 150 000 yuan.

Interestingly, a key role in trendsetting appears to be played by the new private restaurants and their proprietors. These restaurants play a public role in the dissemination of information and the conduct of business. Every city now seems to have a handful of extremely successful restaurants in this category. Their proprietors recognise the importance of their clientele and of catering to their demands, not least by establishing a fresh style every year. In Hangzhou during 1992 a hint of foreign décor was deemed necessary for the best of the new private restaurants, though all served basically the same kinds of local dishes. In 1993 the fashion was for small dining rooms modelled on English country houses of the eighteenth century, with palladium arches, statues of Graeco-Roman gods, oil-paintings of the master and mistress of the house, and appropriate table settings. In the process the new-style restaurateurs themselves become relatively wealthy and trendsetters.

An arch-exponent of the English country house style in Hangzhou is Zhang Weishuo. Zhang's previous experience was as a salesperson for a state-run agricultural product company. He started the restaurant with an original investment of half a million yuan, all of which was borrowed. Though the restaurant employs over fifty people it only has seven tables and can only cater for a hundred people when full. Zhang markets exclusivity, and it seems to work. The restaurant is usually fully booked three weeks in advance, with reservations from government and party institutions, state and collective sector enterprises, as well as private business-people. The restaurant provides Zhang with an annual profit of a million yuan, and in 1992 he established a trading company as an additional and separate interest.

Consequences

The emergence of new and variegated economic élites remains a relatively recent phenomenon in the PRC. Though the processes described here had started during the 1980s, and particularly after the introduction of policies of economic reform to the urban areas after October 1984, their full social and economic impact did not begin to be felt until the early 1990s. At the time of the popular demonstrations in Beijing during the spring of 1989 for instance these new economic élites were not for the most part regarded as emerging social or political forces of any particular note.

This observation is important not simply because it draws attention to the rapid pace of change in China but also because an important paradigm for understanding the relationship between social and political change strongly suggests that the emergence of the new economic élites currently being observed in China usually leads to political demands, at least for representation. However, to date the new economic élites have not articulated political demands, preferring instead to concentrate almost exclusively on the search for wealth and status.

This situation may change but at present the explanation would seem to rest with the sustained and continued influence of the party-state system, to which all sections of the new economic élites accommodate in different ways. Many of the new economic élites – the state capitalists, model managers, suburban executives, and substantial sections of the wheelers and dealers and trendsetters – are essentially already part of the party-state system, and concentrate instead on wealth creation. Those who are not, see their relative independence as an advantage in the search for wealth and status and they prefer to cultivate an ambiguous relationship with the party-state. There is often even an avowed reluctance to join the CCP, even though it is recognised as the most important social network of power, and when membership is sought or accepted it is frequently for instrumental reasons. The relationship between the new economic élites and the CCP presents the latter with one of the key dilemmas of the reform era. To maintain its leadership of and close relationship with the new economic élites, the CCP will need to adjust its policies and change its organisational structures and relationship with society. However, in that process it will also run the risk of jeopardising its own future as a ruling communist party.

Note

1. The information on China's new economic élites presented in this chapter is derived from research currently under way at the Asia Research Centre on Social, Political and Economic Change, Murdoch University, Western Australia. Longitudinal studies of some 1200 entrepreneurs in Hangzhou, Taiyuan and Foshan started in 1991 and is continuing.

    Unless otherwise indicated all statistics are official PRC statistics derived from the State Statistical Bureau's *Zhongguo tongji nianjian* and related publications.

    The yuan is the unit of currency, usually translated as a dollar.

12

Industry and the Urban Economy

Xiao-zhuang Zhou

'Going too far is as bad as not going far enough'

In the second half of 1988 the new Department of Industrial Policy of the State Planning Commission drafted 'the first systematic industrial policy of [PRC]'. In March 1989 the policy was promulgated in 'The Resolution of the State Council on Current Industrial Policy'. The policy promotes a range of industrial sectors crucial to China's sustained economic development and international competitiveness. They include the machinery and electronic industry, especially high-value-added machine and electronic products; high-technology industries, particularly space and aviation, new materials, and biological engineering industries; high-foreign-currency-earning export sectors; infrastructure, including transportation and telecommunications; and basic industries, such as energy, steel, and chemical industries. At the same time, a range of industrial sectors will be limited. These include those machine-building industries with low-end technology and those over-developed light and processing industries in textiles, plastics, watches, and some 'new' consumer industries like washing machines and vacuum cleaners (Zhang 1992: p. 21).

China's economic reforms, first in agriculture and then in industry and the whole urban economy, began in the late 1970s. A decade later much has changed. Whereas it had been a highly administered, planned economy with a predominant state sector, it now operates through the market with a pattern of diversified ownership. The state sector and the non-state sector compete with

145

but also complement each other, in the effort to achieve balanced economic development.

These structural changes have been accompanied by remarkable economic performances. Between 1979 and 1992, China's GNP grew at an average annual rate of 9.0 per cent, exports increased 16.7 per cent annually (*Statistical Yearbook of China*, hereafter 'SYC' 1993: p. 21). *Per capita* income for urban families was 316 yuan in 1978, and increased to 1826 yuan in 1992; the corresponding figures for rural families were 133.6 yuan and 784 yuan (SYC: p. 279). The household bank deposits to GNP ratio increased from 5.87 per cent in 1978 to 48 per cent in 1992 (SYC: p. 18, p. 285). Also in the same period, inflation was kept within a single-digit range except for three years (11.9 per cent in 1985, 20.7 per cent in 1988 and 16.3 in 1989) (SYC: p. 237), and the government budget deficit accounted for about 2–3 per cent of GNP (Qian and Xu, forthcoming).

How did these tremendous changes in China's industrial and the urban economy come about? What distinguishes China's reform strategy from that of other socialist countries in Eastern Europe and the former Soviet Union? These are the questions this chapter will address.

An overview of China's industrial and urban economic reforms

The period 1949–79 was one of rapid industrialisation. This was based on the ability of a command economy to concentrate national resources in its priority sectors. Yet high industrial growth was being purchased at increasing investment costs. As these high investment costs were directly born by consumers, people's living standards stagnated in the 1960s and 1970s. The chaos of the Cultural Revolution further aggravated the situation.

After the end of the Cultural Revolution in 1976, the Chinese Communist Party (CCP) leaders felt the need to catch up economically and to improve people's living standards. Chairman Hua Guofeng launched a 'Great Leap Outward' to promote high-speed industrial growth by developing China's oil reserves and exporting them in return for advanced technology. However, when the excessively optimistic estimates of oil reserves were revised downward in 1978, the plan collapsed.

Faced with these problems, the CCP leadership needed to formulate policy solutions. Some senior leaders, such as Chen Yun, preferred a reform strategy that would improve planning rather than replace it with market competition. In contrast, Deng Xiaoping favoured a more radical strategy that aimed at creating a socialist market economy. After Deng defeated Hua and became the pre-eminent leader in 1980, his opinion dominated the reform process. But Chen's more conservative reform strategy continued to attract substantial support and provide checks and balances throughout the reform decade.

First stage, 1978–84

Before the reforms, China's industrial enterprises were organised to generate revenue for the administration rather than to function as autonomous economic entities. Urban economic reform, therefore, has mainly targeted these industrial enterprises to give them financial incentives and operational autonomy so that they can respond efficiently to market demands.

Four major reform measures put into practice during the first stage are detailed below.

1. *The revival of the enterprise fund, and the profit-retention system*
The enterprise fund which had existed in 1953–57 and 1961–67 was reintroduced in 1978. State enterprises which met planning targets were allowed to create a fund equal to 5 per cent of their total wage bill to be distributed as collective welfare and individual bonuses.

At about the same time, there was an experimental profit-retention system in Sichuan province. Provincial officials realised that the requirement for state-owned enterprises to turn in all their profits to the state removed any incentive for efficient and profitable operation. In consequence in October 1978 the Sichuan officials selected six industrial firms to test a profit-retention system based on expanded enterprise autonomy. The experimental enterprises, after fulfilling their planned output quota, were allowed to sell and resource additional output on their own at flexible prices. These enterprises could retain 5 per cent of the planned profit, plus about 20 per cent of profits above the planned level.

The Sichuan experiment was welcomed in Beijing and immediately popularised nationwide. By the end of June 1980 the number of experimental enterprises had grown to more than 6600, producing 60 per cent of total national output value (*Records of Industrial Events of PRC* (hereafter *Events*) 1991: p. 22). This was the beginning of the legalisation of the market and the beginning of a two-track price system.

2. *Readjustment*

In early 1979, Chen Yun was put in charge of the newly established Finance and Economics Commission. Chen proposed to take three years to readjust the economy, shifting priority away from heavy industry towards light industry and agriculture. Chen's readjustment idea became formal policy in April 1979. By 1980 the growth rate for light industry was 18.9 per cent, and that of heavy industry only 1.9 per cent. As light industry grew so did consumption which increased profits per yuan of investment. In heavy industry, the reduction of output quotas combined with high profit targets forced enterprises to develop new products for farmers, light industries, and consumers.

3. *Profit-contracting and tax-for-profit*

At the end of 1981, the Chinese leaders believed that readjustment had balanced the economy and that the time had come for growth and further reform

Heavy industrial enterprises were demanding more autonomy and more profits. In response, central government allowed most enterprises to shift to a new profit-retention method called profit-contracting where each enterprise negotiated a 'base figure' of profits which it was required to deliver to the state, and retained a high proportion of all profits above this figure.

However, because the 'base figure' was negotiable, managers devoted more of their energies to bargaining for preferential base terms than to improving performance. As a result, the ratio of central state revenue to national income dropped from 37 per cent in 1978 to 25 per cent in 1982 (SYC 1993: p. 33, p. 230).

Faced with the decline in central revenues in 1982, the Ministry of Finance and the State Planning Commission considered substituting enterprise tax payments for profit remission (tax-for-profit). They believed that 'a uniform tax system with the force of law would move enterprises toward full responsibility for profits and losses' (Shirk 1993: 234), while guaranteeing a steady flow of central revenues. Tax-for-profit became official policy in February

1983. The transition from profit remission to tax payment was divided into two stages. First, only small enterprises would switch to paying the state through an eight-grade progressive income tax. Large and medium-sized profit-making enterprises would pay 50 per cent of their profits as income tax, and after-tax profits would be shared with the state according to an individually negotiated profit-sharing scheme. In the second stage, when prices had been adjusted, all financial obligations would be converted to tax payments. The first stage of the tax-for-profit reform proceeded smoothly in 1983. The Chinese leaders realised, however, that price reform was too complicated to be done in a short time. So they decided in mid-1984 to advance the second stage and proposed to levy tax on enterprises producing different products at different rates on each product to reduce the distorting effects of irrational prices and so use this stage as a substitute for price reform.

4. *The development of the non-state sector*

Before economic reform, state-owned enterprises predominated in both the industrial and the commerce/service sectors. Urban collective-owned industrial enterprises accounted for about 20 per cent of the total industrial output and employed workers. From 1978 to 1984 the non-state sector, including urban collectives, rural industries, urban/rural individual/household businesses, and joint ventures, expanded rapidly. This was not intended by the central government; it occurred mainly through local initiatives to alleviate unemployment.

The unemployment problem amongst urban youth was partly due to the return of 10 million young people who had been rusticated during the Cultural Revolution. In addition, there were about 3 million new school-leavers looking for employment every year.

In the countryside the household production responsibility system greatly raised productivity and released a large amount of surplus labour. As the urban areas could not absorb it, developing rural industry under the auspices of townships and villages became the natural way of providing new jobs.

Both urban collective industrial enterprises and rural industry concentrated on light industry, which needs less capital and relatively simple technology, with a short production cycle and high prices. Consequently, they became the engine of China's economic growth in 1980s, and posed serious competition to state enterprises.

Second stage, 1985–88

During late 1984 and the first half of 1985 the Chinese economy experienced severe overheating. Industry grew too fast, capital investment expanded drastically, wages skyrocketed, prices rose, and fuel and power were in short supply. In these circumstances, the major reform efforts in 1985–88 were the preparation of price reform, and the implementation of various contracted responsibility systems.

1. *Price reform*
Before economic reform, the prices of goods, both agricultural and industrial, were set by a central plan. Agricultural goods and raw materials were priced artificially low and manufactured products high, so that the state could extract revenues from industrial enterprises' profits to support a broad range of state activities and to reinvest in industrial development.

In 1986 some of Zhao Ziyang's economic advisers advocated a comprehensive reform based on price reform by first adjusting, and then freeing, all prices within a short period of time, while at the same time setting up a new government budgetary system and a new monetary system (joint adjustment of prices, taxes, and finance). They believed that only through this could a sound economic environment be established. However, the central treasury simply could not afford the necessary compensation and this programme was abandoned.

The emergence of a buyer's market played a significant role in the price reform of consumer goods. As the production of chronically scarce consumer goods increased dramatically, demands were met and then saturated. The prices of consumer goods that had been set artificially high in the central planning period declined accordingly.

2. *Contracted management responsibility systems*
Some economists believed that ownership was the key to reform. According to them, the overheating of China's economy in

1984–85, was due 'to the absence of a mechanism like private ownership or contracting to give the enterprise a sense of financial responsibility' (Shirk 1993: p. 297). Because full ownership reform, the privatisation of state enterprises, was politically infeasible, they advocated contracting as a way to separate ownership from management. From late 1986 various contracted management responsibility systems were introduced. State enterprises contracted with the state. The right to manage the means of production meant responsibility for both profits and losses. An enterprise's tax obligation was calculated according to the tax rule and then combined with a profit-sharing scheme. This contracted management responsibility system was popularised quickly, so by the end of 1987 75 per cent of all state-owned industrial enterprises were using it.

There was also an internal contract system to specify or sub-contract responsibilities, rights and benefits within enterprises. Under the manager-responsibility system, management was further separated from politics. The manager was granted the right to direct production, marketing, purchasing, investment, wage and bonus policies, worker training, the use of enterprise funds, and so on. Concurrently, the roles of the Party secretary were reduced to the area of 'party organisation' and 'ideological work'. The internal contract system tried to create more effective incentives. It divided the enterprise's contract with the state (profit targets, cost reduction, or output targets, and so on) into separate targets for each division or workshop, and these divisions and workshops were responsible for the fulfilment of their targets and were rewarded accordingly.

Third stage, 1989–93

This period is characterised by rectification and readjustment. The urban economy experienced the most serious inflation in the PRC's history in 1988. A wide-ranging programme of economic contraction was put into effect and in 1989–90 the economy declined to its lowest point since economic reform. A resurgence of the economy started at the end of 1990, continued in 1991, and led to a two-digit growth rate, 12.8 per cent, in 1992. In 1993 real-estate investment overheated and macroeconomic policies were implemented to cool it down. Enterprise reform only regained its momentum after the economic environment stabilised in 1992.

1. *Macro economic policies of rectification and readjustment*

From April 1988 China's urban consumer price index shot upward rapidly. Inflation, fuelled by panic buying, culminated in annual rates near 60 per cent in August. Credit creation was tightened, price ceilings were imposed on a range of urban consumer goods, and many investment projects were suspended or cancelled. It is notable that by the end of September 1989, price increases fell to zero and inflation had been controlled (Naughton 1990: p. 351).

But why did the Chinese economy stumble into such a severe inflation at the end of the 1980s? Naughton believes that it was brought about by the expansionary credit policy the government adopted to finance its investment plan in the face of a substantial decline in revenue, and that the revenue shrinkage was in turn due to the decline in the profits of state-owned industrial enterprises caused by increased agricultural input prices and lowered entry barriers for the non-state sector (Naughton 1991: p. 211). Lo further explains that 'the massive credit expansion was indispensable for sustaining *the particular pattern of growth*' (Lo 1993: p. 16, italics mine). According to him, the chief engine of China's economic growth in the 1980s was the explosive expansion of 'new' consumer industries, e.g. colour television sets, refrigerators, washing machines. Therefore, to establish and sustain these 'new' consumer industries local governments and enterprises demanded massive bank credit. Furthermore, the expansion of these consumer industries was reliant on imported components and basic home industries were left behind. This unbalanced development led to what Lo calls 'structural inflation' – the general price level was pushed up by the rise of industrial product prices, and the latter was caused by the panic shortage of energy and raw materials (Lo 1993: p. 16).

2. *Deepening enterprise reform*

After about two years of rectification and readjustment, China's urban and industrial economy resumed vigorous growth in 1991. Deepening enterprise reform was again put on the agenda. The significant measure in this period was the transformation of the operational mechanisms of state enterprises. In July 1992, the State Council issued 'The Regulations on Transforming State Enterprises' Operational Mechanism', which granted state enterprises autonomy in fourteen respects, including investment decisions, assets disposal, product-pricing and selling, import and export, employee-hiring. Various ways have been tried to transform state enterprises' operational mechanisms.

Of these, the shareholding system is widely regarded as the most promising. It clarifies property right relations and responsibilities and truly separates ownership from management. The stocks of the shareholding company usually consist of state shares, enterprise shares, and individual shares. State shares are managed by the State Asset Management Bureau or state agencies like ministries. Individual shareholders may be workers or members of the general public if stocks are issued on the open market. Other institutions may also become shareholders. In shareholding companies, the arbitrary interference of the state and its agencies has been reduced, although in many cases they are still the biggest shareholders. Managers are no longer officials dispatched by supervisory state bodies to enterprises. They are now supposed to serve the interest of shareholders and are directly answerable to the board of directors. Worker shareholders have a stronger feeling of ownership and motivation to perform efficiently. Many experimental companies reported that their economic performance had been improved since they adopted the shareholding system (Lee 1993: p. 190).

China's reform has two distinctive features in comparison with the economic reform of other socialist countries in the former Soviet bloc. First, China's reform has not followed a coherent programme. Trial and error and accommodation of different opinions on reform strategy have shaped the gradual and piece-meal characteristics of China's industrial and urban reform. In contrast, Eastern European countries and the former Soviet Union have been trying to carry out a comprehensive economic reform programme suggested by Western economists and international organisations. They advocate a big-bang reform programme, whereby stabilisation will reestablish fiscal and monetary balance, and thus provide preconditions for price liberalisation – allowing the market to determine prices and privatisation to establish a clear structure of ownership and control. In January 1990 Poland took the lead in implementing this big-bang reform programme; two years later Russia followed suit.

The second distinctive feature of China's economic reform is its experimental and bottom-up nature. Practically every enterprise reform measure popularised nationwide was first given a localised dry run with local authorities and enterprises taking the initiative in the experiment. The development of a non-state sector also came from local initiatives. This is partly due to China's more decentralised industrial administration structure and fiscal system in the pre-reform era. Progress by experiment better serves China because of its vast territory and the diversity of its economic development.

China's economic performances during the reform era have been remarkable. As stated at the outset, the average annual growth rate of GNP between 1979 and 1992 is 9.0 per cent. People's living standards have improved significantly. China's success is often attributed to ownership reform and the development of the non-state sector, in particular the household responsibility system in agriculture and rural industry. Nevertheless, recent studies have revealed that the total factor productivity of state industry had also risen at an average annual rate of 2.4 per cent from 1980 to 1988 (Jefferson, Rawski and Zheng, 1992), and that a substantial portion of the losses of state industry has little to do with its efficiency .

First, industrial success can be theorised in various ways. The two-track price system has many advantages and under certain conditions will function in much the same way as complete price liberalisation (Perkins 1991, p. 164). Also it has several advantages. It is simple. Enterprises can quickly get a taste of market demands on which to base decisions. It avoids the instability caused by one-stroke price liberalisation. It offers a feasible path to a market economy. For this to happen, according to Naughton (1990: p. 354), the output plan must be kept unchanged, financial incentive mechanisms must be consistent, arbitrage between plan and market prices must not be permitted. Despite the fact that these conditions have not held precisely in China and have thus generated arbitrage and corruption, periodic rectification by the central government has prevented many misuses of the system. So the two-track price system played a positive role in China's urban industrial reform.

Second, there is the debate about enterprise reform versus ownership reform. The rationale underlying the proposal of ownership reform is that privatisation can make state enterprises subject to 'hard budget constraint', that is, responsible for their expenditures and losses. More relevant to China's experience is the question whether enterprise reform, state-imposed market-like incentives, and competition could achieve a similar objective.

According to McMillan and Naughton (1993), China's enterprise reform from the beginning allowed enterprises to buy and sell above quota on the free market. As production grew, state enterprises were forced to face active product-market competition and improve productivity. Competition between state and non-state sector and among state enterprises had reduced the monopoly on profit of state enterprises. Driven by the need for revenue, the state increasingly made profit remittance the primary obligation of enterprises and tightened financial discipline. And in the contracted management responsibility system the Chinese government has begun auctioning off top management jobs instead of auctioning off enterprises. Moreover, managers' pay is based on their enterprises' performance, so they conclude that privatisation is not crucial in reforming state enterprises, competition is. In fact, the success of China's urban industrial reform is the accumulated result of many steps rather than any single reform measure.

Thus far, China's gradual and piecemeal reform has achieved unexpectedly good results. While China's experience might suggest an alternative to the big-bang reform programme, the exact sequence of reform events in China cannot be replicated elsewhere – it has its unique institutional roots. China's pre-reform industrial administration structure was significantly different from a Soviet-type economy. It was more decentralised, with large, key enterprises under central planning, receiving supply allocation from and handing over their output to the central government, and less important enterprises subject to planning and management at the provincial, prefectural, and county level. The explanation for this devolution of authority to the local level is the unusually large number of enterprises and the predominance of small enterprises. In 1978, China had a total of 348 000 industrial enterprises, of which 344 000 had less than 1000 workers. In contrast, the Soviet Union had only 40 000 factories in 1979. Until 1980, only 3 per cent of Chinese state-owned enterprises were directly administered by central government ministries. The rest belonged to local governments, received their plan quotas mainly from local governments and remitted their profits to local governments (Shirk 1993: p. 30).

China's pre-reform fiscal system was officially described as 'unified leadership, level-by-level management'. 'Unified leadership' meant that the central government determined provincial expenditure budgets, 'level-by-level management' meant that the profits of enterprises run by central ministries went to the central government and the profits of locally run enterprises went to local governments. If a locality's revenues were insufficient to meet its expenditures as determined by the centre, the locality was given a share of the industrial–commercial tax and other taxes generated by local economic activities. If revenues from local enterprises exceeded local expenditure needs as defined by the centre, then the locality remitted a surplus to the centre. Most provinces gave the centre more than they received from it. If a province fulfilled its revenue collection targets and spent within the expenditure target, it was permitted to retain a small share of above-budget revenue.

The origin of China's more decentralised fiscal system can be traced back to 1950s. Mao Zedong started to talk about 'drawing lessons from the Soviet' at the end of 1955, since events had occurred in the Soviet Union after the death of Stalin which made Mao and other CCP leaders doubt the wisdom of the Soviet model (Bo Yibo 1991: p. 472). Mao said ' we must not follow the example of the Soviet Union in concentrating everything in the hands of the central authorities, shackling the local authorities and denying them the right to independent action'. The more decentralised fiscal system was put into practice during the Great Leap Forward. Provinces were delegated greater fiscal and administrative power, and granted a larger share of their revenues, greater discretion over tax rates, expenditures and planning authority, and the 'ownership' of almost all central enterprises except large and important ones. Although after the failure of the Great Leap Forward, the centre recentralised the fiscal system, funds and financial authority remained more dispersed than they had been before the Great Leap Forward. The Cultural Revolution brought about another wave of fiscal decentralisation. Provincial governments were granted authority to set their own budgets and, after transferring a lump sum to the centre according to contract, were able to keep and use all remaining revenues.

After the Cultural Revolution ended, fiscal system reform came ahead of other reforms. In 1976 and 1977, several provinces proposed revenue-sharing experiments with total provincial revenues split between centre and province and the percentage remaining unchanged for several years. The Ministry of Finance welcomed the experiments and proposed to popularise them nationally since the revenue-sharing scheme would guarantee central income and clarify resources and responsibilities of each tier of government. This further decentralised fiscal system strengthened provincial governments' motivation to promote their most profitable enterprises and collect revenue from them.

The Chinese government has been making economic policies based on a decision rule of 'delegation by consensus' at least since the early 1980s (Lieberthal and Oksenberg, 1988). That is, the CCP leadership sets the overall policy line of economic reform, but delegates to the State Council the authority to make specific economic decisions. The State Council leaders then delegate to their subordinate commissions, ministries and provinces the authority to decide if they reach agreement. If the subordinates cannot agree, the State Council leaders will step in.

This delegation of policy choice to bureaucratic agents exploits the superior information of these agents, expertise, and specialisation. It also gives all the agents who will implement the policy a voice in its formulation, so the central leaders can learn in advance under what conditions the agents will support the policy and thus can estimate whether it will be possible to meet all these conditions through compromise and side payments. The risks of delegation by consensus are minimal because the CCP leaders and the State Council can veto any policy they oppose.

However, under delegation by consensus, policy is less likely to get passed than under majority rule since any agent can practically veto the proposal by holding out against it. For example, the proposal for a big-bang price reform in 1986 was abandoned because manufacturing industries did not like it – they wanted the central treasury to compensate them and the Ministry of Finance could not afford to do so. In sum, the central decision rule of delegation by consensus gives ministries and provinces a real say in decision-making but their divided opinions makes it impossible for China to implement radical economic reform programmes. To speak of reform with Chinese characteristics is then not far off the mark.

13

The People's Liberation Army and the Market Economy[1]

Godfrey Kwok-yung Yeung

'Down to the sea'

'Down to the sea' (*xiahai*), or taking on money-oriented commercial activities, has become a fashionable term in China. One of the largest institutions, the People's Liberation Army (PLA), 3-million strong, is following the trend towards frantic commercial activity which is proliferating all over China.

This chapter discusses the entrepreneurial state paradigm as an explanation of the PLA's commercialisation programme during China's economic reform era. The entrepreneurial state refers to the way in which the state apparatus or its affiliated agencies engage in economic activities directly and behaves like a private enterprise through having aims of entrepreneurship and profit-generation, which are contradictory to the conventional bureaucratic notion of the state and inefficiency of state-owned enterprises or parastatals (Blecher 1991: 267–69). In this chapter the PLA's commercialisation programme is defined as 'the military apparatus taking on non-military profit-generating economic activities which are irrelevant to national defence in any direct way'.

The success of the PLA's commercialisation programme not only affects the economic reforms in China both directly and indirectly, since the PLA is one of the most important factors for national stability, but also influences the possible political developmental paths in China. The PLA then is an institution having intimate and complex interactions with the Party and the state.

Background and rationale for commercialisation

Before testing the entrepreneurial state paradigm via the PLA's commercialisation programme, it is crucial to have a brief discussion of its politico-economic background in the 1980s and the rationale behind the decision.

After the disastrous Sino-Vietnam War in 1979, Deng Xiaoping, as chairman of the Party's (CPC) Military Affairs Committee and the Central Military Commission (CMC), streamlined the PLA by reducing it by 1 million troops and combining the eleven Military Regions into seven in 1985. Apart from these dramatic changes, the defence budget was reduced, although there was a slight increase in the budget to secure the loyalty of the PLA after the 1989 Tiananmen crackdown.

Despite being one of the objectives of the Four Modernisations,[2] the military was accorded the lowest priority in the reform decade. The living standards of low-ranking soldiers had deteriorated. As the procurement of equipment accounts for the lion's share of the defence budget, some of the officers who are worst off, have complained that the importing of expensive military hardware is at the expense of their welfare. High-ranking military officers have been frustrated by the shrinking defence budget during a period of rapid economic growth and high inflation. The triumph of the state-of-the-art electronic weapons in the Gulf War has accelerated the sense of inferiority among those officers responsible for modernising the obsolete equipment with the tiny amount of foreign exchange at their disposal.

The PLA's social status has also deteriorated in the materialist-oriented Chinese society. The traditional image of the People's Army vanished under the Tiananmen crackdown. Under these circumstances, not only is morale low, but recruitment problematic. The official *People's Daily* reports that fighting, gambling, robbery and hooliganism are not uncommon among some new recruits while fewer and fewer youths are willing to be conscripted since there are alternative job opportunities available in various enterprises in the rural areas, the traditional recruitment base of the PLA (Woodward 1992: 234–35).

The small number of military officers who refused to carry out the Tiananmen crackdown triggered alarm bells among the political leaders who had counted on the unquestioning support of the PLA. The most prominent act of disloyalty was when Major General Xu Qiannian, the former commander of the élite 38th Group Army deployed in Beijing, was reported to have feigned illness and to have refused to dispatch his troops to be deployed in Beijing city centre.

As a strategic response to the deterioration in army welfare under the austerity budget period, the CMC issued guidance for PLA units to engage in self-reliant agriculture and sideline production aiming to make up the shortfall in central government's food subsidy from the mid-1980s.

Despite this encouragement from the CMC, army-run farms cannot achieve total self-sufficiency for the 3 million troops. In 1991, the PLA-run farms supplied more than 70 per cent of the vegetables and 42 per cent of the meat for the troops. Nonetheless, an extra-budgetary subsidy from local military regions is needed to make up for the inadequacy of the central government's food subsidy. Obviously, the PLA has to find other ways to make up for the shortfall. The commercialisation of the PLA is the answer proposed by the CMC.

The PLA as an entrepreneurial state

The PLA and its associated units are regarded as institutions in the entrepreneurial state model (Figure 13.1). In this model, all units or institutions under the authority of the PLA are directly engaged in various kinds of economic activity in different magnitudes. Therefore, the entrepreneurial institution is established within the PLA's boundaries and its daily operation is under the direct management of the corresponding unit(s) of the PLA. In other words, every PLA unit has a dual identity in this model: national defence and enterprise.

The PLA's commercialisation programme can be considered as a two-step strategic policy: (1) the military–civilian conversion of the PLA-run arms industry and (2) the PLA-run non-military enterprises.

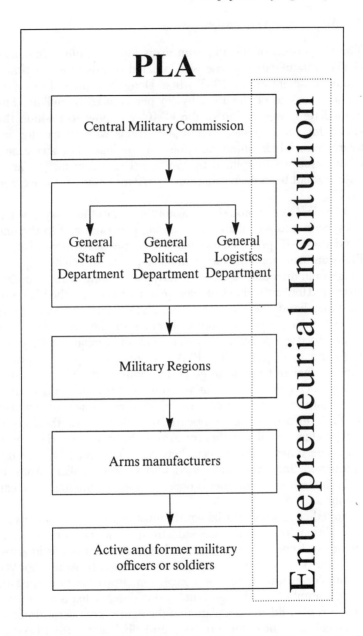

Figure 13.1 A simplified entrepreneurial state model of the People's Liberation Army (PLA)

1. Military-civilian conversion

The conversion of the PLA-run arms industry into a military–civilian manufacturing base was initiated shortly after 1979 and gained momentum in 1985 when Deng Xiaoping decided to reduce the size of the PLA by 25 per cent to 3 million. The immediate consideration of the CMC was how to cushion the effects for the 1 million redundant troops without causing intolerable social discontent and political problems. The seriousness of the issue was amplified by the fact that orders for the arms industry had been decreasing since 1979 and many firms were in deficit.

The CMC's response was a twofold strategy of military–civilian conversion and a civilian skills training programme. On the one hand, the CMC provided a loan to accelerate the conversion of the PLA-run arms manufacturing units to producing civilian goods. This would maintain the operations of the existing arms manufacturers and lower the shock of massive redundancies in the PLA. On the other hand, the CMC organised large-scale civilian training courses to increase the competitiveness of the redundant and demobilised troops before they went back into civilian life. Between 1983 and 1991, 7.4 million PLA personnel took part in various types of civilian training projects. In addition, the PLA provided dual-capacity training – that is, combined military and civilian skills training – for their newly recruited troops. The conversion of the PLA-run arms industry appeared to be successful as the share of civil production value within the arms industry increased by more than nine times to 76 per cent between 1980 and 1992 and the production lines were diversified into various civilian products from household consumer goods to high-technology nuclear products.

Nonetheless, these official figures must be treated speculatively. In addition, the 'actual' cost-effectiveness of the conversion is unknown. Reports of unsold household consumer goods in army warehouses may indicate that some converted firms are not yet profitable. Furthermore, the conversion project is presumed to enjoy a number of privileges, such as low-interest loans and therefore, it is plausible to speculate that the figures are over-estimates.

To enhance the competitiveness and efficiency of the PLA-run arms industry, the CMC initiated a large-scale migration scheme to move the 'Third Line' military industrial bases from the remote south-west inland regions to the coastal areas after 1991. During the early 1960s the 'Third Line' arms manufacturers were part of Mao's dispersion strategy for war preparations but suffered from geographical isolation, unreliable information and lack of entrepreneurial experience. Yet Mao's dispersion strategy appeared to be successful as the average annual output of the migrated plants was reported to have increased by 59 per cent and their profits increased by 32 per cent in 1991.

2. *PLA-run enterprises*

As the combined military–civilian conversion and civilian skills training strategy proved to be a success, the CMC subsequently moved to the second stage: the establishment of enterprises within the PLA.

The most aggressive strategic move by the CMC during 1988–89 allowed the PLA to run enterprises with a high degree of autonomy. The enterprises are financially independent and their managers have autonomy in daily managerial and production decisions. Like the board of directors in a private company, the CMC's guidance on major business decisions, such as mergers, is the only managerial constraint on the PLA-run enterprises. Basically, the operation of the PLA-run enterprises emulates private enterprise and profit-maximisation is their prime objective.

From the top to the bottom the hierarchy of the PLA – CMC, General Logistics Department, military regions, arms manufacturers, individual military officers – has established or are engaged in various enterprises. The air force has opened its military airbases for civilian airlines whilst their officers work as pilots and crews for the PLA-run civilian airline, China United Airlines. Since 1990, various military regions have opened their underground air-raid shelters, built in the late 1960s, for commercial usage, for example, warehouses, car parks, markets or even hotels. In February of 1993, the Niutianyang economic development zone, the first-ever development zone operated by the army, in Shantou Special Economic Zone (SEZ) of Guangdong province, was opened. The general picture of army-run enterprises seems promising as there are currently more than 1000 army-run firms of various sizes employing 3 million workers to produce all types of civilian products. Some foreign experts have estimated that the

PLA-run enterprises produced about 10 per cent of China's total industrial output.

The peak of this commercialisation phenomenon is perhaps located in Shenzhen SEZ, adjacent to Hong Kong where more than 500 army-run science and technology enterprises are based. In 1992, these 500 PLA-run enterprises accounted for 10 per cent of the total industrial output value in Shenzhen. This has been a rational economic decision taken by the army-run enterprises and it is not a phenomenon which existed in the conventional state-owned enterprises.

To enhance the economic efficiency of PLA-run enterprises under large-scale unified management, the CMC formed the Shenzhen 999 Enterprise Group, the first-ever Multinational Corporation in China, by incorporating thirty four army-run enterprises in 1992. The Shenzhen 999 Enterprise Group diversified into all types of profitable business in the domestic and overseas markets. The diversification of the investment portfolio is a typical rational strategic decision by a multinational to enhance competitiveness and lower the risks of over-dependence on a single core industry – the famous 999 series of medical products manufactured by Nanfang Pharmaceutical Factory.

In addition, the CMC sets up overseas companies to raise foreign equity for new investment. In one case, the China Poly Group, which is owned by the General Staff Department, acquired the Continental Mariner, a public company listed on the Hong Kong Stock Exchange, via 'back-door listing' to avoid the time-consuming and tedious administrative procedures necessary for a public company (Holberton, 1993). The CMC also encourages foreign capital investment on their new projects – either in the form of joint ventures or joint production – and technological cooperation with foreign companies. From 1979 onwards, more than US$ 5 billion foreign capital has been invested in PLA-run enterprises. This indicates that PLA-run businesses do mean business.

Politico-economic implications

The politico-economic implications of the PLA's commercialisation programme can be discussed from two perspectives: (1) Professionalism versus commercialism, and (2) State, Party and Military.

1. The professionalism-commercialism dichotomy

The issue of commercialisation presents a dilemma for the military. On the one hand, the PLA would like to maintain its professionalism – as a professional defensive institution – and is reluctant to engage in non-military commercial activities. The task of a professional soldier is to protect the nation from foreign invasion and therefore, the state should shoulder the financial burden of the PLA. This type of wishful thinking may be more pronounced among the Red Army veterans who participated in the Long March. As pillars of the revolution in the establishment of the People's Republic of China, and still commanding tremendous political influence, the resentment of these Red Army veterans against the commercialisation programme cannot be ignored. Some military officers who are enthusiastic about the professionalisation of the PLA may think that the combative abilities and spirit of the PLA have been ruined by the commercial activities. The PLA's commercialisation programme encourages the misallocation of resources and privilege-seeking and, therefore, the dedication to selflessness, patriotic pride and the sacrifice of the spirit are all in doubt. In fact, commercialisation may be a 'hot-bed' for the generation of conflict between the younger and well-educated higher-ranking military officers and those older but less-educated lower-ranking soldiers who have little or no civilian work experience. The phenomenon of 'red-eye disease' (jealousy or envy), semi-official bribery, profiteering, bureaucratic racketeering of, and associated with, better-off colleagues are unavoidable (Cheung 1993: p. 18).

On the other hand, the PLA desperately need the hard currency generated by economic activities either to procure advanced military hardware to upgrade their out-dated equipment or to improve the general living standards of the army. Some military cadres argue that professionalism and commercialism are complementary. They point out that commercialisation is the only, if not the best, way towards self-reliance for a modernised PLA and that it generates job opportunities for demobilised and retired soldiers. The triumph of the allied forces in the Gulf War demonstrated that a modernised PLA would have more combat-effectiveness than a bulky one equipped with antiquated weapons. By using the hard currency generated from the PLA-run businesses to import advanced weapons, the PLA can allow the living standards of the soldiers to remain intact or even improve because the CMC is able to allocate more resources to soldiers' welfare out of the retrenched military budget. The 80 per cent of the official defence budget generated from army businesses in 1992 demonstrates the potential economic benefits of the commercialisation programme. Furthermore, it is extremely inefficient to divert tremendous amounts of scarce resources to maintain a large military arsenal in the post-Cold War era and there is no reason to go against a worldwide trend of civilianising the military apparatus. In fact, the dual-capability training of the PLA and the military–civilian capability of the arms industry are the best ways to maintain a strong and modernised PLA with maximum military deterrence at minimum cost.

2.   State, Party and Military

In the tripartite relationship between the state, party and military, PLA commercialisation raises the issue of 'the Party holds the gun' or 'the Party with the gun at its head'.

The PLA's commercialisation programme is a double-edged sword for the Party. First, the programme provides economic incentives to smooth over the discontent among PLA officers, especially the younger generation with a better education, so that the *gun is under the control of the Party* and the PLA supports the CCP's leadership. Rather than wholly relying on ideological indoctrination, the CPC uses economic incentives as a centripetal force upon the PLA. Second, the commercialisation programme generates foreign exchange to procure advanced military hardware abroad and carry out military research.

Nonetheless, 'the Party holds the gun' argument can be criticised since the commercialism of the PLA is part of an irresistible tendency towards economic reform as the 'actual' process of commercialisation involving military officers is well ahead of the official promulgation of the commercialisation programme. The central government was forced to legalise the commercialisation programme after commercial enterprises became common. Moreover, the central government was also forced to increase the autonomy of the PLA as the majority of ex-military personnel have little education or other civilian work experience. The economic hardship suffered by this 'reserve army of the unemployed' could be converted into a highly organised syndicated criminal network with military training. Thus, 'the Party with the gun at its head' may be the case as the PLA maximises its room for manoeuvre with the CCP.

In sum, the tripartite relationship between the state, CPC and PLA, the commercialisation project can be interpreted as an instrument to strengthen the hegemony of the Party's leadership by buying the loyalty of the army via economic means, whilst it can be also be interpreted as a sign of the deterioration of its authority and hegemony over the PLA after the Tiananmen crackdown of 4 June.

Conclusions

It may be premature to draw any final or concrete conclusions about the success of the PLA's commercialisation project at present. The commercialisation of the PLA in China's economic reform era is a phenomenon of an entrepreneurial state. In other words, the PLA as an institution engages in economic activities and behaves like a private enterprise by aiming at profit-maximisation and entrepreneurship, which is contradictory to the conventional stereotype of inefficiency and bureaucracy associated with the state-owned enterprises. This can be interpreted as a special, if not unique, feature of socialism with Chinese characteristics.

It is suggested that other countries currently reducing their military capacity should cautiously scrutinise the conversion experience of China before deciding to adopt it without reservation. First, the commercialisation of the PLA is a *political gamble* of the CPC since the stability and loyalty of the military are mainly relied on in the present economic situations in China. If there is an economic down-turn, there may be a disintegration of some units of the PLA and this would lead to political instability since one of its important unifying factors – economic incentives – would have evaporated. Second, the official figures presented in this chapter are likely to exaggerate the magnitude of success of the PLA's commercialisation. As the PLA-run enterprises and military-civilian conversion projects are expected to enjoy a number of privileges, such as low-interest loans guaranteed by the CMC and guaranteed supply of scarce raw materials, and tremendous resources and commitment from the hierarchy of PLA, the 'actual' cost effectiveness of the PLA-run enterprises and military–civilian arms industry may not be as promising as indicated. Therefore, other disarming countries may not be able to replicate the 'success' – if it is a real one – of the PLA.

Finally, recent reports suggest that the government will attempt to curtail the PLA's business activities in the future because of deteriorating morale, the potential effect on combat ability, and because its speculative activities, such as real estate, fuel inflation. This will mean an increase in the military budget although it is unclear where the money will come from. It is more likely that the form or nature of the PLA's commercialisation will change rather than its business activities halt, for its involvement is so extensive.

Notes

1. I am grateful to Robert Benewick, Gordon White, Adrian Wood and Robin Luckham in the preparation of this chapter. The interpretations and any errors of fact are, of course, my own responsibility.
2. The four prime areas – industry, agriculture, science and technology, and military – to be modernised in China.

14

Trade and Development: The Political Economy of China's Open Policy[1]

John Thoburn and Jude Howell

'When an arrow is on the string it must go'

China's opening up to the outside world has been a feature of the economic reforms since 1949. From that date until the late 1970s the country was completely closed to Western foreign investment. International trade continued after 1949, despite American embargoes, but was tightly and centrally controlled. But China in the reform period is a major recipient of direct foreign investment and exporter of light manufactured goods. The presence of foreign firms and of imported consumer goods brings an exposure to Western and Japanese culture and business practices. International trade increasingly means that exporters must conform to international standards of quality, and domestic producers face import competition. For the planners, international trade means that world prices influence the domestic price structure and the economic-decision making of consumers and enterprises. Such changes have profound political implications too. The Chinese communist party (CCP) in the reform era has sought legitimacy in economic terms – its ability to deliver the goods – rather than in ideological terms. Western ideas of democracy, the 'fifth modernisation', contributed to the demonstrations which ended in the Tiananmen crackdown of 4 June 1989.

This chapter starts with the politics of the Open Policy. It then considers China's experience with foreign direct investment and with the trade reforms. A further section looks at foreign borrowing. We also discuss the implications of these reforms for the structure and operation of the Chinese state.

The politics of the Open Policy

If we look at the evolution of the Open Policy since 1978 we find that it has not proceeded in a simple linear fashion. The pace, extent, forms and direction of opening have vacillated over the past fifteen years with advances and retreats which have their origins in both economic and political factors. Here the focus will be on the political dynamics of opening up.

The Open Policy has significant distributive consequences. It provides opportunities and benefits for those regions, institutions, and social groups granted preferential rights and privileges and bold enough to take up the entrepreneurial gauntlet. Ideological differences and power struggles within the top leadership of the Chinese Communist Party as well as tensions between those who see their interests furthered and those who perceive themselves losing out have shaped the evolution of the Open Policy.

It is not easy to position top leaders in particular groups. However, the following patterns can be identified. Between 1978 and 1982 the key divisions with regard to the Open Policy were between the 'reformers' centred on Deng Xiaoping, the 'whatever-ists' ('whatever Mao said must be followed') led by Hua Guofeng, and the 'Ultra-leftists'. Hua Guofeng favoured opening up, but not on the scale or in the way envisaged by the reformers. He preferred the restoration of trade policies adopted in the 1950s with some minimal reform. The ultra-leftists, who had come to power during the Cultural Revolution, were even more sceptical about the reformers' ambitions and took an isolationist stance. They called for self-reliance and condemned the Special Economic Zones (SEZs) as enclaves of imperialism. Opening up for them was equivalent to following the capitalist road and succumbing to dependency.

With the ousting of Hua Guofeng and his allies divisions among the reformers became more significant, centring on the pace, timing and extent of opening-up. Three major groups can be identified:

1. the radical reformers, who advocated a rapid opening-up of China to the international economy. Hu Yaobang and Zhao Ziyang belonged to this group.
2. the moderate reformers such as Chen Yun, who sought a more moderate pace and a significant role for planning and who were concerned about social developments in the SEZs.
3. the conservative reformers, who were sceptical about opening up on a grand scale so quickly and were particularly concerned about ideological aspects such as 'spiritual pollution'. They had their base in ideological institutions such as the Propaganda Department of the Central Committee and were behind both the Spiritual Pollution Campaign of 1983 and the Anti-Bourgeois Liberalisation Campaign of 1987 which linked opening-up with spiritual decline, prostitution, drug-smuggling and crime.

Since 1982 the relative strength and composition of each of these groups, and their impact on the policy process, has varied. In 1984, for example, the influence of the radical group was particularly strong. After the Tiananmen crackdown, however, the influence of the conservatives increased enormously. Not only did the boundaries between the moderates and conservatives blur, but Deng Xiaoping distanced himself from the radical reformers. However, since the Fourteenth Party Congress of October 1992, when Deng Xiaoping called for more and faster opening and guaranteed an Open Policy for the next hundred years, there has been a revival of more radical ideas.

The Open Policy has also been shaped by the tensions between and within institutions. Reform has weakened ideological authorities and planning institutions. Light industry, such as textiles and electronics, has been promoted in preference to heavy industry such as steel. Within institutions there are divisions between 'politicocrats', that is, those cadres who owe their positions to their political credentials, and 'technocrats', cadres whose authority rests upon their technical and professional skills. The politicocrats have frequently dragged their feet in the implementation of the new policy, taking too long to approve foreign investment and trade contracts. At the same time, however, some have been keen to reap the benefits of the new policy, such as overseas trips and opportunities to increase their earnings. This has resulted at times in poor decisions regarding technology transfer.

Regional interests have also shaped the course of the Open Policy. Two axes of tension are significant here: central and coastal local governments, and inland and coastal areas. The decentralisation of authority to approve foreign trade and foreign investment contracts has encouraged greater initiative at the micro-economic level. However, it has also led to central loss of control over foreign exchange. Whilst the central government has sought to redress these economic imbalances through recentralisation, coastal local governments such as Guangdong and Fujian have been reluctant or unable to heed central commands. The crucial role of these two provinces in the reunification process with Hong Kong and Taiwan, coupled with their relatively thriving economies, has boosted their bargaining power *vis-à-vis* central government.

The Open Policy and reform have clearly favoured the development of the coastal areas. This contrasts starkly with Mao's attempts to minimise regional differences. Officials, academics and individuals in the inland areas have responded ambiguously to the rapid growth of the coastal board. On the one hand they have supported some of the attacks upon the SEZs. They have also tried to protect their own industries by blockading products from the coastal areas. On the other hand, some enterprises, units and individuals have been quick to take advantage of new opportunities. Whilst these regional tensions were not so prominent in the initial stages of opening up, from the early 1980s onwards some top leaders were already drawing attention to the problem of regional differentiation.

Foreign direct investment

During the fifteen years of the Open Policy an increasing area of China has been opened to foreign investment. Starting with the SEZs in the south of the country, China subsequently opened fourteen large coastal cities, then special open zones and open provinces. By 1987 the areas open to foreign investors included nearly 30 per cent of China's population, and generated over 60 per cent of the country's industrial output (Kueh 1992, pp. 640–41), though most of this output was still from domestic enterprises. The 1990s have brought a further expansion of the Open Policy in the inland border areas of Heilongjiang, Xinjiang and Yunnan. Moreover, the current prioritisation of the Yangtse delta provides a challenge to the previous weight given to the SEZs. In particular, Shanghai's Pudong Development Zone, which has been called the 'head of the dragon', is designed to spearhead development in the main cities along the river, comprising the dragon's body. In mid-1992 several more cities, including Chongqing, were designated to operate in a fashion similiar to the open coastal cities. Although the Chinese have tried hard to attract Western and Japanese investment, some 66 per cent of the inflow has come from Hong Kong.

Special Economic Zones and Open Areas

The SEZs have been the most visible aspect of the Open Policy. Set up between 1979 and 1981, the four original zones were located with a view to maximising their attraction to investment from ethnic Chinese living outside China. Shenzhen, the largest, was located in Guangdong province immediately adjacent to Hong Kong. Zhuhai was set up beside the Portuguese enclave of Macau, also in Guangdong. Shantou, in the north-east of Guangdong province was established in an area with many links with Southeast Asian Chinese communities and Xiamen SEZ in Fujian province was intended to attract Taiwanese investors.

Although the Chinese leadership was undoubtedly influenced by what it knew of export processing zones (EPZs) set up in other Asian countries, the SEZs were different. The SEZs, like EPZs, gave generous tax concessions and duty-free import privileges to foreign investors, and provided extensive infrastructural facilities. However, the SEZs were much larger, and the greater freedom they gave to enterprises to trade has also attracted many domestic Chinese enterprises and organisations to invest there. The SEZs were additionally designed to be 'windows' on foreign technology, knowledge and management practices, and for experimentation with, for example, increased use of contract labour instead of the jobs-for-life of workers in state enterprises.

Initially, SEZs were set up in the south not only to capitalise on links with Hong Kong and South-east Asia, but to confine the SEZs' economic experimentation to locations away from established industrial areas. The open cities and other open areas have gradually given new areas access to foreign investment. Shanghai is now setting up a large zone, Pudong, to rival the southern SEZs. Hainan island in the far south was made an SEZ in 1988.

Nevertheless, the attraction of foreign investment is still largely confined to China's coastal regions. Guangdong province alone attracted nearly half of the accumulated foreign investment stock from 1979 to 1990 (Kueh 1992, p. 652). In the early years much foreign investment went into service sectors such as hotel construction, but since the mid-1980s it has been going increasingly into manufacturing.

Through the establishment of the Shenzhen SEZ, China's Open Policy has been used to hasten the integration of Hong Kong into China in 1997. Similarly, the Zhuhai SEZ opposite Macau and the location of an SEZ at Xiamen look towards the possibility of integration with Macau and Taiwan.

Experience with foreign investment

Chinese leaders have stressed the importance of foreign investment as a means not only of earning foreign exchange but also of introducing 'advanced technology'. These two aims have proved incompatible to a large extent. There has been a rapid growth in exports from southern China, but this has been in low-technology operations, such as toys and plastics, in which Hong Kong has been losing its competitive advantage as a result of rising labour costs (Thoburn *et al.* 1990, 1991). Western and Japanese companies in higher technology activities have been more interested in the Chinese domestic market of 1.2 billion people. Such companies have little interest in transferring technology to future competitors (Leung *et al.* 1991), and have been discouraged by past difficulties in remitting abroad profits earned in Chinese domestic currency.

From the viewpoint of Western and Japanese companies, the Chinese 'climate' for foreign investment is widely perceived as difficult. Although there is a legal framework for foreign investment, often the law is not applied. Much negotiation may be necessary even to secure local services such water and power supply. Established state companies, with workers with jobs-for-life, have often proved intractable partners in joint ventures. For these reasons, Hong Kong companies have been better able to negotiate their way through the Chinese system than have Western companies, and sometimes Western companies choose Hong Kong intermediaries.

Benefits

The benefits of foreign investment for China spring mainly from the export-orientated operations in southern China. For individual localities, and for Chinese enterprises, partnership with foreign investors offers access to foreign exchange, to the outside world, and increased freedom from the planning system. So foreign investment has been actively sought by a wide variety of economic actors, and there has been intense competition between localities, particularly those in the south with good links to relatives abroad, especially in Hong Kong. Often it has been possible, by a variety of means, for these areas to offer concessions such as tax holidays which are as generous as those of the SEZs.

A distinctive feature of the Chinese foreign investment scene has been that foreign investors have an unusually wide choice of contract. Processing and assembly arrangements, where the foreign investor brings in materials from abroad for processing in China and then exports the output, have commonly been used by small towns and villages in Guangdong and Fujian to attract investment in labour-intensive consumer goods. These generate local employment and foreign exchange in the form of processing fees, without relying on the domestic market for supplies. There have also been large numbers of small export-orientated joint ventures, usually involving Hong Kong companies making light manufactures. Though 'low-tech', these small-scale export operations generate valuable experience of overseas standards of product quality and quality control. Hong Kong investors, through improved management techniques, are often able to get much larger outputs from the same equipment and size of labour force than could Chinese enterprises.

However, for joint ventures and wholly-owned foreign ventures in China, export earnings in the late 1980s and early 1990s have been less than total payments for imports (Kueh 1992, pp. 668–9). Doubts have been raised within China as to whether the capital inflow from foreign investment in the SEZs has been greater than the cost of infrastructural investment met by the Chinese. Although by the early 1990s China was the Third World's second-largest recipient of direct foreign investment, it still received less than Singapore.

Foreign trade

China's trade expanded following the establishment of better relations with the USA in 1972, and grew further in the early 1980s.
But major changes were delayed until the mid-1980s, and were
made as part of a more general price reform. During the reform
period foreign trade decisions have been decentralised and the
monopoly of the national foreign trade corporations has been
broken by the establishment of several thousand individual trading
companies which can buy exports from enterprises and sell imports
on the domestic market. Competition between such companies has
meant a much closer relation between world prices and domestic
prices. According to Lardy (1992, pp. 704–5), by 1991 90 per cent
of goods imported into China were sold at prices based on world
prices, and by the late 1980s the pre-reform pricing system applied
to only 20 per cent of China's exports.

These changes, though significant, have not transformed China
into a free trade economy. There is a wide range of tariffs and
non-tariff barriers protecting domestic industry , and many controls remain on the export side. Individual foreign trading
companies too may be run by local authorities and act in the
interests of those authorities.

Exchange rate policy

Once a decision was taken to allow the Chinese prices of imports
and of exportable goods to reflect prices in world markets, the
exchange rate became crucial. China maintains an officially fixed
rate of exchange. This can be achieved in principle by the monetary authorities intervening in the foreign exchange market by
purchases and sales of foreign currency, and in practice access to
the purchase of foreign currency is restricted for Chinese citizens.

For virtually the whole of the reform period, and still today to
some extent, the Renminbi (RMB) has been overvalued even
though China has devalued the RMB on many occasions since the
start of the reforms. This raises the price of foreign exchange in
terms of RMB and thereby raises both the price of imports and the
Chinese currency price enterprises receive for exports. However,
rather than devaluing the RMB to a point where excess demand for
foreign exchange is eliminated, the Chinese government has let the
excess demand be channelled to a separate free market. There,

foreign investors wishing to remit out of China profits earned in RMB can buy foreign currency if they are willing to pay a higher price for it. This parallel market started life as a black market, but gradually acquired semi-official status and transactions take place at designated 'swap centres' in major cities. The Chinese government's frequent devaluations of the RMB tend to move the official exchange rate towards the swap market exchange rate. The Chinese have attempted to control the swap market rate, and this led to a divergence between the swap market and the black market. When the controls were removed in mid-1993, there was an immediate and sharp depreciation of the RMB on the swap market, though this lasted only a short time. The government intends to supplant swap markets by a state-bank monopoly over hard-currency dealing.

At the start of the 1990s, despite rapid economic growth, China enjoyed a substantial surplus on the current account of its balance of payments, reflecting both successful export performance, some macro economic restriction of imports in 1990–91, and China's exceptionally high proportion of savings out of national income (43 per cent in 1990), which served to restrain import demand. As the economy has expanded further, however, the balance of trade has moved into deficit.

Trade expansion and foreign investment

The trade reforms have seen a major expansion in China's exports. Exports now generate about 20 per cent of national income. Though this percentage may be slightly overstated, undoubtedly trade opportunities are now a significant influence on economic decisions. The share of manufactures in China's total exports have risen to about 75 per cent. Nor are these exports simply the result of attracting foreign investment. Even in Guangdong, the province with the most foreign investment, exports from domestic firms accounted for nearly 66 per cent of export earnings, and only in Shenzhen SEZ were they clearly more than 50 per cent of exports generated by foreign-invested enterprises. Over 20 per cent of China's exports are provided by rural industries (Zweig 1991).

However, partial reform of the trading system, as elsewhere in the Chinese economy, gives significant opportunities for black-market trading.

Foreign borrowing

In addition to inflows of foreign capital for direct investment by foreign companies, China has borrowed directly from international capital markets, international agencies, and foreign governments. The country's total outstanding long-term debt in 1990, according to World Bank statistics, was the fourth largest in the Third World – nearly as large as that of Argentina and Indonesia, and about half that of Brazil, the world's largest debtor. This indebtedness must be seen against the great size of the Chinese economy. In 1990 the cost of servicing the debt took about 10 per cent of the country's export earnings, and was equivalent to nearly 15 per cent of national income, both low figures compared to other Third World countries at China's level of development. Debt has been used to finance technology and equipment imports, and in part to cover China's large budget deficit, which is largely caused by expenditure on urban food subsidies and losses made by state enterprises.

The impact of the Open Policy on the Chinese state

With the opening of China and domestic economic reform the Chinese state has entered a period of transition. The introduction of market forces has spawned elements of a new 'market-facilitating state'. The key features of this are as follows:

1. it promotes entrepreneurship and engages itself in risk-taking and profit-seeking activities;
2. it legally defines relations between economic actors in the market-place and seeks to resolve economic disputes through the law;
3. it is staffed by people with professional and technical skills;
4. it now seeks to regulate the market at the macroeconomic level rather than the microeconomic level.

These elements are most apparent in the SEZs where the concentration of foreign capital is highest and domestic economic reform has proceeded furthest.

This transition towards a market-facilitating state can be observed in the restructuring of state institutions, changes in their operational mode and social composition. Restructuring has involved the adaptation of existing institutions and the creation of new institutions. Trade and financial institutions, customs, the trade unions, CCP and PLA have all had to adapt their structures and ways of operating to accommodate foreign capital.

The Open Policy has not only engendered the adaptation of existing institutions but also the creation of new institutions. The establishment of the SEZs for example led to the creation of a SEZ Affairs Office under the State Council as well as special administrative offices at provincial level. Efforts to coordinate the management of foreign investment prompted the setting-up in 1986 of a special Leading Group in the State Council with parallel structures at the local level. Foreign capital's concern for legal protection has contributed towards the development of a legal structure dealing with external economic relations.

As well as this restructuring of the state, the Open Policy has also led to changes in the way the state operates. In order to encourage greater entrepreneurship the reformers have (i) decentralised some authority over foreign economic relations from central to lower levels and (ii) encouraged the formation of quasi-state-type institutions.

Since 1978 there has been a proliferation of foreign trading companies at provincial level and below. Central government has also loosened its control over the amount of foreign exchange retained by provincial governments. Similarly, the reformers have extended the authority to establish foreign-invested enterprises from the SEZs and coastal cities to inland and border areas.

Quasi-state institutions mediate between the state and foreign capital. They are quasi-state in that they are set up and owned by the state but are supposed to operate like business enterprises. The China International Trust and Investment Company was one of the first such hybrid institutions to sprout at the national level. A good local example is provided by the Xiamen SEZ Construction and Development Corporation, which can set up joint ventures, and engage in trade and leasing.

The type of person working in those parts of the state dealing with the external economy has also changed in the reform period. Technical qualifications and education have eclipsed political credentials in importance. Whilst Party membership is still an asset, particularly for going overseas, additional qualifications are increasingly being required.

The elements of a new market-facilitating state coexist uneasily with the institutions born of the previously centrally-planned system. While the crackdown in 1989 strengthened the hold of the old command institutions, the commitment towards greater reform at the Fourteenth Party Congress in October 1992 heralds a greater role for the market-facilitating state.

Conclusions

Since the beginning of the reforms, China has become a major force in world markets and a large recipient of foreign capital, both as direct foreign investment and as foreign borrowing. Trade has opened up possibilities for export-orientated industrialisation, especially in the south of the country. Although foreign firms producing in China have been important in helping the export drive, domestic firms have played a larger role. China's 'socialist market economy' by no means implies that China is a free-trading nation like Hong Kong, though. The Chinese state is still in a transitional phase, with a mix of institutions from the communist era and new 'market-faciliting' ones.

Note

1. We are grateful for very helpful comments from Chen Yao of the Chinese Academy of Social Sciences in Beijing and from Zhang Leyin of the University of Greenwich, UK. Of course, any errors are our own.

15

Gender in China

Shirin M. Rai

'To educate a daughter is like watering another man's garden'

Changing lives

The Chinese communists were acutely aware of the oppression of women in their society, and were committed to the cause of women's equality. From the start they were insistent that China's modernisation could not be complete without the inclusion of women in the public sphere. Like most other state socialist countries, at the time of the setting up of the Chinese state, the 'woman question' was debated within the materialist framework set out in Engels' Family, Private Property and the State. The key feature of this position is that the roots of women's oppression lie in the denial of property and, through that, access to the public sphere as independent actors. The question of the private/public dichotomy has particular significance in Marxist politics. The division between the two is regarded as signifying the alienation of individuals in society. The obliteration of the private/public dichotomy is one of the goals of communism.

In China there was a conscious reinterpretation of these arenas. 'Public' work came to mean work for the state and 'private' work encompassed the rest. The simplicity of this analysis of women's oppression allowed socialist revolutionaries to formulate concrete policies to mobilise women into waged work.

An equally significant result of the above analysis was the critique that the communists developed of Chinese social relations. Civil society (see Chapter 6) was cast as the arena where the oppression of women was perpetrated, tolerated and sanctioned.

Civil society was identified as the repository of 'feudal values', and thus inherently oppressive. The attack upon civil society was therefore legitimised as the communists set about creating a 'new socialist man' [sic] and society. This attack soon became a generalised onslaught upon all forms of social relations and organisations unacceptable to the communist regime and led to a virtual freezing of civil society. For women the consequences of this freeze were significant, and particular.

Women under the revolutionary state

The first initiatives: rights and education

This materialist analysis of women's oppression led to a huge mobilisation of women into waged work after 1949. The other most significant area of reform was the family. The Marriage Law of 1950 prohibited concubinage, introduced monogamous marriage, and gave women the right to marry the person of their own choice, and the right to divorce and maintenance. The Land Law allowed women to hold property in their own name and a right to a share in the family inheritance. In 1958 the Great Leap Forward was launched to speed up China's progress towards communism, and this led to the communisation of agricultural cooperatives and the setting-up of communal eating places, laundries, and crèches. By 1959, an estimated 4 980 000 nurseries and kindergartens and more than 3 600 000 dining halls had been set up in the rural areas (Croll 1978, p. 268). Women entered commune production as individuals in their own right and earned their own 'work points' giving them economic independence within the male-headed family. One can speculate that a reason for peasant non-cooperation with the communists during this period was that the challenge posed to the patriarchal family by community provision of domestic services and the crossing of the private/public boundary by the state could not have been palatable to the male heads of family who also provided the party-state with most of its rural cadres. The Great Leap Forward failed and was followed by a disastrous famine which claimed millions of lives. As a result of the failure there was a greater emphasis on social stability and economic recovery. The party-state withdrew from the more radical measures, such as the public dining halls and launderettes which attacked the traditional family. The family-based social provision was back.

Education was regarded by Mao and the Communist Party as crucial to building a new China. Moreover, education for women was regarded as an important means of granting them access to better jobs and a more independent life. While no special measures were taken to ensure that women were equally represented at all levels of the educational pyramid, the emphasis on flexible patterns of education in the countryside during the Cultural Revolution did allow vast numbers of girls and women to get some formal education. It is no surprise that the expansion of female education in China occurred mainly in two periods: 1950 to 1958, and 1966 to 1976, both periods of high mobilisation of women in the public sphere (see Table 15.1). At a more informal level, the chaos of the Cultural Revolution allowed many women to leave their homes and travel all over China as Red Guards. For many this was an exciting and liberating experience. Also, the campaign against the Chinese philosopher Confucius launched during the Cultural Revolution criticised his derogatory attitude towards women.

The critique that follows cannot in anyway detract from the material improvement in women's lives. A closer look at the way the 'woman question' was addressed in China shows the limitations

Table 15.1 Number of female students as percentage of total enrolment

Year	Higher education	Regular secondary schools	Primary schools	Teacher training
1949	19.8	—	—	—
1951	22.5	25.6	28.0	26.0
1955	25.9	26.9	33.4	27.1
1958	23.3	31.3	38.5	31.5
1973	30.8	33.0	40.7	—
1975	32.6	39.3	45.2	—
1976	33.0	40.4	45.5	—
1978	24.1	41.5	44.9	29.8
1983	26.9	39.5	43.7	37.2
1987	33.0	40.8	45.4	—

Sources: State Education Commission, *Statistics* 1984: 40 and *Chinese Education*, Vol. 7, Summer 1989.

of the materialist approach and reveals how the nature of the state in China did not allow the autonomous assessment and articulation of women's needs. A paternalistic party-state gave women rights it thought appropriate; self affirmation and an independent setting of agendas was not allowed.

Patriarchy, paternalism, and the party

One of the reasons why the Chinese party-state did not allow independent women's organisations and movements political space was ideological. The class-struggle analysis of historical movements meant that Marxists had always been suspicious of separatist organisations. Special interests were thought to weaken class solidarity. Lenin, in creating the monolithic party apparatus, further strengthened this opposition to independent interests. 'The leadership of the party' was to be the golden rule of communist organisation. If the party was cast as the repository of the 'most advanced ideas' in society, it knew what was best for the people. While in China there was no debate about whether there should be an All-China Women's Federation, as there had been in the Soviet Union in 1917–18, its constitution makes clear that the Federation's role is to help to implement the party-state policies on women, and that it functions under the 'leadership of the Communist Party of China'.

Critics of China's policies on women contend that the CCP colluded with the patriarchal system for peasant support for the revolution. They argue that as Marxism lacks a conceptual framework within which to analyse the nature of an autonomous 'sex-gender system' (Stacey 1983, p. 263) Chinese leaders of all political convictions labelled discrimination against women in socialist China as a remnant of a 'feudal ideology'. It also meant that the debate about women's equality remained within the confines of communist ideology and did not become a gender issue challenging the various modes of power within Chinese society. Women were not allowed the public political space needed to debate and frame their own demands.

A final point on how the 'woman question' has been considered in China: in August 1937 Mao had written, 'whatever happens, there is no doubt at all that at every stage in the development of a process, there is only one principal contradiction that plays the leading role ... while the rest occupy a secondary and subordinate position'. And it was only the Communist Party which could decide the principal contradiction. In grading social contradictions in this way it becomes clear that the issue of gender inequalities could not be given the status of a primary contradiction. Apart from the fact that the leadership of the CCP was predominantly male, they were operating with no clear ideas on patriarchy other than the famous Engels' text. The gender-blindness of the CCP leadership combined with the organisational pre-eminence of the party meant that the marginalisation of issues of gender was almost a foregone conclusion. Further, 'universal priorities' – whether the making of the revolution, or the reconstruction of the economic system or its modernisation, had priority over 'partial interests'. Engendering these 'universal' agendas was never attempted; the specificity of women's needs was not taken on board. An examination of Chinese policies on women in the context of the above discussion reveals a complex picture of Chinese women's lives under communist rule.

Marriage, monogamy and morality

Harriet Evans points out that although the Chinese communists presented the Marriage Law of 1950 as a protection for women against concubinage, such a restricted explanation of the law did not allow for a general debate about gender relations within marriage (Evans 1992, p. 149). The only distinction that was made within the framework of monogamy as a social relationship was between bourgeois and socialist monogamy, the latter being naturally superior to the former because of the more independent economic position of women under socialism (Evans 1992, p. 151). As a consequence of this emphasis on monogamy social stability came to be linked to social morality which in turn was made dependent on the monogamous family. 'The implications for women were striking ... women's interests were no longer to be served by prioritising their new marital rights, but by making concessions to conservative opinion in order to preserve family and marital stability' writes Evans (1992, p. 151) – by inference, any form of sexual relations between men and women that did not allow for a more general debate about gender relations within marriage. The question of family property also remained unresolved. Exogamous marriages remained the norm, and there was no systematic challenge to the male as traditional head of family.

This emphasis on monogamy and sexual morality continues today as a bulwark against social instability that might result from the dramatic changes in the Chinese economy.

Women under the modernising state

Four Modernisations: a new context for women

Mao Zedong died in 1976 leaving behind a mixed legacy for China – the potential for becoming a superpower, but a stagnant economy and a volatile and oppressive political system. The need for change was felt by many within and outside the party-state. The 'Four Modernisations' – of agriculture, industry, defence, and science and technology – informed the new agenda set out by the reformers led by Deng Xiaoping after defeating the radical faction of the 'Gang of Four'. The market was to regulate and guide changes in China's economy. According to the then General Secretary of the CCP, the role of the state was to be slowly reduced to the formulation of macroeconomic policy and the use of 'economic levers such as price, finance, taxation and credit for intervention and regulation'. The implications of these changes for women's lives were and continue to be significant, both in the private and the public sphere.

One of the key areas of change in Chinese public life has been the relationship between the state and civil society. A functioning civil society is only just beginning to emerge in China, and is primarily linked to the rise of the private entrepreneur both in the city and the country. Moreover, the party-state no longer includes, other than at the rhetorical level, social transformation on its political agenda. As China moves away from its goal of a communist *nirvana* and declares itself as being at the 'primary stage of socialism', it seeks only the transformation of the economy; all other contradictions are subordinated to the resolution of the 'economic question'. This withdrawal of the state from the transformative agenda and rise of a civil society has created a complex set of realities and options for Chinese women.

For both Chinese and foreign observers of the Chinese situation and its impact on women's lives, the weakening of the economic monopoly of the state and the introduction of the market are the focus of study. The market represents choice, mobility, and an incipient civil society for some, and insecurity, lack of social support, unfair competition, and a threat to participation of women in the public sphere for others. The picture, of course, is complex. The impact of the introduction of the market has not been the same on all social groups. Even within groups the reforms have touched the lives of members in different ways. Further, the 'evolving pattern of social interests ... has an important impact on the course and content of the reforms' (White 1993, p. 198).

Modernisation, markets and work

The division of labour in the public sphere has never been questioned by the Chinese party-state. Women have generally been concentrated in low-skilled and low-paid jobs. Whenever women's work and women at work has been discussed it has been by 'desexualising' the debate. The rhetoric of women's equality has always had the man as the reference point: what men can do, women can do too. The following examines two different cases affecting women at work in the public sphere to illustrate the different ways in which the reforms are affecting their lives.

The first addresses the question of employment for China's graduate women. These are privileged women with education, and increasingly, educated family backgrounds. Until the mid-1980s graduates were allocated jobs according to a central plan drawn up by the Ministry of Planning with the help of the State Education Commission (see Rai 1991, pp. 174–78). Under this system women students tended to be allocated teaching jobs in schools that were low-status and low-paid. Competition for jobs was introduced gradually and cautiously in the 'free' market. Yet it has not worked quite as expected.

The paternalistic state in the Maoist period set about liberating Chinese women by mobilising them into the workforce. The modernising state in the post-Mao period is giving women choice – by allowing them to go back to being mothers, and wives. While the massive task of economic reconstruction in the 1950s needed the labour of women, growing urban unemployment in the 1990s means that the state is wasting education and training to ensure the *status quo* in gender relations that is seen as necessary for China's social stability. In 1986 it was reported that 'among the unemployed young people in the country, the proportion of women rose to 61.5 per cent' (Chinese Education, Summer 1989, p. 28).

On the shop-floor pressures of profitability and economic efficiency are forcing women out of jobs. Crèches have been closed down and managers do not want to give maternity leave benefits to their women employees. 'The losses *caused by women* bearing children for the regeneration of the human race should not be borne by factories ...' (Chinese Education, Summer 1989, p 86, my italics). In many areas women are being encouraged to take retirement at the age of 45. As contractual work begins to replace tenured employment, managers can refuse to renew their contracts, and are doing so. The ethic of the market is also used by managers to 'prove' the unsuitability of women in the public sphere – they are not competitive, and are plagued by divided loyalties. Women, under these conditions, are finding the market a hostile place.

The response of the party-state to this attack upon women's right to work has been muted. As a protector of women's social position, the state has exhorted industrial enterprises to recruit women, but without confronting the question of the sexual division of labour. At the same time, for example, it has acceded to the demands of the managers that the state subsidise maternity benefit. Delivery and Child-Bearing Funds have been set up in many cities with contributions from both the enterprises and local governments to support women workers during their maternity leave.

Second, in rural China, the situation is different. The de-collectivisation of agriculture and the introduction of the 'family contract system' has resulted in a significant expansion of cash from both the agricultural and the non-agricultural sector. 'Between 1978 and 1984 grain acreage decreased by 8 per cent and the acreage sown to economic crops increased by 47 per cent. At the same time, the proportion of the total rural labour force used in crop farming declined from 75.2 per cent to 62.7 per cent' (Jacka 1992, p. 124). Further, the new system of production has formalised family-based production. While even under the commune system, a woman's wages were merged with her husband's or father's at the time of distribution, the accounting of individual wages was generally practised. Now the male-headed family is the only recognised economic unit, other than in exceptional circumstances. Another feature of rural reforms has been the increasing concentration of middle-aged women in food production. Food production is a notoriously labour-intensive, low-paid area of work and has been traditionally women's work. As in the case of urban women, in the countryside the state is responding to this shift in women's work by encouraging and 'enabling' them to do better and earn more. For example, in 1989 a campaign to improve the productivity of rural women workers engaged in food production was launched called 'Competing and Learning' under the auspices of the All-China Federation of Women. During this campaign there has been no questioning of the gender division of labour and its consequences for women's lives. However, younger women are not so bound to the land as are middle-aged family women. The informal relaxation of travel permits has allowed young women to move to the cities in search of better paid work, or to travel as traders. This migration of rural women has created other problems for them – sexual and economic exploitation in a largely unregulated market.

There has been an important shift in political rhetoric. The language of social transformation and responsibility is being replaced by that of individual initiative and opportunity. The individual is beginning to separate out from the collective and now carries responsibility for her situation and social status in society. As the experience of women in other market societies shows this new ethos is a mixed blessing.

The public and the political

New agendas for women

The current situation in China is full of promise as well as conflict. People are organising around their interests but the status of these organisations is not yet clear. Much greater independence is being given to established self-governing mass organisations such as the All-China Federation of Women to set their own agenda. However, the continued refusal of the party-state to consider significant power-sharing does not allow the deepening of political reforms. Yet resistance to particular features of state policies has been significant, and in the main tolerated by the party-state. Further, the 'opening up' of China to the rest of the world has meant the influx of new ideas and vocabulary. Chinese women, for example, are beginning to examine theories of women's social oppression not bound to the materialist model. In this political context Chinese women have been protesting against the new inequalities and discrimination that they are facing.

The publications of the Women's Federation have been inundated with angry letters written by women who feel that they are being forced out of their jobs, or discriminated against at the time of promotions. One contributor asked: 'in today's attempt to build the Chinese economy and implement the Four Modernisations, do we or don't we need knowledge? Do we or don't we need talent? If the answer is yes, then female university graduates should be respected and utilised.' Such articles make clear that Chinese women do not want to leave work; that it is the pressures of new social reforms that are pushing them in that direction: 'Most women are worried that having no job may jeopardise their position.' A survey by the Shanghai Academy of Social Sciences of 500 married couples in Shanghai found that only '23.7 per cent of married women are willing to return home to concentrate on household matters', and most of them saw this as a contingency measure rather than choice (*Chinese Education*, Summer 1989, p. 50). Significantly, discourses of rights on equal opportunities are beginning to emerge.

However, it is more difficult to judge how much independence the All-China Federation of Women will be allowed in voicing the discontent of its members. The study of the campaign to 'compete and learn' has shown that the Federation is very much part of the party-state's agenda for furthering economic reform, but it has not challenged the gender biases operating in constructing policies on women. The role of the self-governing mass organisations as transmitters of state policies under the Maoist regime has not fundamentally altered in the post-Mao era. Further, despite the greater leeway granted for dissenting from the party line, the history of these organisations does not allow their members to trust them. This will take a long time to develop.

The political waters are even more uncharted for autonomous organisations. These are beginning to form at various levels – from academic women's networks to informal associations protecting the material interests of their members like the Beijing Association of Domestic Workers.

Women are not only facing pressure to retreat from the economic sphere, but also from their already limited access to political life. Rural women have been particularly hit by the changes in agricultural production. The commune system included women on its various committees to give them a representative character; the same was the case with the various revolutionary committees that managed the factories. With the dissolution of the commune system and the disbanding of the revolutionary committees women are being slowly pushed out of the public political sphere. Changes in the system of agricultural production has meant family- and house-based work for women – a 'courtyard economy' is now being encouraged. This has taken away the public space in which they encountered each other and exchanged views. In the cities too the disappearance of crèches and the pressures to leave their jobs is forcing women into leading more 'private' lives. The limits placed on political reforms by the party-state prevent development of free public space within which women can organise in their own interests.

An article on the public and private responsibilities of Chinese women concluded 'Men taking part in politics require opportunity and ability; women taking part in politics require opportunity, ability and family support. The unfairness of this situation demands our consideration.' An editorial in Beijing Review commented on the declining numbers of women in public life: 'in the 1987 re-election of leading bodies at the county and township levels, the number of women representatives was found to be down in twelve provinces and municipalities. In some areas there was not a single woman in county and township government' (Zhang 1992, p. 41). The view that the Women's Federation takes illustrates the way the question is being approached in China today. The official of the Federation interviewed by Zhang made it clear that 'the increase in women's *participatory capability* [in economic production] is central to improving the status and role of women in social production' (Zhang 1992, p. 51). The Federation continues to consider women's social and political position within a materialist construction of the women's question.

Conclusion

In this chapter I have argued that gender relations in China have been considered by both the Maoist and the post-Mao regimes as subsidiary to the more urgent agendas set by a largely gender-blind party-state. Hence neither regime has challenged the patriarchal foundations of gender-based discrimination. Not only have the communists failed to confront traditional patriarchal social arrangements but they have built upon them to achieve other economic and political goals.

Liberal theorists have insisted on the 'integral relationship between a realm of protected privacy and the quality of political participation' (Bachrach and Botwinick 1992, pp. 132–36). Feminists have argued to the contrary that the protection provided by the private sphere is a gendered protection. Specifically, the family, which provides the social foundations of the 'private' sphere, needs to be 'opened up' to critical scrutiny to reveal the silences imposed upon women within the confines of the 'private'. In her critique of patriarchal liberalism Carole Pateman argues that unless family relations are conceived of and lived equally between genders, whatever the differences that might characterise the sexes, public equality will be gravely undermined (Pateman 1989, pp. 118–40). If we position Chinese women in the context of this debate, their situation is doubly difficult.

The Maoist state did not challenge the patriarchal assumptions of a traditional civil society other than within a narrow materialist framework. Thus, while the private sphere came under attack, it was primarily to bring women into employment and as part of the party-state's attack upon civil society. An emphasis on class politics also refused women the liberty of organising in their own interests. In the post-Mao era Chinese women are again caught in a dichotomous position. An emerging civil society is making the private sphere more of an autonomous space. But the protection from the gaze of an omnipresent state is being bought at a significant cost by women. The 'protection' given by the private sphere to women is only partial, and conditional upon conformity with the norms set by a largely patriarchal society. The party-state's insistence upon monitoring the public sphere makes it difficult for women to promote their interests other than at peripheral levels. The marginalisation of women's issues and struggles continues in the face of the programme of market reforms.

16

Population and Family Policies

Penny Kane

'You cannot wrap a fire in paper'

Population and family policies in China have shown a remarkable degree of consistency for more than two decades. Family planning services had been government policy since 1953, but were originally seen solely as contributing to better maternal and child health and the status of women. From 1970, when population growth targets were included in the Fourth Five-Year Plan, the aim has been to control and reduce population growth rates through a comprehensive package of interventions. These have included efforts to raise the age of marriage and the status of women; to create a small-family 'norm' and to increase old-age security as well as the widespread delivery of contraceptive and abortion services.

In 1970, there were some 830 million Chinese and, as a result of the dramatic reductions in death rates over the previous two decades, the population growth rate was around 2.8 per cent, implying a potential doubling time of some twenty-five years. The perceived problems of meeting the demands – for health care, schooling, and jobs, for example – of those huge additional numbers was not the only issue to concern the country's planners: there was also the issue of the population's structure. High growth rates in the 1950s had been followed, during the disastrous years after the 1957 Great Leap Forward, by low and even (in 1960 and 1961) negative growth (Kane 1988). As the country recovered and death rates continued their long-term decline, there was a second 'baby boom'. Thus the size of each birth cohort varied considerably and the task of designing services to meet their needs was made more complex. Worse, the irregularity in cohort size was not just a temporary phenomenon: as each became adult and married and had children, the surges and declines in the numbers in various age-groups requiring particular services would be perpetuated.

Clearly there was a need to expand contraceptive and abortion facilities beyond the cities to which they had been largely confined, and to accompany that expansion with major promotional campaigns to encourage people to use them. The campaigns initially concentrated on spreading a simple triple message: that couples should marry later, have long intervals between births, and should limit the total number of children they produced. Late marriage was already a feature of China's efforts to increase the status of women by giving them access to further education as well as a greater chance of resisting pressures to accept an arranged marriage. Long intervals between births were encouraged for health reasons; reductions in family size were described as essential in controlling population growth.

The success of the campaigns was extraordinary: by 1975 the growth rate had fallen to around 1.8 per cent, and the Fifth Five-Year Plan (1975–80) included the target of a further reduction, to 1 per cent by 1980. To achieve this, each administrative level introduced its own target, and each local unit was encouraged to discuss – and where necessary modify – the fertility plans and behaviour of its members.

During a period when the production team or brigade in the rural communes had a collective income, and made collective decisions about the allocation of funds for local health care, crèches and schools, the relevance of individual couples' decisions about the timing of their next pregnancy or whether to have a fourth baby was reasonably evident. As a result community pressures could – and often did – have a major impact on the couple's ultimate actions. In addition, local units were easily able to understand the planning difficulties which resulted from fluctuating numbers having children in any particular year, and often attempted to smooth out the bulges by persuading some couples to defer a pregnancy to a less-crowded year.

These ambitious interventions were not underpinned by any considerable body of demographic understanding, let alone demographic theory. It was only in 1975 that population studies, banned from consideration in 1960 along with many other areas of social science, were reintroduced into Chinese universities. Those – mainly statisticians – suddenly allocated to become demographers were starting from scratch, with very little access to foreign texts, and with the additional handicap of having to develop an acceptable Marxist theory.

The first result of their studies was a recognition that the 1 per cent growth target was unattainable, and that future reductions in growth would be extremely difficult. 50 per cent of the population were below the age of 21. Even if all of them had smaller families than had been customary in the past, China would continue to grow for the foreseeable future. Nor would restricting all couples to two children result in a zero growth rate by the end of the century, as had been hoped (Kane 1987).

The one-child family policy

Thus was conceived the most unusual, and most controversial, of China's population policies: the single-child family (Croll *et al.* 1985). It was never intended that *every* child should be an only child, but that the proportion of only children should be considerably increased through a combination of rewards, such as priority in health care, schooling and housing, for families who agreed to stop at one. At the same time, those who had third or subsequent births would have to pay fines or taxes to offset the additional burden they were placing on the community. The original assumption was that the measures should become law, but strong opposition meant that no national legal provisions were ever ratified. Instead, each province drafted its own regulations in support of the policy.

Announced in 1979, the single-child policy became more ambitious the following year, when a group of social and natural scientists began to build population models and project population size in combination with economic development, food and water supplies, and ecological balance. They concluded that China's population – by then only just below the thousand million which it was to reach in 1981 – should actually be reduced, over the next hundred years, to between 650 and 700 million. To achieve this, they recommended enforcing *universal* single-child families until the year 2000 and then gradually allowing more people to have two children again. The sheer impossibility of carrying out their recommendations, as well as the havoc they would have created in the age-structure of the population, prevented a universal one-child family policy from being introduced. Nevertheless, the assumption that one or two generations should make sacrifices now for the long-term benefit of the Chinese people remained an integral part of the policy.

In the cities there was considerable pressure on parents to restrict themselves to a single child. Most of the city-dwelling families had at least one member who worked for the state, whether in industry or the service sector. Such people faced substantial pressures, in the form of fines and deferred promotion as well as delays in access to housing. After the first few years of the policy, such deterrents were the major factor in people's compliance, because the alleged incentives for a single child – such as priority in getting a place in a crèche, in being allotted a larger flat, or in health care, quickly became meaningless. When four out of five children are 'only' children – the situation in the larger cities throughout the 1980s – 'priority' loses all meaning. Cash subsidies for single children which were introduced in many cities, usually for health care, were comparatively significant in the late 1970s and early 1980s. By the early 1990s, however, individual incomes had risen by a factor of five or six at least, and the unchanged cash subsidy represented a negligible contribution.

In addition to official deterrents many city couples had a much longer experience of contraceptive use, along with virtually universal female employment and few labour-saving devices to ease the housekeeping tasks which were still predominantly left to working women. City couples were also less likely to have a parent living with them to ease their burdens or take care of children. Indeed, many of the grandparents were still working. Such conditions had already persuaded an increasing proportion of couples during the 1970s to limit their family to a single child long before the policy was introduced.

In rural areas, however, the single-child policy met a very different response. Despite improvements in mortality rates, rural prospects for child survival remained worse. In Hunan, a province around the middle-ranking for economic development, infant mortality was 65.4 per 1000 live births in 1980 and 60.2 in 1986, four times the level reported in Shanghai (SFPC/CSP 1990). One birth was not enough, even if that birth was of a son. Sons were essential to a family both in the metaphysical sense – only through a son is the name and lineage continued – and in the immediate practical context of support for old age. While a daughter left home on marriage, a son would take over the family land and care for ageing parents.

Official attempts to change peasant attitudes can be traced right through the history of post-Liberation China. Examples of a daughter bringing her husband to be the support of her family were widely publicised, but they remained rare. Old people without surviving children were entitled to the 'five guarantees' (basic food, medical care, clothes, shelter and burial) provided by their unit but accepting such minimal charity was sometimes seen as humiliating. A variety of local pension schemes (see Chapters 17, 18) was introduced in the early 1980s in wealthier rural (largely suburban) areas but the numbers reached were limited.

As economic reforms progressed, it became increasingly difficult to regulate peasant fertility, or penalise those who had large families. With the demise of collective agriculture much of the pressure on individuals to conform to local family size or family spacing norms disappeared. Early efforts to link reproductive goals to the provision of land were relaxed as it became apparent that peasants would not invest in their land without some security of tenure. Increasingly, fines became the main way of attempting to discourage an extra birth. As peasants grew wealthier, however, fines became less of a deterrent. In poorer areas many of the families simply refused to pay them. Local family planning officials, often friends or relatives of the families involved, recognised that there was no point in attempting to collect money which simply did not exist.

The current demographic situation

The 1990 Census gave a mid-year population for China of 1.134 billion, and birth and death rates of 21 and 6.3 per 1000 population. The resulting natural increase rate of 14.7 would, if continued, see the population double in about forty-eight years, or before 2040. During the current Five-Year Plan period (1991–5) the number of women moving into the peak reproductive ages of 20–29 will – as a result of earlier baby booms – be 16.4 per cent greater than in the previous five-year period. Thus the number of births is also increasing and, even if the total number of children born to each couple remains the same, the birth rate will also rise.

The reported mean age of marriage for women declined during the 1980s to just below 22. Despite references in the Chinese press to couples who choose to have no children, fewer than 2.5 per cent remained childless through the 1980s. Intervals between marriage and first birth have declined steadily in the past three decades, with the mean now being 1.33 years. However, while 95 per cent of women in the 1970s continued from a first to a second birth, in the latter part of the 1980s more than one in every five women had only a single child.

Data for decision-making

The figures above should be interpreted with caution. Chinese population statistics have a long tradition and are more comprehensive than those in most developing countries. An ongoing population registration system has been supplemented since Liberation by four censuses and, in the past decade or so, national surveys of fertility behaviour. But there are indications that data has deteriorated. In the late 1970s reporting of births began to deteriorate as pressure was put on local units to achieve low population growth targets (Banister 1987). Even the census of 1982, which had a high degree of overall reliability, seems to have missed some births in 1981 especially births of girls. Officials continued to assume that their data was reasonably accurate until at least 1986, when a national sample survey revealed a total fertility rate of 2.4 births per woman, instead of the 2.1 calculated on the basis of birth registrations. Nevertheless, it was not until 1988 that the government finally admitted that the target of limiting population to 1.2 billion at the end of the century was not going to be achieved. Based on current information, they suggested the actual number in the year 2000 as perhaps being as high as 1.284 billion. The 1990 census (considered slightly less complete than the previous one) produced an end-year population figure of 1.143 billion, and with another 'baby boom' group coming into the fertile ages in the 1990s, the population total in 2000 will undoubtedly exceed 1.3 billion.

There were several reasons why population statistics during the

1980s and early 1990s became increasingly unreliable. Local family planning officials had their neighbours, friends and relatives as clients. Caught between unrealistic targets and local resistance to those targets, false returns were a way out. Pressures on local cadres intensified from 1986, when a 'population management responsibility system' introduced penalties for administrators who failed to meet their quotas. This provided another incentive to adjust reported figures.

Records might also be falsified if the couple should not have been having children at all. The legal age of marriage in China was increased in 1980 from 18 to 20 for women and from 20 to 22 for men; the recommended age has always been several years higher. Those who chose to wed before the approved, or even the legal, age often underwent traditional ceremonies and settled into their homes with community acceptance, simply postponing the registration of the wedding. The 1987 fertility survey suggested that 10 per cent of all births that year, involving 2.5 million children, were to couples who had not yet reached the legal marriage age.

As the economic reforms accelerated, the number of migrants increased. The 1987 one per cent sample census identified 30.5 million people who had moved to other areas since the 1982 census. 50 per cent of all the migrants were aged 15–24 and most of the remainder were 25–44; in other words they were a floating population of young people in the fertile ages. As the survey included only those who had legally registered in their new location, or had been there for six months, it undoubtedly underestimated the actual numbers. With the phasing-out of rations, particularly the grain allocated to city-dwellers, and the introduction of a range of new housing opportunities from temporary shanties alongside building sites, to private flats, there were few inducements for migrants to identify themselves. Avoidance of income tax, and family planning workers, were good reasons for continuing to 'float'. In 1992, there were said to be 60 million migrants. By 1993, estimates – still probably underestimates – of the 'floating population' had risen to 80 million people, or more than 10 per cent of China's working-age population.

As individual businesses or private companies have spread, and more state factories are transferred to new forms of management, as well as a growing body of city workers who can afford private housing, parents are not subject to fines or lack of promotion prospects if they exceed the single-child quota and often have significant financial, as well as fertility, reasons to avoid registration.

China's missing girls

Most of the births which appear to be missing from the registration system and even from the censuses are of females. Trends in reported sex ratios at birth have risen from 108.4 males (1982) to 111.75 (1990) for every 100 females. The maximum feasible biological difference in the numbers born is thought to be 106 males to every 100 females. While the Chinese sex ratios were normal for first and second births in 1981 and only became heavily skewed for higher-order children, figures for more recent years show increases in sex ratios amongst second children (Hull and Wen 1992).

There has been considerable debate internationally about the implications of these alarming sex ratios. Some (for example, Hull 1990) view them as evidence of widespread use of Ultrasound B and X-ray machines for early identification of the sex of a foetus and its subsequent abortion. Use of the equipment for sex preselection is illegal in China but the frequency with which this has to be said suggests fear that it happens.

Other studies (such as Coale 1984, Banister 1992) suggest widespread and rising levels of infanticide and/or early death of girl babies from neglect, usually the result of differential feeding and access to health care. Death from neglect among infant girls has been comparatively common in much of Asia and remains so in South Asia; Hull and Wen (1992) suggest that the sex ratios of deaths in children under the age of one in the 1990 Census provide some confirmation for this hypothesis. A report on orphanages in China (Johnson 1993) suggests that very few boys – except the severely handicapped – are found in them, and that overwhelmingly it is girls who are brought to them or abandoned nearby in the hope that they will be taken in.

Other girl-children are informally adopted out or given away. Johansson and Nygren (1991) found that the very high proportions of girls reported in the 1988 fertility survey as adopted into a family accounted for most of the 'missing' girls. Although doubts have been cast on this explanation (Hull 1990) the Guangdong Provincial Family Planning Regulations were revised in 1992 to include an explicit condemnation of the practice of informal adoption. The abnormally low levels of infertile marriages reported in China also suggests considerably more adoption than is admitted. There is anecdotal evidence that many couples are even willing to move to a distant place to ensure secrecy in their decision to adopt.

The most likely explanation for most of the missing girl-children is that their births are not being registered. Migrants and those in the private sector may be willing, for future legitimacy or other advantage, to record a son but are much less likely to report a daughter. In addition they provide a possible kin network through which others can hide a daughter from local investigation.

The growth of private schools and private medical care have combined to make it easier to avoid a child being picked up by the system at a later stage. Private facilities do offer hope that at least some of these girl-children may not miss out throughout life even if they have missed out on official existence. The worst result of the current one-child policy may be the development of a subclass of women who have no formal standing, little or no education, poor health resulting from inadequate health care, and few prospects.

Government responses

Government reaction to difficulties in implementing the one-child policy has taken several forms. On the one hand, each report of unsatisfactory family planning achievements has been met by a new implementation campaign. Each of the periods of intensification has led to reports of local abuses such as forced abortions and sterilisations, despite official reiterations of the programme's voluntary nature.

Increasingly, demographers in China have joined outside observers in suggesting alternative policies to meet the same objectives in limiting population growth. Most alternatives involve increased emphasis on a higher age of marriage and on the timing of births – especially the first birth; some have also suggested deliberate expansion of urbanisation and a faster pace of economic reform.

So far Chinese policy-makers have insisted that the current policy must remain in place, especially because swings and reversals in many domestic policies have created widespread scepticism; thus, unless the one-child policy remains sacrosanct people will assume that any replacement can be safely ignored. In addition, the one-child policy is a model or target to be aimed for, rather than actually achieved. If, with a target of one child, it is difficult to keep actual family size to between two and three children, a target of two might raise family ambitions to three or four.

Nevertheless, there are encouraging signs of change. Guang-dong, which has had a mediocre record on family planning despite being the first province to introduce regulations for the one-child family, revised those regulations in 1992. Significantly, limits imposed on the total number of births permitted have disappeared. Instead, the regulations simply state that unplanned births are forbidden. Emphasis, in other words, appears to be on ensuring births are spaced, planned, negotiated and approved within local communities according to local quotas.

Such an approach may also be legitimising informal rules which have partly accommodated the desires of local couples. A recent study in rural China concluded that women had 'actively contested policy elements they did not like, forcing local cadres to negotiate' (Greenhalgh 1992).

A further encouraging sign is that women have also become more vocal and better-informed about contraceptive service provision. Quality of services has been uneven, with inadequately informed family planning workers offering a limited choice of methods. In many areas the choice has simply been sterilisation or an intra-uterine device (IUD). Some of the contraceptives – like the steel ring IUD – are inferior. With assistance from the UN Population Fund and other donors, better-quality condoms are being produced in greater numbers, the steel ring has been replaced by a modern copper IUD, efforts are being made to ensure a wide variety of contraceptive choices in rural areas and to retrain family planning workers to discuss those choices adequately.

Finally, family planning workers report changing attitudes among clients which have made family planning and small families – if not the one-child family – more acceptable. Even rural Chinese marrying and having children in the 1990s are the sons and daughters of parents who participated in the fertility declines of the 1970s. These young people have grown up in smaller families, which their parents achieved through contraception, and they begin to take both for granted.

These are signs that Chinese population policy may become less inflexible. That it will change fundamentally is improbable.

Conservative estimates are that some 17 million people will be added to China's numbers annually to the end of this decade. The population will continue to grow until into the twenty-first century. The implications for China, and for the world, are incalculable.

17

Family Strategies: Securing the Future

Elisabeth J. Croll

'A leaf before the eye shuts out Mount Tai'

In 1978, on the eve of reform and after the long years of revolution and its promises, it was the immediate association of riches with reform that sold the idea of radical and rapid economic transformation and acted as an incentive to those about to adopt such changes. One of the most important questions of the first decade of reform was whether the government could satisfy the rising expectations it had set in motion. In those first years it seemed more than possible, for one of the most important and much-publicised immediate repercussions of reform was the dramatic increase in new economic opportunities, cash incomes and the standards of living of peasant households. Indeed, throughout the countryside a combination of economic reforms and new pricing policies caused the largest overall rise in peasant incomes since the early 1950s. The number of newly rich and in particular 'ten-thousand-yuan' households became the chief rationale and criterion for measuring the efficacy of reforms and not only in the popular imagination. Officially too, the association of riches with reform permeated government reports, policy documents and speeches and constituted the overriding criterion of policy success. 'Get rich quick', 'You too can become rich' and 'Riches for all' were slogans and popular sayings which encouraged widespread emulation of the 'ten-thousand-yuan' households.

In the first years of reform the accumulation of wealth depended largely on the degree to which peasant households or families could individually take advantage of new, diverse and specialised opportunities for income generation, meet the new demands on their resources and manage new responsibilities for production, processing and marketing. One of the most important repercussions of reform was the generation of a completely new set of demands on individual peasant households including the procurement of raw materials, production inputs, technical knowledge, capital, transport, storage and markets. These were demands which had formerly been the responsibility of the collective. Despite the inexperience of the farmers and the weakness of the service infrastructure, the journeys I made during the first years of reform were made captivating by the hum and liveliness of activity as farmers took advantage of the new opportunities for generating income by expanding cultivation, raising livestock, handicrafts and every conceivable form of entrepreneurial activity, spilling out onto courtyard, street and market. Farm, workshop and small factory all generated new goods, services and business, creating new wealth and new and greater choices for households and villages.

Change of sky

Significant and sometimes dramatic rises in the national *per capita* rural incomes were widely celebrated in the first years of the reform. By the end of the first decade however it was clear that not all regions and households had benefited similarly from the reforms, and that initial rises in peasant incomes had been commonly eroded by rising costs and inflation (World Bank Report 1992). New opportunities had been tempered by constraints and aspirations, and expectations modified by uncertainties and anxieties in the face of new risks. The generation of new opportunities for and demands on the peasant household have been well-documented. What has received less attention has been the new sense of risk and increasing insecurity experienced by many peasant farmers as they embraced the new opportunities. Before reform, and encompassed by collective and plan, the peasant household had few autonomous responsibilities or choices beyond the most marginal; with reform, new and individual responsibilities multiplied with immediate repercussions for the profits and losses of their farms. Making the most of the new opportunities, exercising choices and accumulating wealth were primarily dependent on securing pre- and post-production services, sufficient supplies of inputs and reliable markets all of which were frequently outside farmers' experience, understanding – and certainly their control.

It has been increasingly acknowledged that problems in the supply of inputs and their rising costs have diminished, or in some cases even reversed, the gains of the early years of reform. For example, the supply of fertiliser, which is the most important of inputs in maintaining and improving yields and therefore incomes, has frequently been in short supply and of poor quality. The press has repeatedly taken up this cause on behalf of farmers because 'chemical fertiliser markets in many localities are in a mess and a major factor adversely affecting agricultural production and standards of social conduct'. In these circumstances the returns from the land have declined. In many of the villages where new mechanisms of collective supply have not been established, many of the farmers interviewed complained bitterly about the costs and difficulties of obtaining supplies of fertiliser and feed. They felt that these responsibilities were increasingly heavy and for some outweighed the advantages gained from the reforms. Several peasant farmers openly expressed a wish to return to collective farming for the simple reason that they had previously not had the responsibility of procuring agricultural and other production inputs. It became increasingly clear in some regions that unless there was some government aid in procuring inputs, the majority of farmers would be caught in a downward spiral.

Newspapers also reported instances of farmers encountering marketing problems because of poor information and their misunderstanding of supply and demand. Often farmers were unable to sell their products because of over-supply and falling prices or insufficient quotas on purchases. Year after year, there have been reports that state contracts to purchase grain and promises to purchase agricultural sidelines remained unfulfilled. Neither the state nor the market reliably matched supply and demand, and because farmers often had no alternative means of selling, storing or processing their products, much went to waste. Farmers increasingly protested: 'How can it be a commodity economy where there is no market for principal farm and sideline products?', 'We cannot grow things that can make money and what we have grown is worthless' or 'One cannot buy what one wants and one cannot sell what one has.'

One of the most bitter of interviews I have undertaken in the past few years, but symbolic of upward and downward spirals in mobility was in a household which was on the verge of bankruptcy in a village near Beijing in 1989. The farmer had developed a specialised operation raising chickens in the early 1980s and subsequently established a large and successful chicken farm with some 1000 chickens. By 1984 he had become an envied 'ten-thousand-yuan' householder. However, his success was short-lived for first the costs of chicken feed rose, supplies dwindled and quality declined. Second, not only was he left with rising costs and poor stock, but once neighbouring farmers copied his successful example, the local market was flooded, resulting in falling prices and unsold baskets of eggs. He travelled to distant markets where eggs were in short supply, but was fined for illegally crossing provincial boundaries to sell his produce. At the time of my stay in the village, there were hundreds of undernourished and be-draggled, smelly chickens, a rusting small truck once used for transporting eggs and eggs piled high in every corner of the house. Two to three years ago this household would have been presented as the local success story. Now this failing enterprise caused a great deal of bitterness and resentment, primarily directed towards village cadres who, unusually, were nowhere to be seen during my visit. Not only was the farmer bitter, but the household was dismayed by the unexpected losses and downward mobility.

New hardships

Throughout China, production and living costs have both been affected by inflation which, exacerbated by an overheating economy, has also reduced the value of peasant households' savings which rose sharply during the reform decade. Household savings are usually accumulated for a particular item, occasion or as a reserve to meet unexpected expenses and as a cushion against ill-fortune. Inflation has also been accompanied by differentials between rich and poor which have widened in recent years and there has been an increase in the number and amounts of local fees and levies legally and illegally exacted in the villages as charges for services which may be provided or simply used to make good shortfalls in local government funds. Lack of available cash has been increasingly apparent as grain stations continue to issue IOUs to peasant households in return for contracted grain. Local post offices, too, have failed to cash the remittance slips from absent relatives working in towns and cities. The spectre of rising rural unemployment is ever-present, with an estimated rise in rural surplus labour of 10 million each year. It is currently estimated that 100 million out of 900 million peasants are now unemployed despite the growth in rural industry and that half of these are 'floating' or on the move in the search for work. For the poor and downwardly mobile, there are few guarantees or little more than minimal safety nets in place either in cash or of the kind formerly provided by some collectives. As a result of these economic, political and social factors, riches for many still seem as far away as ever and even for those newly rich, incomes have levelled off and have been increasingly threatened by rising costs, inflation and an uncertain market.

With new opportunities came new choices, riches and risks; with increasing constraints have come increasing disappointment and decline. The Chinese press frequently admits that while there are many 'joyously grasping the opportunities', 'hundreds of thousands of others feel that challenge and crises are inevitable' as disappointment and declining incomes more openly mark peasant experience of reform. While some enjoy risk-taking and become very practised, others find the new risks and responsibilities so onerous that they wish for a return to the familiarity and the security of the commune. The new and increasing hardships imposed upon peasant households are being openly described as the 'peasants or farmers' burden'. By 1993 the dimensions of the burden had led to growing government concern and outbreaks of peasant unrest and revolt which in turn made for a greater sense of social instability, vulnerability and insecurity.

Down to the sea

For many the future looks less promising and more unpredictable, especially in comparison with the messages and images promoted during the years of revolution. After 1949, countless slogans privileged the future in relation to the present. To make the present more tolerable, slogans such as 'Three years of hardship for a thousand years of happiness' reiterated the message that tomorrow will always be better than today. Chinese ideology has continually demoted the present to a liminal state or a state of transition *en route* to an imaged future marked by limitless possibility, prosperity and equity in distribution with equality and security for all. Although this future might be distant or even recede from time to time, it was supported by a rhetoric which planned and charted the future and in certain circumstances was a substitute for living in the present. Gratification was deferred and the experience of the present denied.

After 1979 however, concern was with the present rather than the future and largely focused on immediate incentives, enrichment and gratification rather than deferring needs and rewards. The very rationale for, and platforms of, reform were based on policies and promises intended to improve and secure livelihoods and even a consumer lifestyle *immediately*. But when reform failed to deliver on these promises, farmers were left without the security and certainty of a planned or imaged future to frame, define or counterbalance their experience. An important insight and field-finding of the past few years, and, I suggest, a predominant theme of post-reform China, is the widespread absence of a dream or a concept of the future as a common point of reference.

While there was and still is some excitement at the new opportunities created by economic reforms, there is also a sense of loss or bereavement that has not so much to do with a wish to return to the past as with the onset of uncertainty, unpredictability and anxiety. Since the mid-1980s there have been no promises of a better future or any certainty that tomorrow would be better than today. Chinese leaders, including Deng Xiaoping and Jiang Zemin have admitted that China 'has no clear idea of the future' and is 'a country without a concept' (Branson 1990). It is not without significance that the term currently in vogue for taking up the new business opportunities or 'leaping into the tide of private business' is *xiahai* or 'going out' or 'down to the sea':

> Some say the sea symbolises an immense realm, and going to the sea is an action that incites bold people. Some say that there are more chances of harvest in the sea than on the land. People watch the sea from the shore with some desire, some fear and some mystery. The waves are turbulent, so there may not be plain sailing ahead (Xiao Ming 1993; see also Chapter 13).

To continue the analogy, while some venture into the water boldly and some more timidly, some may swim, some may flounder, some may be saved and some may drown – for is not all venturing a risk? What is interesting is that it is the sea which has become the colloquial euphemism combining as it does smoothness and

turbulence in the single waters which are uncertain or even uncharted. In the villages it is now often said of the economy that 'the
only thing certain is uncertainty and change'.

Peasant dreams

In the face of greater uncertainty and vulnerability, many of the
time-honoured sources of security are also at risk. For generations,
peasant farmers in China had dreamed of land and more land for
security of family and property. The relationship of peasant to
land, be it ownership, management or cultivation, has traditionally
been the most important determinant of peasant livelihood and
security. Promises of land redistribution made in peasant rebellion,
revolution or reform have always been central in soliciting peasant
support. In reform, the new production-responsibility system by
which land was redistributed to peasant households had been both
popular and productive. However for villagers as for government
spokesmen, land has remained 'the central issue in China's rural
areas'. For the government 'the success of China's farm production
is very much dependent on the development of a rational land
policy'. For villagers fears of an insufficient land base have centred
on decreasing available arable land and increasing shortfalls in
investment and production inputs, insecurity of tenure and inequality in distribution. In many areas of China, the arable land is
still of such a quality that it does not provide a year's grain supply,
redistributed household-plot sizes have proved unsuitable for
large-scale farming, and in a country where arable land is already
scarce the removal of land for housebuilding and village and
township enterprises is a serious matter. Long-term household land
entitlements make for security of tenure but also mean that land
distribution has failed to keep pace with changes in household size,
making for paucity of land support for many dividing and expanding peasant households. Although diversification of farm activities
into non-agricultural pursuits has frequently caused land to
become a less-important component of farm economies, given the
risks associated with the production and marketing of varied side-
line farm products, land and crops are still seen to be both practically and symbolically the most important and long-term
guarantee of food supply and livelihood.

  If peasant households dreamed of land, they also dreamed of
having a sufficient number of sons to continue the family line and

work the land. For generations fathers and grandfathers had dreamed of sons and grandsons who would support them in their old age, maintain or expand their landholdings and guarantee their well-being in this world and the next. Sons were not only for dreaming and continuing the family or ancestral line, for in very practical ways they represented future prosperity and security. Indeed without sons there was no family future about which to think, plan and dream so that for generations in the Chinese household – be it large and extended or small and nuclear – there had been a traditional birth preference in favour of sons. During the first years of reform however, dreams of son-security were increasingly threatened by the introduction of stringent birth control policies including the single-child family policy which potentially cut short age-old forms of security.

The implementation of the single-child family policy also showed, however, that the truncation or abandonment of these age-old dreams and guarantees for the future is not taking place without a struggle and, in the face of continuous resistance, the government has had to modify the policy to take account of the preference for sons. In recent years two children have frequently been allowed. Single-daughter households have often been permitted one son and increasing wealth has made it possible for households to pay the necessary fines and raise an out-of-plan son. Sons were not only preferred in the interests of long-term security, but daughters have increasingly been sacrificed in the same interests. Daughters might be under-registered or subjects of discrimination either at birth by infanticide or through neglect shortly thereafter, or increasingly before birth by gender-selective abortion (Hull 1990). Censuses and surveys since the mid-1980s commonly display a large increase in sex ratios at birth most especially in agricultural households and among higher-parity births especially where the first child is an only daughter (see also Chapter 16). This discrimination against girls lies in the quest for old age insurance which only sons as the permanent members of the family can provide. Indeed *Nongmin Ribao* (*Farmers' Daily*) recently pointed out that the only way to correct the growing imbalance between births of boys and girls was to provide proper social provision for farmers so that they need not fear an impoverished and insecure old age. Hence various national programmes in the 1990s have advocated the introduction of new forms of insurance which will ease the anxieties and enhance the long-term prospects of the single-child family and especially the family with an only daughter. Already in the countryside, in a move symbolic of an era marked by the individual search for new sources of long-term security, farmers have turned in substantial numbers to a new means of providing protection against risk – insurance.

Insuring the future

In the face of uncertainty and as a guarantee against ill-fortune, peasant households have begun to take out a variety of forms of individual insurance to secure their future:

> the insurance industry has entered Chinese society and altered their views about living … it's not only a saving but also a prevention for any unexpected changes in the future … so that insurance pensions have become an integral part of some family's expenses (Wang Ningjun 1993).

Insurance has been sold in a sustained effort to encourage households and businesses to shift from dependence on the state or collective to having their own insurance to secure long-term aid and make good losses resulting from accident or ill-fortune. Staff of the new and expanding insurance companies have been instructed to inform people that 'having insurance offers security and benefits to others', 'new types of insurance could ensure society's stability and families' safety' and that 'families could and should shift risk on to insurance' (Yuan Lili 1993). In the past ten years insurance companies have proliferated and the oldest and largest, the People's Insurance Company, has revived. China now has over 300 kinds of insurance, encompassing property, life, disability, agriculture and credit. Family insurance can include health, children's education, marriage, housing, old-age, unemployment as well as various types of property cover. The insurance companies are breaking their own records in response to clients and premiums paid per person and per household reflect an insurance trade increasing by 30 per cent each year (Wang Ningjun 1993). Published figures for Beijing, Shanghai and Fujian province suggest that many millions of households have taken out a form of insurance. There are many stories in the media of families taking out insurance to secure property, health, education and personal possessions. The most popular forms are life insurance and those for securing pensions. These insurances are said to be especially popular among those with only daughters as a new means of relieving their fears and anxieties about the future in the absence of a son. One woman was quoted as saying:

> Now the money a son gives his parents every month is 30 odd yuan at most. But after we joined an insurance company we got more than 200 yuan for an elderly pension. This is much more than a son's 30 yuan. So it's more reliable than relying on a son for old age (Wang Ningjun 1993).

Another, younger, 31-year-old mother of an only daughter was quoted as asking, after she had arranged for a retirement payment of a monthly pension of 80 yuan per month 'so why do I have to rely on a son when I am old?' (Li Wei 1993). Families are thus encouraged to purchase insurance as an alternative to previous guarantees or dependence on sons or the state.

Securing the future in the years of reform has not only involved individual households in the shifting of new risks on to new forms and guarantees such as insurance, but has also involved the spreading of risks on to revived kinships and other-world, or heavenly, networks. Kin network has long been one of the most important forms of security providing support in hard times, but after collectivisation in the mid-1950s, the economic and political significance of kinship ties was reduced as households were incorporated into the all-embracing collective. However, collective cohesion might take advantage of and rest on pre-existing kinship ties and small kin clusters might remain the focus of various informal economic and ritual forms of cooperation. In contrast, during the reform years, in the absence of collective production structures, relations between post-household division and close-kin-related households have been reinvested with economic and political significance. New production responsibilities and demands frequently proved beyond the capacity of the individual household and collective safety nets were reduced at a time of increased entrepreneurial and market instability. This tendency towards economic association and cooperation between small neighbouring closely-related kin-based units was officially encouraged. It was seen as a means of augmenting the limited resources available to individual households to diversify and facilitate agricultural and non-agricultural production, processing and marketing. In and beyond the villages there have developed complex exchanges of labour, services and funds to facilitate the entire production process from cultivation or construction and processing to marketing, and to foster well-being and safety nets in times of crises. These complex exchanges were normally based on small aggregated groups of neighbouring kin-related households which I have elsewhere termed the aggregate family (Croll 1987), but they also extended to include larger male-linked kinship networks outside the village and affinity links or links made through the wife's kin. Recent village studies suggest that membership of the neighbourhood aggregate family engenders a greater degree of welfare, well-being and security based on corporate interests and mutual claims for assistance. In the absence of past collective or sufficient new village support, the more distant patrilineal kin and affinity links for providing gifts and loans to peasant households, whether it be in meeting basic needs or extraordinary expenses, are deemed to be an important resource without which households feel themselves to be severely disadvantaged.

One of the most interesting social phenomena in the countryside is the new importance attached to spatially extended kin or other networks by households or family aggregates beyond the immediate village environs. This gives them privileged access to materials, markets and information, generating income and spreading risks. The argument could also be extended to include all forms of relations or *guanxi* (connections) which, during the reform era, can be mainly seen as generating exchanges of resources or gifts thereby instituting new and larger claims or obligations for immediate assistance or to be called upon in the future. Indeed *guanxi* is not confined to ensuring or maintaining relations in this world. It may be extended to 'other world' networks for new religious acts of overt supplication to ancestors and to the gods in the interests of securing fortune and good luck can also be directly linked to an increased sense of risk, uncertainty and fears of downward mobility (Feuchtwang 1991). Almost every home has an ancestral altar where incense is offered to the deceased and the gods (or fortune-tellers, soothsayers and shamans speaking for the gods) are importuned and placated for luck, fortune and well-being, thereby giving support and security to the villagers in coping with the unpredictable and arbitrary.

Perhaps in this new era of uncertainty, materials and markets seem as far away as the gods and certainly as capricious. In a thriving market town in Guangxi, I was impressed by the preponderance of the most common for sale – meat and incense. One could have been forgiven for thinking that these were the two staple items of consumption. Perhaps they were, for symbolically they signified the two most common types of *guanxi* or relationship deemed necessary to safeguard family income and fortune: one for feasting and establishing *guanxi* in this world and the other for appeasing and supplicating those in the other world. Both these relations, alongside the new material interest in insurance have become common family strategies important in securing the future.

18

Social Welfare Reforms

Joe C. B. Leung

'When the city gate catches fire, the fish in the moat suffer'

Social welfare in China is intricately interwoven with political and economic activities. A term '*she hui bao zhang*' corresponding to 'social security' is often used to refer to measures of social protection and social provision. It consists of three main programmes:

1. Social insurance: occupational and state social security programmes usually provided by the work units covering the loss of income in contingencies.
2. Social welfare: social services provided by work units, the neighbourhoods, and the government.
3. Social relief: assistance provided by the government and the collectives to ex-servicemen, poverty-stricken households, and victims of natural disasters.

To the party-state social welfare is an instrument to facilitate economic productivity, to maintain social stability, and to enhance the legitimacy of the Communist regime. Social welfare has become a vital mechanism to mitigate conflicts instigated by rapid modernisation high economic growth, and market-oriented reforms.

General background

With a GNP per capita of US$ 370 in 1991[1], China is ranked as one of the poorest nations in the world. Yet great strides have been made in social development, for example,in life expectancy (79.5 years), mortality rate (6.7 per 1000 population), infant mortality rate (31 per 1000 population), literacy rate (69 per cent). Moreover, the World Bank (1991) reported that China has attained the level of the middle-income nation group, while a social development report produced by the United Nations in 1991 ranked China at 82 among 160 countries.

China recorded a population of 1.171 billion in 1992, with the annual natural growth rate at 13 per 1000 population (see also Chapter 16). Despite the implementation of the single-child policy since 1979, the impetus for population growth created by former policies will result in a population numbering 1.29 billion by the end of this century. The proportion of older persons (65 and above) will increase from 5.6 per cent in 1990 to 12.9 per cent in the year 2025, whereas the proportion of young people (0 to 14) will decrease from 27.7 per cent to 20.7 per cent in the same period. The number of employees retiring in 1992 reached 25 million (as compared with 3 million in 1978). Average household size in 1990 was 3.96 persons (4.24 persons in 1982), and about 65 per cent of these households consisted of two generations only (see Chapter 17).

With the rapid liberalisation of the economic structure, social concerns such as poverty, family breakdown, rural migrants, school drop-outs, unemployment, prostitution, drug addiction, juvenile delinquency, the care of abandoned children, the elderly, the physically disabled and the mentally ill have become more critical. While the official (and underestimated) unemployment rate was 5.8 per cent in 1979, which was reduced to 1.8 per cent in 1985, and then increased to 2.3 per cent in 1991 (State Statistical Bureau, 1992, p. 100). It is estimated that annual new entrants into the labour market will reach 20 million, and that the existing surplus labour force is 200 million in the rural areas and 20 million in state-owned enterprises.

Inequalities in incomes and living standards between the rural and urban areas, between geographic regions, and between employees in different economic sectors are widening. For example, the ratio between the annual per capita income in the cities and in the rural areas dropped from 3.47:1 in 1957 to 1.24:1 in 1978, but has increased to 2.31:1 in 1992. In addition to income differences, urban residents enjoyed state subsidies in daily necessities which are progressively being phased out. But over four decades to 1990, state financial subsidies took up approximately 20 per cent of expenditure. Almost 60 per cent of this went to consumer goods, while the rest subsidised the losses of state-owned enterprises.

If the annual per capita net income of 300 yuan is used as the poverty line in the rural areas, 9.2 per cent of the rural population (80 million people) were living in subsistence poverty in 1991. In the urban areas, if the annual per capita net income of 600 yuan is used as the poverty line, 5 per cent of the urban population (about 15 million people) were poverty-stricken. In 1992, the number of poverty-stricken households relying on government assistance reached 7 million, and annually there are over 100 million victims of natural disasters requiring help from the government. Other vulnerable populations include 52 million people with different kinds of disabilities, and 180 million illiterate people.

In short, the welfare responsibility of China is tremendous and escalating. Yet economic reforms in the 1980s have restructured, and to some extent, dismantled the basic welfare system. People now find either that their emerging needs cannot be satisfactorily met, or that welfare services are inaccessible to them. Even though the Chinese constitution has recognised some essential rights of the citizens including the right to welfare, individual rights are subsumed under the interests of the state and the country. Besides being a gift from the state, welfare entitlements are to be earned.

Social welfare policy under Mao Zedong

For decades after coming to power in 1949, China adopted a Soviet model of social welfare centred on the workplace. Whether a factory in an urban area, or a cooperative (later commune) in the countryside, the collective work unit functioned as a self-sufficient 'welfare society' within which an individual received employment and income protection, and enjoyed benefits and services such as housing, food, education, and health care. Through central planning, wages were kept low, and jobs were created to absorb the unemployed with little consideration for efficiency. Welfare benefits were a form of social wage to compensate for low wages. Notwithstanding inequalities between collectives, disparities among members within the same collective were limited. Within the ideology of self-reliance, these collectives were expected to solve their economic and social problems with their own resources.

While the right to welfare was not based on legal entitlement, the moral obligations of the collectives ensured a more or less equal distribution of benefits and the paternal protection of members in times of difficulty. In a sense, the model resembled the structure of the clan and extended family in traditional Chinese society. The difference is that the party leaders replaced the clan elders as the figures of authority and paternal benevolence.

As this welfare system is 'collective-centred' rather than 'state-centred', the role of the state at the macro-level was to provide a stable order within which the collectives could develop and fulfil the functions of political education, economic production, and welfare protection. The collectives were controlled by the state through central planning and redistribution, and also were some-what protected. For example, the state would provide subsidies or credits to cover losses. At the individual level, the state ensured that citizens belonged to a collective through household registration which limited rural–urban migration, and job assignment which controlled the recruitment and mobility of workers. For the few people outside a collective, the state provided a remedial welfare programme for the 'three nos': those with no family, no source of income, and no working ability.

Under Mao, social problems such as prostitution, begging, ve-nereal diseases, illiteracy, delinquency, drug addiction, and un-employment were either eliminated or substantially reduced. Through policies of full employment, reduced income differentials, control over wages and prices of essential commodities, the CCP attained high levels of public health, education, and social welfare. These achievements were better than those of countries with similar levels of economic development. Thus, social welfare under Mao provided the CCP with a mandate to govern, and political stability.

Welfare reforms under Deng Xiaoping

With the market-oriented economic reforms after 1978, the egalitarian-oriented and need-based welfare system established by Mao has come under severe criticism. The major assaults are on the 'iron rice bowl', or job security, which is regarded as an impediment to the promotion of economic productivity and work incentives. Distribution, according to Deng Xiaoping, can no longer be based on need, but on labour effort, supplemented by other means of distribution such as ownership of land and capital. Furthermore, differences in pay should be widened so as to encourage individual enthusiasm and speed up the development of production, and the major policy is to allow some people to become wealthy first, as part of the goal of common prosperity (*Beijing Review*, 15–21 April, 1991, p. v).

The disbandment of the communes in 1983 created a welfare vacuum. Some collective programmes such as the Five Guarantees and cooperative medical insurance are in disarray. Only those villages that have benefited from the economic reforms through the development of rural industries can afford to provide social services, such as homes for the childless elderly and employment for the disabled (Leung 1991). Recently, the government has encouraged those affluent areas to organise contributory retirement insurance, but the coverage is extremely small. Now, the ideology of self-protection and family responsibility is highly promoted (see Chapter 17).

Reforms began in the early 1980s for the granting of more autonomy and decision-making power to the state-owned enterprises. These include a profit-retention scheme, taxation and responsibility for their losses and profits. As each enterprise has to cover its own welfare costs, there is little sharing of costs among the enterprises. In particular, some of the old enterprises are finding it increasingly difficult to pay for escalating pension and medical costs. To share the costs and the risks, the government has encouraged enterprises to fund their pension schemes jointly. In 1986 the government promulgated regulations on bankruptcy, recruitment and dismissal of employees, contract labour, and unemployment insurance. The government thereby endorsed the principles that:

- enterprises that are not profit-making should declare bankruptcy;
- employees should be dismissed for unsatisfactory employment;
- new recruits should be hired on contract rather than on a permanent basis.

From now on, the unemployed should be taken care of by the newly-developed unemployment insurance scheme.

Trends in welfare reforms

Rising welfare costs

In 1990, social security expenditures amounted to 110.3 billion yuan,[2] which was 6.2 per cent of GNP compared with 10.6 billion yuan and 3.1 per cent in 1978. Of this amount, 85 per cent was for the welfare of employees in urban enterprises. The increase is mainly due to rising payment for pensions and medical care which constitute 50 per cent and 21 per cent of the total expenditure respectively. But welfare responsibility is now perceived as an economic burden rather than as a political asset (Leung 1992).

Towards welfare pluralism

To cope with mounting welfare costs, notably in the state-owned enterprises where over 33 per cent are running at a loss, the Eighth Five-Year National Plan for Economic Development (1991–95) and the Ten-Year Development Programme (1991–2000) postulated:

> A social insurance system for the aged should be established for people of different occupations in cities and towns, with the state, collectives and individuals sharing the cost in a rational way. The scope of insurance for people waiting for jobs should be enlarged, and a multi-level social insurance programme be practised.

The notion of contributory insurance is becoming popular (see Chapter 17). Insurance can cover retirement, medical care, work injury, and unemployment. Enterprises and village governments, depending on their financial situation, may contribute to the funds. The essential issue remains as to what extent the employees or villagers can afford to make contributory payments. Even though the employees have received unprecedented wage increases, particularly in bonuses, increases in the cost of living due to the relaxation of price controls have affected the quality of life for urban residents. For the peasants, the economic situation has deteriorated, and the real income has remained stagnant. Furthermore, they have been plagued by local officials trying to squeeze funds from them in the form of taxes, fines and contributions to public work.

Economic liberalisation has produced a diversified economic sector with different forms of ownership. State policy on welfare only applies to state-owned enterprises which employ about 18 per cent of the economically active population. Welfare reforms accommodate regional differences and policy instructions from the state council are only guidelines. This is in line with the economic policy of allowing the enterprises and local governments to have more autonomy. With increased local autonomy and reduced direct control from the central government, the term 'social welfare with Chinese characteristics' is becoming less precise. It is more relevant to refer to social welfare with regional characteristics such as 'Guangdong characteristics', or 'Beijing characteristics', or 'Sichuan characteristics'.

Social services cannot rely on government funding, and have to look for other means including charging fees and revenue from profit-making businesses. Privatisation on a small scale can be found in education, housing, and medical care and since 1987 lotteries have been introduced to raise funds for welfare programmes.

Widening inequalities

With a decentralised welfare system, inequalities are inevitable. Yet under the present economic policy, the party-state has little intention of reducing the disparities in welfare provision. Even so there are implementation problems, and taxation as yet cannot deliver adequate levels of redistribution

Emerging role of non-governmental organisations

Non-governmental organisations (NGOs), or to be specific, organisations without the patronage of the party-state are rare. NGOs include mass organisations for youth, women, workers, and residents (see Chapter 6). Whilst reducing their traditional role in political education, these organisations are becoming active in the provision of social services to their constituencies. These services include personal and family counselling, career guidance, job training, recreational and cultural activities, and voluntary work.

Playing down the policy on self-reliance, China is beginning to welcome foreign donations and assistance in charity and relief work through such organisations as the Foundation for

Underdeveloped Regions in China. But so far, only a limited number of international organisations such as World Vision and Oxfam are able to operate regular relief projects in poverty-stricken areas.

Growing importance of welfare policy in maintaining social stability

Welfare reforms in both urban and rural areas are met with strong resistance from people who experience a deterioration in their quality of life. There have been reports of unprecedented industrial action over redundancy and working conditions and rural violence against government. Given the importance of welfare to the maintenance of political stability, it is likely that the iron rice bowl in state-owned enterprises will remain largely intact.

Conclusion

Social welfare policy has only been considered a controversial issue since market reforms were introduced in the 1980s. Modernisation has revealed many social problems and unmet social needs. In order to rationalise the economy while maintaining political stability, welfare reforms will have to be cautious. They will be marked by an incremental and pluralistic orientation, coping with immediate problems rather than having a grand design. This means that the party-state will continue to issue instructions and guidelines from the top, while encouraging innovative and flexible responses at the local level.

In the future social welfare will become an important mechanism for understanding the legitimacy of the party-state. Although general living standards have improved dramatically, the issue of income redistribution will be high on the political agenda, and social inequalities will constitute a major threat to political stability. Social welfare therefore will have a new meaning in the formulation of social policy in China.

Notes

1. The use of the foreign exchange rate to calculate GNP has not been satisfactory. Recently, the International Monetary Fund, using 'the purchasing power parity' method of calculating the wealth of nations put GNP per capita of China at US$ 1450.
2. This figure does not include housing subsidies of 30 billion yuan.

19

Chinese Literature and Film in the 1990s

Anne Wedell-Wedellsborg

'Rather be a shattered vessel of jade,
than an unbroken piece of pottery'

By the early 1990s the cultural scene in China was more diversified than ever since the founding of the People's Republic, and for the first time commercial, rather than political, factors were determining the majority of what was published and produced. Guidelines from party leaders were no longer the main agents of cultural change. As the market economy made its way into literature and the arts, ideological control weakened (despite the Tiananmen crackdown). Along with the rapid development of the media and publishing industry, literature split into many genres and levels, each appealing to different audiences.

The most conspicuous phenomenon has been the unprecedented growth of works produced with the explicit purpose of sheer entertainment and commercial profit. There are, of course, still a considerable number of highly talented authors writing according to their individual aesthetic standards and personal visions of Chinese culture, past and present. Some of their works have lent plots and themes to those films that have marked China's re-entry into the realm of top-quality world art. This chapter will present some of the trends and a few of the particularly significant writers and film-makers that have stood out during the past few years. But first a broad outline of the cultural climate of this period.

The changing cultural climate

Following the Tiananmen crackdown, the Minister of Culture since 1986, the writer Wang Meng, stepped down. He had presided over the hitherto most liberal period for literature and the arts in the history of the PRC. The choice of his successor, veteran leftist He Jingzhi, signalled a tightening of control and return to power of the old guard in the literary establishment. Following the crackdown the press launched fierce attacks on literary figures such as Su Xiaokang, one of the creators of the highly controversial television series of 1988, *Heshang (River Elegy)* which had portrayed Chinese civilisation (including socialist) as stagnant and harmful to progress. Su had fled to the West, as had a number of other prominent intellectuals who had openly sympathised with the student-led protesters. They were accused not only of the political offence of 'bourgeois liberalisation' but also, more seriously, of national betrayal and of instigating unpatriotic behaviour. Though a few major literary magazines and periodicals maintained an independent line, others were taken over by hardliners. The literary journal, *Beijing Wenxue*, which in the late 1980s under the editorship of the perceptive and charismatic critic, Li Tuo, was a breeding ground for *avant-garde* literary experiments and new criticism, was put in the hands of Hao Ran, a literary star of the Cultural Revolution.

But this short-lived offensive on the part of the more orthodox writers had limited effect. By the early 1990s there was a definite revival of creativity, even in the most official publications, and it was clear that the return of some leftists to posts in literary and art organisations would have little long-term influence.

In retrospect, the Tiananmen crackdown does *not* mark a watershed in China's cultural life, just as it did not basically alter the ongoing economic and political development. In a somewhat paradoxical way the Tiananmen events enhanced rather than halted the separation of literature and politics. The absence of an overt, consciously political, problem-literature which in the immediate aftermath of the crackdown was a result of suppression, now simply seems a fairly natural reflection of the general apolitical, money-centred and spiritually disillusioned atmosphere in Chinese society of the mid-1990s. A number of those controversial writers and critics who took part in the literary movements of the 1980s are now in the West. They include critical and socially concerned writers such as Liu Binyan and Su Xiaokang, and also people mainly associated with artistic experiments, like Bei Dao, Gao Xingjian, Liu Suola, Liu Zaifu and Ah Cheng, whose activities and writings in the context of the then-prevailing spiritual climate nevertheless acquired political implications. Many of the artists and writers inside China, not least those of the youngest generation, now evince a remarkably apolitical stance. Even the party has played down its role, asking writers in vague terms to serve socialism and modernisation, not politics.

That the relationship between politics and literature is taking on new dimensions is also apparent in the response of the writer and former Minister of Culture, Wang Meng, to a blatantly political critique of one of his short stories, published in the official party paper for literature and arts, *Wenyibao* in 1991. A pseudonymous critic, drawing upon Taiwanese comments, alleged that a two-year-old short story, 'Hard Thin Gruel', by Wang, was a veiled attack on Deng Xiaoping. Wang reacted by instituting a civil action against both the critic and the paper.

The significance of this case is not whether Wang Meng had allegorical intentions nor which elements of factional struggle were attacked in the story, but rather in his self-confident assertion of basic civil rights against political assaults. Wang was not the first writer to take this action, but he was the most famous and politically important, and the incident was widely publicised. This move was an overt and conscious attempt at demarcating the different spheres of the political and the artistic. Though the Beijing Intermediate People's Court rejected Wang's suit, he nevertheless came out as the 'winner' in the eyes of the public and of his colleagues. And in the following months a number of stories and essays on the topic of 'gruel' written by Wang and some of his friends appeared in various magazines as provocative tokens of their stance.

Although Chinese publishing and art production is far from being free and market-directed in the Western sense, increasing commercialisation is the most radical factor of change in the field. Economic reform has reached far into cultural institutions. As subsidies are reduced or withdrawn, magazines, publishing houses and film studios, most of them actually belonging to state organisations, are forced to cater to popular demand or seek additional financing through business transactions. The fact that the CCP has not entirely relinquished censorship and political control only serves to make the situation more complicated for officially-produced culture. Didactic, ideologically-sanctioned works of socialist realism have little appeal. Stories of crime and violence are much more successful as moralising entertainment. For example, there is a series based on actual criminal cases, written by writers with access to the archives of the Public Security Bureau, and published with considerable profit by it.

Many new state-owned literary magazines have sprung up, mostly carrying popular fiction – martial arts stories, detective thrillers or romances, sometimes reprinted from Taiwan and Hong Kong. Firms and enterprises will run side-line publications featuring whatever can be sold for a profit : from folksy almanacs and popular religion or superstition to how-to-get-rich-fast and do-it-yourself entrepreneur manuals. Another result of the general structural break-up and loosening of controls has been an increase in illegal publishing. The appearance of private bookshops and the growing number of street stalls circulate a variety of material and undermine strict state-control of reading habits. Quite a lot of fiction is written by groups of writers, including well-known serious authors under pseudonyms.

The literature of the 1990s

The literary scene in the 1990s is characterised by the presence and interaction of many styles, themes and 'layers' of literature. There is a not-very-interesting, but widespread, layer of officially endorsed literature by writers who used to belong to the literary and critical establishment. A more élitist, 'pure' literature addresses a limited readership of many students or people of the literary world. The writers of these works emerged as the *avant-garde* of the late 1980s, backed up by a host of 'new critics' employing Western theories. Recently these established writers have had to compete for the term *avant-garde* with artists of the rapidly growing youth subculture and authors of fringe literature/rock lyrics and so on. Surrounding them is the vast sea of popular entertainment. Of course these groups overlap and intermingle, and cutting across them is an increasing number of regional and local varieties. Finally the voice of exile literature, from writers of the 1980s *avant-garde* now in the West, is gaining some attention in literary circles.

Despite these layers, however, one of the interesting features of the current cultural scene is the occasional blurring between élitist and mass culture. Intellectuals have commented on the way that the songs of the popular rock singer, Cui Jian, undermine official rhetoric by miming and parody. A novel by the serious writer, Jia Pingwa, has generated immense interest and sold tens of thousands of copies, no doubt a result of its reputedly pornographic contents. The most obvious example of this trend is the Beijing novelist, Wang Shuo, whose stories in the late 1980s were read and dissected by sophisticated critics, and who by the early 1990s is the most widely read and discussed popular writer in urban China.

One recurring trait running through all this diversity is cultural self-consciousness. Although its reverse, Westernisation, may be the first to meet the eye – in the shape of innumerable translations, the widespread use of Western jargon in literary criticism and the adoption of Western literary techniques and genres – the increasing focus on Chinese culture is a deeper and more interesting phenomenon. In both literature and film this is further reinforced by the emergence of regionalism, in efforts to capture local dialects, habits and landscapes. A number of the best works are informed by the interplay between the search for the individual self and the exploration of Chinese history and tradition. The urge for self-realisation has merged with a quest for cultural identity. The scope and variety with which this theme has been treated in recent Chinese literature can be illustrated through the introduction of five writers – Can Xue, Yu Hua, Su Tong, Mo Yan and Wang Shuo – who each have a highly distinctive style and aesthetic perception.

The problems of individuality *vis-à-vis* Chinese culture and society is at the centre of the writer, Can Xue's, weird stories. Can Xue (born 1953) is from Hunan and she began writing in the early 1980s. Her prose abounds with subjectivist images of the web of mutual suspicion and interference that bind families and neighbours together. There are no psychological explanations or narrative dynamics in the ordinary sense, but her language progresses as relentlessly and unpredictably as metastases. She has written a number of stories, but only one long novel, *Breaking out performance* (*Tuwei biaoyan*, 1988). The latter is a piece about the woman *X*, who does not subordinate herself to the collective. It is concerned with predicament of the individual in a conformist society and parodies the ways of life in a system of mutual surveillance.

Cultural critique is also prominent in the fiction of Yu Hua (born

1960). In several of his stories from the late 1980s the narrative, or part of it, is carried on through the perceptions of an insane person. In '1986' (*Yijiubalin nian*, 1987) a middle-school teacher who disappeared after being persecuted during the Cultural Revolution suddenly returns to his home town. He has gone mad and become obsessed with his old hobby – methods of punishment and torture in ancient China: from cutting off the nose and castration to being torn apart by five horses, all of which he manages to inflict upon himself in a mixture of reality and fantasy. The detailed descriptions of killings and mutilations in his stories, together with the conspicuous lack of individual identity in his characters and the absence of direct social motivation, give the impression of a violence so deeply entrenched in Chinese history and culture as to be beyond rational explanation.

Violent and dramatic events with hints of allegory are part of most of Mo Yan's tales, from his family saga, *Red Sorghum Clan* (*Hong Gaoliang Jiazu*, 1987) to his grotesque satire entitled 'Alcohol Country' (*Jiuguo*, 1992). In the former novel (made into a film by Zhang Yimou) Mo Yan (born 1956) depicts his grandparents' generation in strong colours and with a touch of magical realism, as people capable of intense desires and violent acts. Many of his other stories of the tragedy and hardship of life in the countryside can be read as starkly contrasting counter-images to those presented by the socialist–realist writers of the 1950s and 1960s. And in Mo Yan's world the role of the Communist Party remains marginal. The inhabitants of 'Alcohol Country' – a parody on a China seized by the materialist craze – indulge in sex and wine, and the gastronomic speciality of the region is 'steamed child'. This reference to cannibalism as part of Chinese culture, whether understood in the spiritual sense or quite literally, also features in works by other contemporary writers. The protagonist in the story is a dwarf, full of unbridled sexual lust and entrepreneurial energy, a millionaire and 'model worker', ironically embodying, as the narrator tells us, the spirit of the times.

Another original and richly imaginative writer is Su Tong (born 1963) often choosing historical settings of the 1920s to 1940s for his fiction. Su Tong's narrator in *The Diaspora of 1934* (*Yijiusansi nian de taowang*, 1987) also traces the story of his grandparents. The novel concerns the violent disintegration of a family in southern China, caught in the difficult transition from the values of a traditional rural community to the flux of urban life. However, the I-narrator's interest in the past is aroused by the monotone of present-day city life. The contrast between a rich, though violent, history and a dull contemporary life is inherent in most of Su Tong's narratives. This part of his writing has been termed 'meta-historical', and is to be read not only as artistic experimentation, but also as a contribution to the general rewriting of Chinese history that gained momentum in the late 1980s.

Su Tong, who is a native of the southern province of Jiangsu, has also written several stories in which the spatial framework is the modern city. The city culture of the south, especially of Shanghai and Guangzhou, is much more developed than in the north, and the journals based there promote urban literature. However it is the Beijing novelist, Wang Shuo (born 1958), who is the recorder *par excellence* of the new popular culture of the lower-class urban milieu. Indeed Wang can be considered the most remarkable phenomenon on the literary scene in recent years. The creator of a series of sardonic and entertaining novels, as well as television plays and film scripts, Wang is perhaps the only contemporary freelance writer to be able to live off his royalties in relative affluence. Scorned by some, and calling himself a producer of mass-literature, he is actually, as pointed out by the Australian sinologist, Geremie Barmé (1992), 'a witty writer of serious intent who uses the present Chinese cultural order as the basis for a fictional world of great humour and insight: a literature of escape and sublimation'. Part of Wang Shuo's genius is his deft handling of language, his ear for Beijing slang, and his ability to parody or invert Communist Party language. He turns irreverence into an art form. The subversive effect of his immensely popular writing, which surprisingly has escaped censorship, is regarded by many as even stronger than that of the straightforwardly dissident writings of the early 1980s. Geremie Barmé sees Wang as the major exponent of a modern '*liumang* culture' – *liumang*, originally meaning 'hooligan', indicates the opposite of officially accepted behaviour and implies a disrespectful attitude to authorities and to prescribed moral standards. Wang Shuo portrays an anarchic unofficial world, where the lives of prostitutes, petty criminals, salesmen and homeless vagrants, with all their frustration and daredevil mockery of the sacred icons of communist ideology, are treated as normal existences. He exposes absurdities, but offers no alternatives and does not call on his readers to protest.

The four-volume edition of Wang's work published in 1992 had a print run of 30 000 copies and was reprinted. Among his best novels are *I am your Father* (*Wo shi ni baba*, 1991), a subtle study of the relationship between father and son, and *No Man's Land* (*Qianwan bie ba wo dang ren*, 1989). The latter comes closest to the theme of national character/identity, expounded in Wang's devastatingly satirical manner, and is inspired by the debate surrounding the Taiwanese writer, Bo Yang's, essay 'The Ugly Chinaman' which was widely read in China. It is a pitch-black, almost surrealist, comedy on the specific Chinese combination of megalomania and self-deprecation, and is filled with the unprecedented, provocative, mocking and twisting of party rhetoric.

Several of Wang Shuo's novels have been made into popular movies, none of which have been of international standard. But works by Mo Yan and Su Tong have been the basis for two remarkable films by Zhang Yimou, and Zhang's latest project is the filming of a recent novel by Yu Hua.

The new generation of film makers

It is film-makers like Zhang Yimou and Chen Kaige who are mainly responsible for winning international acclaim for Chinese film. Both belong to the 'fifth generation', which refers to the first group of film-makers to graduate in the post-Mao period, i.e. 1982. The previous generations of film-makers are: the pioneers of the early part of the century; the left-wing people of the 1930s who became known as the second generation; the third were the first to make films under the People's Republic; and the fourth generation are those trained in the PRC or who graduated just before the Cultural Revolution. While several fourth-generation directors, like Xie Jin and Wu Tianming, are still active, it is the fifth generation which has made films that combine a Chinese vision with a completely modern use of cinematic technique.

Recently a sixth generation, the class of 1989, has entered the scene. Their film-language and world-outlook are as different from their immediate predecessors as are the products of the new literary subculture from the serious fiction of the 1980s. They are realist, consciously turning their backs on the refined cultural aestheticism of the famous fifth generation, often taking as their subject-matter daily life in the big cities. They have a keen eye for social ironies at the same time as being politically disillusioned and profoundly anti-moralist. One of them is Zhang Yuan, whose first film 'Mama' (1992) was a sensitive portrait of a mother's difficult life with her retarded son in a small apartment. His next film, 'Beijing Bastards' (1993) has amateurs, including the singer, Cui Jian, playing all the roles and an improvised dialogue with lots of slang, giving a documentary impression, characteristic of sixth-generation films. His films remain close to contemporary Chinese reality whilst depicting problems of urban life common to many parts of the world.

Starting with Chen Kaige's 'Yellow Earth' (1984) photographed by Zhang Yimou, and later Zhang Yimou's own 'Red Sorghum' (1988) which won the Golden Bear Award at the Berlin Festival, the fifth generation startled the established Chinese film world, and for the first time called international attention to Chinese film. Though other fifth-generation directors, for example, Tian Zhuangzhuang, have created original and artistically experimental works, the series of films by Chen and Zhang are the most mature and interesting of the group's achievements. Chen Kaige's early films, including 'King of Children' (1987) based on the story by Ah Cheng, tend towards abstractions in their poetic understatement, heavy symbolism, and daring lack of melodrama (which have also made them largely incomprehensible to the average Chinese audience). But 'Farewell, my Concubine' (1993) confronts the audience with violent emotions and vibrant tensions. Set in the world of Beijing Opera, with homosexuality as a secondary theme, the film recounts China's recent history through the individual fates of its protagonists.

The fascination with national culture and mentality which runs through the films of both Chen Kaige and Zhang Yimou is the cinematic expression of the inquiry going on within contemporary literature. In 'Red Sorghum', 'Judou' (1990) and 'Raise the Red Lantern' (1992), based on stories by Mo Yan, Liu Heng and Su Tong, and all set in pre-PRC China, Zhang Yimou explores the visual beauty and violence of the traditional order. His main characters are all women (played by actress Gong Li) whose sexual instincts and emotional desires bring them into conflict, or even disaster. In China there has been a great sensitivity towards the vaguely allegorical implications of his films and their possible references to contemporary political issues. But Zhang's only political film is 'The Story of Qiuju' (1992). With its contemporary plot of a peasant woman seeking redress for her husband, it stands apart from his other films and has even been seen by some as propaganda for recent legal reforms. With the exception of this film, all Zhang's other films have been temporarily banned in China, or shown only briefly for a select audience.

Thus for all their international prizes, the fifth-generation films have faced many obstacles at home. Several of them have had to seek financial support in Hong Kong, partly because of official opposition, but also because of a general crisis in the Chinese film industry. As television and videos keep people away from the cinema, commercialisation prevails and censorship operates unpredictably, film studios are in a difficult position. Of China's sixteen studios, only three receive support from the state, the rest are dependent on the market. If a film is banned, the money spent making it will be lost, so the temptation to play safe and produce purely entertaining movies is strong.

Despite the undisputed quality and high artistic standards of serious Chinese literature and film today, the situation is problematic for both. For experimental writers and film-makers, the blessings of greater freedom are accompanied by the loss of a wide audience, or even problems of publishing or shooting films. Chinese writers, in particular, are used to enjoying an elevated status and occupying a central position in society, as conveyors of moral values and and, at times, as the conscience of the nation. Many of them now feel lost and uncertain as to their role.

If there is a silver lining, it is to be found in the regional diversity springing up after the socio-economic changes of the 1980s. Vast as China is, valuable subcultures can thrive in provinces and cities. They are less disturbed by politics, and if they can manage the market, they might just get more of a hearing abroad too.

20

China's Foreign Policy in the Post-1989 Era

Rosemary Foot

'Feeling the stones while crossing the river'

The dramatic and unforeseen developments in international relations since the middle of 1989 have led to profound changes in the distribution of power in the global system and in our thinking about what constitutes the basis of power in that system. Moreover, the nature of the emerging regional and global orders is difficult to discern, and determining foreign policy in the context of such fundamental change is problematic. For China such uncertainties have been compounded by their coincidence with domestic unrest that led in June 1989 to the killings and arrest of political protestors. Such a response damaged China's relations with Western Europe and Japan and introduced serious points of friction with the USA, the country that China has perceived as central to the success of its modernisation efforts. The disintegration of the core of the socialist world begun with the Tiananmen crackdown raised questions about the legitimacy of the Chinese Communist Party, and generated fears among Chinese leaders about the long-term stability of the political order in the PRC. Beijing quickly had to determine its response to a set of events that demonstrated – initially at least – China's international and domestic vulnerability. One author has used the apposite Chinese proverb 'feeling the stones while crossing the river' to describe China's search for equilibrium in an uncertain era (Shambaugh 1992). A discussion of that search forms the focus of this chapter.

Foreign policy in the early reform era

It could be argued that the period from April 1984 to May 1989 represented the most productive era in the history of the PRC's foreign relations. Punctuated at the start by the Reagan visit to China and at the end by the Gorbachev summit in Beijing, it was a time when China enjoyed good or steadily improving relations with both superpowers and thus unprecedentedly high levels of national security. After 1984, bilateral ties with Washington in military, cultural and economic fields proceeded apace. With respect to Moscow, there was discernible progress under Gorbachev on what China referred to as the 'three obstacles' to the normalisation of the relationship, thus the Sino–Soviet border dispute moved towards resolution and troop levels on both sides were cut drastically, Soviet pressure was put on Vietnam to withdraw from Cambodia, and Moscow prepared to extricate itself from the costly conflict in Afghanistan. At the 1989 summit Moscow and Beijing restored formal party-to-party ties, and official talks were begun on arms control and confidence-building measures.

More generally, China's approach to its foreign relations became less ideological and more pragmatic as it sought friendly relations with all states on the basis of the 'five principles of peaceful coexistence' (a set of principles expounded by Premier Zhun Enlai in the 1950s which called for mutual respect for sovereignty, non-aggression and non-interference in each other's internal affairs). Nor did Beijing offer much by way of tangible or rhetorical support for the Third World's goal of establishing a new international economic order. China's leaders no longer supported the thesis that world war was inevitable, though lesser conflicts were not ruled out. In the mid-1980s, China described its foreign policy objectives as maintaining world peace, developing friendly cooperation with all countries regardless of social system, and promoting common economic prosperity. Its stance on external issues would be determined according to the merits of each case. Developed and developing countries alike were to be encouraged to contribute to the maintenance of peace, stability, and economic progress within the existing global system.

Partly as a result of its membership of the World Bank and International Monetary Fund from 1980, its application to rejoin the GATT in 1986, and its promulgation of a major foreign-trade reform document in September 1984, China had become a major actor within that system. The foreign-trade reform, together with a reduction in the scope of the foreign-trade plan, and the initiation of price reform and currency devaluation led to significant increases in China's trade, much greater than the overall increase in world trade. Attitudes towards foreign investment and aid also underwent dramatic change. Virtually non-existent in 1978, the cumulative total of foreign investment in China reached US$20 billion by 1990. In the mid-1980s, the country became the largest borrower from the World Bank; by 1989 Beijing had overtaken New Delhi in becoming the world's largest recipient of official bilateral and multilateral aid, receiving almost US$2.2 billion a year.

A more active stance within international political organisations complemented this integration into the world economy. Almost totally excluded from the world of intergovernmental organisations in the period 1949–70, by 1977 China had joined twenty-one and by 1988 thirty-seven. Its participation in non-governmental organisations (NGOs) also rose dramatically from only seventy-seven in 1977 to 574 in 1988. China's attitude towards the United Nations also changed. In 1965, depicting the United Nations as a 'dirty international political stock exchange in the grip of a few big powers', the Chinese had called for the establishment of an alternative, revolutionary international organisation. By 1985, however, China's then premier described the UN as 'irreplaceable in the historical mission it shoulders and the impact it exerts on the world'. Beijing also started to become involved with the UN's peacekeeping operations, sending PLA officers to join the UN's truce-supervisory organisation and applying for membership of the UN's Special Committee on Peacekeeping Operations.

In sum, China's approach to foreign relations in the 1980s was flexible and nuanced. Its relations with nearly all its neighbours had improved, it was more active globally and neither of the two superpowers posed a security threat. Its primary objective was to enjoy and sustain a peaceful and stable international environment in order to be able to concentrate on its drive for modernisation.

Tiananmen and the ending of the Cold War

The collapse of the Soviet empire and then of the Soviet Union itself, straddling the eruption of serious political protest in China brought a new situation into being. Beijing was forced to reassess its place in the world, its relationships with the major states, the pace and nature of economic reform, and the linkages between domestic economic decentralisation, global integration, and political unrest.

The Tiananmen crackdown led to a severe crisis in China's relations with the West, particularly with the USA. Public opinion polls indicated that more than 75 per cent of the American people had followed the events of 4 June closely or very closely (Harding 1992). Reflecting and responding to the horror expressed by the American people, the Bush administration immediately imposed a ban on military sales to Beijing and on high-level military exchanges. Two weeks later, Washington suspended all official exchanges with China at or above the level of assistant secretary, and recommended that all further lending to China by international financial institutions also be suspended. It further urged its Western allies and Japan to impose similar sanctions. The European Community followed suit, confirming decisions already taken by national governments, and at the G7 meeting in Paris in July, Japan brought its policies into line. The Asian Development Bank and the World Bank halted new lending, negotiations over China's GATT application were suspended, and the IMF deferred work on its technical assistance projects. China's reformers considered these governments and international institutions to be crucial for the country's search for 'comprehensive national strength'. As such Beijing had a major foreign and domestic crisis on its hands.

As noted earlier, these events coincided quite closely with the collapse of Communist rule in Eastern Europe. China had offered advice and support to at least two of these governments prior to their downfall. For example, Politburo Standing Committee member and Security Chief, Qiao Shi, had visited Bucharest close to the eve of the violent coup, and voiced support for China's longtime ally, Nicolae Ceausescu. When the Romanian military overthrew him, police and army units in Beijing were put on alert. Chinese leaders also mistimed their visit to East Germany: during political unrest in the autumn of 1989, Politburo Standing Committee member, Yao Yilin, allegedly advised Erich Honecker to suppress the demonstrators in Leipzig (Lieberthal 1992). As the repressive regimes of Eastern Europe tumbled and began to transform themselves, China no longer appeared to be at the forefront of reform within the Communist world, a status its market reform policies had once accorded it.

The collapse of the Soviet empire, in addition to undermining the confidence of Chinese leaders, also had wider international ramifications. It marked the final demise of the 'strategic triangle', a geometric metaphor that had awarded China a significant place in the management of the global balance of power. The ending of East–West rivalry had the effect of reducing China's importance as a global actor, and extending the possibilities for Western diplomatic and economic pressure without the fear that such pressure would push Beijing into Moscow's embrace. Moreover, the end to a rivalry based primarily on nuclear and conventional military strength gave a primacy to different forms of competition, based on economic might and levels of scientific and technological achievement. In this kind of competition, countries such as Japan naturally eclipsed China within the Pacific–Asian region (see Chapter 21).

With the dissolution of the Soviet Union and its empire, Beijing also had to face the fact that the USA now remained the sole superpower. Moreover, this occurred at a time when Washington had stepped up its criticism of Beijing over human rights, trading practices, and missile sales, to name but three of a number of irritants in the bilateral relationship.

The Gulf War of 1991 further bolstered the perception that the USA dominated the global system, even though Washington had to rely on some of its richest allies to help to finance the war effort. Despite such reliance, it was Washington that was able to muster the coalition of forces, transport large numbers of troops and their equipment thousands of miles, and target Iraqi troops and sites. Conservative hardliners in Beijing used the new evidence of American hegemony to argue that China was the object of a US strategy of 'peaceful evolution' reminiscent of the days of John Foster Dulles and designed to undermine Communist Party rule and substitute a capitalist system. While it was welcomed that the United Nations had been strengthened as a result of its involvement in the Gulf, there was also the fear that in this post-Cold War era the West was using the new opportunities to impose its views and policies upon others.

This concern about US dominance and the dangers of a unipolar world was gradually modified as the Chinese leaders regained some of their confidence and as they began to restore ties with their erstwhile foreign partners. One consequence of this was a return to the position that the distribution of power in the world was multipolar, the poles made up of the USA, Europe, Japan, Russia and China. Nevertheless, fears of Western interference have continued to resurface, for example, in debates over whether political conditions should be attached to multilateral aid, and in discussion of conflicting positions at international gatherings such as the UN World Conference on Human Rights, where China saw the West as attempting to 'propagate their views on human rights ... to legalise and institutionalise their interference'. Moreover, where the USA is concerned, Chinese commentators argue that, despite evidence of multipolarity, in terms of overall power the USA still ranks first. All the signs are that while Washington might be willing to cooperate with Beijing on certain specific issues, it would also not shy away from pressurising Beijing on a wide range of political, economic, and strategic matters.

China's responses after 1989

China has had four main approaches to dealing with the un- certainties of the post-Tiananmen era: to remind other states – especially the USA – that it still retains global importance; to emphasise its positive contribution to the resolution of regional conflicts in Asia; to offer regular and timely concessions to the West; and to accelerate the improvement of its ties with its Asian neighbours.

China retains global significance for a number of reasons. It has become a significant trading nation – by 1992 the eleventh largest trading nation in the world – and by its action it can bolster or undermine the GATT trading norms. It is also a nuclear-weapons state which in 1992 finally adhered to the Nuclear Non-Prolifer- ation Treaty. Nuclear status, together with its position as a major exporter of arms to the developing world, put it in a position to advance or impede the spread of nuclear and conventional weap- ons technology. As a developing country with the world's largest population, its policies can help to protect or destroy the global environment. China is also one of the five permanent members of the UN Security Council and can exercise veto power. That position accords it a role in any major security question that comes before the UN.

The value of that role as one of the five permanent members was illustrated during the Gulf crisis which China handled with enough dexterity to accelerate the removal of a number of Western sanctions that had been imposed after Tiananmen. Some economic sanctions had already been removed as a consequence of the lifting of martial law in Beijing in January 1990 and the release of several hundred political prisoners. Nevertheless, the Gulf war was used to demonstrate how valuable a cooperative China could be: it voted for all ten UN resolutions that ordered military and economic sanctions against Iraq and abstained on resolution 678 that permitted the use of force to compel an Iraqi withdrawal from Kuwait.

Such cooperative or, rather, non-obstructive behaviour reaped a number of diplomatic and economic rewards. At the foreign ministers meeting at Luxembourg at the end of October 1990, the European Community decided to resume political, economic and cultural relations with the PRC. In early November, Japan formally announced the resumption of its development aid to China, releasing US$ 240 million under the Third Yen loans programme. The day after Beijing's abstention on resolution 678, Foreign Minister Qian Qichen met President Bush at the White House, effectively putting an end to the ban on high-level diplomatic communication; and in December the World Bank voted to extend the first 'non-basic-needs' loan to Beijing since the Tiananmen crackdown.

China has also been emphasising its role in the resolution of regional conflicts in Asia. A one-time supporter of the Khmer Rouge and arch-opponent of Vietnam, it has since retreated from its former ally and normalised relations with Hanoi. It has given concrete and verbal support to the UN activity in Cambodia, backing the negotiated settlement and electoral process, and sending an engineering battalion to work under UN auspices. On the Korean peninsula, it has put pressure on the North to continue its dialogue with the South and with the USA, and has pressed Pyongyang to accept inspection of its nuclear facilities and to remain a signatory to the Non-Proliferation Treaty. Full diplomatic relations have been established with South Korea, and it has supported joint membership of the United Nations for both Seoul and Pyongyang. Along its borders with the former Soviet Union and Mongolia it has sought to contribute to stability in the area through the establishment of diplomatic and economic ties with these new states, even as it keeps a wary eye on nationalist trends in Inner Mongolia and on Islamic fundamentalism in Xinjiang.

Elsewhere in Asia, China has sought to deepen ties that have been improving since the mid-1980s. The response of these countries to the Tiananmen crackdown was notably muted. The general tenor of its Asian neighbours' reactions was that this was an internal matter. India's leaders, for example, responded in this manner. Together with New Delhi's unequivocal, pro-Chinese stance on Tibet, this has helped to accelerate the improvement of Sino-Indian relations, leading to increases in cross-border trade, the shelving of the border dispute, and the development of confidence-building measures to ensure that war does not break out inadvertently.

Although China clearly retains a preference for acting unilaterally, or at most bilaterally, in the field of foreign affairs, it has also sought to conciliate ASEAN (Association of South-east Asian Nations) by pledging support for its efforts to enhance security cooperation in East Asia. Thus, in July 1993 China attended the ASEAN ministerial meeting held to discuss security issues in the region. In November 1991 China joined what is currently the most significant multilateral organisation in Pacific Asia, APEC (Asia Pacific Economic Cooperation) and, in doing so, also demonstrated its greater flexibility towards Taiwan's international representation since Beijing, Taipei and Hong Kong all joined APEC at the same time.

On the debit side

Nevertheless, although China has benefited from its positive behaviour in the United Nations and with its neighbours, there are underlying difficulties and tensions. While China's power is maximised in the UN because of its veto, a more assertive and interventionist UN in the post-Cold-War era could pose problems for a China that seems particularly concerned to maintain the distinction between domestic unrest and threats to global peace. Beijing could find itself isolated and subject to external pressure. Such fears have led the Chinese to attempt to reinforce the global norm of state sovereignty and non-interference and to shore up a somewhat outmoded distinction between domestic and international affairs. Some Chinese comment has recently described the 'new internationalism' that has emerged as a new form of colonialism in disguise, an interpretation for which Beijing has sought support among developing states.

China's relations with its Asian neighbours also have their negative aspects. ASEAN's more energetic attempts to establish a security order in East Asia have been made not only as a result of the demise of the Soviet Union as a Pacific power and the resultant reduction in the American presence, but also because of the disputes its members have with China over ownership of islands in the South China Sea. In February 1992, the Chinese passed a maritime territorial law affirming their sovereignty over the Paracels and the Spratlys. Beijing also claimed the Diaoyutai islands in the East China Sea which puts it into contention with Japan and Taiwan. The maritime law empowered China to adopt 'all necessary measures to prevent and stop the harmful passage of vessels through its territorial waters'. Three months later, Beijing granted a concession to an American oil corporation to explore for oil between the Spratlys and the Vietnamese coast and reserved the right to use force to protect the corporation's drilling activities. In June 1992, Qian Qichen tried to defuse the issue by offering to shelve the territorial dispute for resolution at a later date, and suggesting joint development of the islands' resources. He also pledged not to use force to resolve the matter. But ASEAN member states remain watchful, especially as China enhances its naval and air capability to a point where its sovereign claims in the area will be difficult to challenge. The Chinese have purchased Russian SU-27 combat aircraft which, operating from Hainan island, will be able to range over much of the South China Sea; and the development of its blue-water capability and strategic nuclear forces is partly designed to prevent encroachment in an area believed to be rich in natural and mineral resources.

Similarly, China's relations with Taiwan have a dual aspect. Economic and cultural ties have been deepening, especially since the mid-1980s. Taiwanese investment on the mainland has been rocketing and direct quasi-official talks were held in April 1993 in Singapore, the first encounter between the organisations established to handle day-to-day contacts between the two authorities. Yet certain trends could undermine these promising developments. Political liberalisation in Taiwan, together with its global economic position, has served to increase Taiwan's international

status and the ruling party's determination to see that status translated into membership of organisations such as the GATT and the
United Nations. Western ties with Taiwan have also been upgraded, and arms sales have increased. Such developments tend to
reinforce calls in Taiwan for self-determination, and Beijing's
contemplation of the use of force to prevent or reverse moves
towards independence. International reaction to the use of force
against Taiwan is difficult to gauge but external support for the
island in the event of fighting has to be a part of Beijing's
calculation.

Conclusion

International changes have been sweeping and fundamental since
1989. The familiar Cold War structure has been replaced by an
order that is incomplete and difficult to discern. The Chinese
leadership's fears about its interaction with other governments and
peoples who mostly view communism as an outmoded invention of
the past, has led to an intense internal debate that has not been
resolved and which has yet to be conducted in a post-Deng era.
The hardliners in Beijing argue for slowing down the pace of
reform and keeping a tighter control over the scale of interaction
with the outside world. Reformers want to accelerate the pace of
reform and to re-establish, even enhance, China's integration with
the international political economy. Where his opponents argue
that China's past poverty and backwardness can be explained by
the rapaciousness of imperialist powers, Deng claims that this came
about because of the country's self-imposed isolation.

At the root of the reformist economic strategy is a commitment
to export-led growth. This implies the need to maintain good
access to the diverse markets of the West and Japan, and to the
USA in particular which currently takes over a quarter of China's
exports. In the past, it was evident that it was the USA that was in a
position to obstruct China's economic development, to deny it
access to international economic institutions, to prevent its uni-
fication with Taiwan and restrict its political recognition. Still
today many Chinese researchers believe that the goal adopted by
the Fourteenth Party Congress in October 1992 of creating a
socialist market economy cannot be realised if relations with the

USA deteriorate sharply (see Glaser 1993). This implies a conciliatory stance on China's part.

But accepting that degree of dependence on any country, and
especially the USA, makes China uncomfortable. Moreover, it is a
difficult policy to manage, with an administration in Washington
that appears assertive and combative on issues such as human
rights, missile sales, access to China's market, and Taiwan. If
Chinese leaders accept that the country must remain integrated
with the world economy – and that policy would now be difficult to
reverse – then China will no doubt continue to respond to US
pressure. At the same time it will probably attempt to build firmer
economic links with other parts of the developed and fast-de-
veloping world, and to reinforce the norms of non-intervention and
non-interference in each state's internal affairs. In most respects, its
policies in the 1990s are likely to resemble those of the mid-to-late
1980s outlined earlier; but at a time of leadership transition,
societal change, and uncertainties about the shape of the new world
order, even this level of prediction might be unwise.

21

China and the Pacific Rim

Paul Wingrove

'Sleep in the same bed but dream different dreams'

A Pacific Rim?

This is a chapter which questions its own title, but to good purpose. Whilst there is much fashionable talk about the 'Pacific Rim', it is arguable whether that term is of much value in describing a real-world phenomenon. By this I mean that in a conventional, geographic, sense a Pacific Rim exists. But in an economic or political sense it is difficult to find such a unified entity. Rather, we see a highly differentiated, fragmented and potentially conflict-ridden Pacific Rim. There are indeed unifying factors – rapid economic growth and new trading patterns have emerged to promote links between the countries round the Pacific periphery. There are emerging patterns of economic interdependence – possibly, according to some, hints of integration which define a 'Pacific Rim' and perhaps even contain the seeds of a future integrated Pacific economic community. But there remain, if not objections, then qualifications to the use of the term 'Pacific Rim'. For example, the geographical definition of the term is debatable. Realistically, we need to stretch the concept some distance to encompass not only the rapidly growing economies of North-east Asia but also those of some of the South-east-Asian states which, while not evidently part of a geographical Pacific community still participate in the pace and pattern of growth in and around the Pacific region. From another point of view states such as Russia and

North Korea, both a part of the geographical Pacific Rim, are not in the same economic league as some of the other fast-growth, high-tech Pacific economies, and for different reasons are to some extent politically apart from it. So there is a variance and variety here which undermines the notion of a region somehow united by economic similarity, political concordance or simple geographical propinquity.

The point may be put more strongly: even though we may discern the beginnings of some localised degree of Pacific interdependence in economic affairs, this is a region riddled with political conflicts and the memories of political conflicts, which still survive to threaten or impede economic progress or to give some subdued direction to its development.

One significant and overarching transformation has, of course, profoundly affected developments in the region: the ending of the Cold War and the downfall of the former USSR, have removed a number of barriers to economic and political development.

Conspectus

Considered broadly, three factors determine the past and future political complexion of this region:

1. The political history of the region has seen the legacy of colonialism overlaid with the tensions of the Cold War. The struggle for independence, occasionally down the path of revolution, has been the experience of many of the East and South-east Asian nations and many sensitivities about independence underlie the politics of this region. Nor have these struggles for independence simply resulted in conflict with the West: China, for example, in the 1950s and 1960s turned against the USSR, its formal ally (under the 1950 Sino-Soviet Treaty) in the 'socialist camp', at least in part because Moscow seemed to be recreating a paternal, semi-colonial style in its relations with Beijing; and socialist Vietnam also found itself in conflict with socialist China in 1979.
2. The world's larger powers have had, and continue to have, major economic and security interests in the region. The former USSR (and now Russia), the USA, China and Japan,

even – to an extent – some of the states of Western Europe, have confronted or occasionally cooperated with each other in this motile, dynamic Pacific arena. Different cultures and different ambitions have clashed and created a complex and volatile mix of political interests. Two superpowers (admitting Russia for the moment), one 'half-superpower' (China), one uncertain aspirant (Japan) and a handful of unresolved political problems (North Korea, Taiwan, Hong Kong) have provided the basis for a complex geo-political scenario. At the height of the Cold War, in particular, this was a potent brew.
3.   National, religious and cultural differences divide this region deeply. Even within the borders of the Chinese state created in 1949 there are the subdued nationalist and ethnic aspirations of, for example, Tibetans, Mongolians and Muslims. Interestingly, beyond China's borders the Chinese diaspora in East and South-east Asia shows deep cultural differences as new environments have transformed traditional Chinese behaviour and loyalties. But other nationalisms and cultural differences make this region one of many political sensitivities.

Economic determinants

The developing economic framework of the Pacific Rim is its most notable feature, but is less tidy than one would imagine, although this depends to a degree on the criteria which determine who is counted in the Pacific Rim club. Rapid growth and well-developed economies characterise, or have characterised, a number of countries – Japan, Taiwan, Hong Kong, Singapore, South Korea. But one can find variations and exceptions which make the Pacific region more complex. In particular, China has also enjoyed rapid growth in recent years of something in the order of 10 per cent per annum, and is one of the world's largest economies, but in some crucial ways it still remains relatively backward compared with the 'tigers' of the Pacific economy. Vietnam is also in this position, but more so. Other nations have barely started their economic development.

This unevenness in development is compounded by the fact that what there is by way of regional economic interdependence is offset to an extent by the fact that much of the advanced Asian Pacific economy looks outwards towards the advanced countries of the

West perhaps as much as to the Pacific economy itself, and is therefore only partly regionally committed. As for the larger Western powers who sit around the Pacific Rim, the USSR has until recently been only relatively weakly linked to the Pacific, while the USA participates in the booming Pacific economy, but sees it as both threat and opportunity.

In fact, looked at more closely what we can see in this region is more like the uneven, localised, often bilateral and fragmented development of an East and South-east Asian economy, rather than an economy of the 'Pacific Rim'.

The key relationship

In this fluid, developing system, Japan is China's key economic partner, taking this role from the onset of China's economic reform programme. Capital and trade are the prizes for China, while the China market is the prize for Japan. Yet this has not been an easy relationship by any means. This is a multifaceted political relationship in which many things may go unsaid, but are still deeply felt, and occasionally surface to ruffle feathers in Beijing and Tokyo. Japan undoubtedly feels some guilt over events in the Second World War, but is infuriated when reminded about those events by China, as happens occasionally, often in response to a Japanese attempt to rewrite the history of the Second World War. China perhaps feels a sense of cultural superiority towards Japan, but also recognises its own technological backwardness compared with its neighbour. Japanese capital is welcomed by China, but Beijing is irked by Japan's limited involvement in joint enterprises and no doubt worries about overdependence on Japanese capital and expertise. Japan is distressed by the changes of course in China's economic policy (including occasional cancellations of major projects), but turns the other cheek in the interest of the long game.

The Tiananmen events resulted in transient and low-key economic punishment from Japan and a formal statement that Japan hoped that political normality would be restored, with no repetition of the action taken by China. This probably represents Japan's main worry about the China market – that it may be under the guidance of an unstable political system, one that offers no guarantees after the demise of Deng Xiaoping, and one where even the possibility of resurgent anti-Japanese feeling cannot be

excluded. This, perhaps, explains in part Japan's limited commitment to direct investment in China. Japan seems to have placed
something of an insulating barrier between itself and a valued but
possibly unreliable partner. Anxieties about China's political stability were displayed even some time after Tiananmen when, in
August 1991 Japanese premier Kaifu raised the issue of human
rights and arms control during a visit to Beijing, and by implication
political stability. This is clearly a central consideration for Japan
and understandable when one bears in mind the violent and barely
controllable lurches in policy that characterise post-1949 China.
For China, on the other hand, Japan's leading role in the developing Pacific economy and its crucial provision of capital and
expertise, cannot be ignored. Hence it must ensure that it does not
alienate this close neighbour and former enemy.

The semi-detached

Recent Chinese relations with the USA have become remarkably
cool since the high point of the late 1970s when a President and an
enthusiastic Secretary of State tried to co-opt China against the
Soviet Union. By the time of the advent of Mikhail Gorbachev it
became clear that China had little to offer politically to the USA,
since the USSR no longer presented a major threat and the
'strategic triangle' had lost its geo-political appeal. Moreover, in so
far as the relationship with the USA now turned much more on
economics, in this respect China had become something of an
irritant. Its textiles, in particular, threatened the American market,
and brought on the same protectionist responses in the USA that
Japanese computer-chip imports also inspired. Hence, given the
fairly complete mending of fences between the USSR and China in
1989 as a result of Gorbachev's visit to Beijing China, for the USA,
has become just another Asian nation, offering substantial economic and trading benefits, but also some competition. It is that
context which made the American reaction to the Tiananmen
events so powerful. Given that China was no longer necessary to
America's global strategy, and was even something of an economic
competitor, it could more easily be publicly condemned and internationally pressured. This is not to devalue the revulsion that
Americans felt at the events of June 1989. There was clearly a deep
public and political reaction to this flagrant abuse of human rights.

This was reflected in the actions of Congress which used its annual review of China's 'most-favoured nation' trading status as an occasion for condemning that country's human rights record. Only President George Bush seemed out of touch with the mood of the American people when, within a matter of months, he decided to send secret envoys to renew contacts with China. Thus, in so far as the USA plays a role in the Pacific Rim, at least in relation to China, it is now a role of cool calculation in which hard-headed, often economic, interest has replaced the old ideological dogmas or geo-political strategies of the Cold War era. And for many Americans China after 1989 has, in any case, proved itself to be a brutal, authoritarian regime, pretty much on a par with others of the sort, in and beyond the Pacific. The old sympathies for China, particularly evident on the west coast of the USA, have evaporated. Still, the importance of the economic relationship became evident in June of 1994 when President Clinton (spurred on no doubt by the thought of some extremely valuable pending contracts) renewed China's most-favoured-nation trading status, downplayed all his earlier talk about human rights, and made it clear that this annual Congressional human rights spat would be brought to an end.

On the other side of the Pacific, Russia's role in the region has largely been determined by historical security interests which developed as a consequence of the expansion of Tsarist Russia into the Far East and collision with the other states also pursuing ambitions in the region. Thus, in the Russian Civil War (1917–21) Japan opportunistically seized Russian eastern territory. Again in the 1930s Japan menaced, only to turn south towards China. And in the post-war period both the USA and China have, at different times and in different ways, appeared to present a threat to the interests of Russia in the Pacific region. Admittedly, there does seem to be some weak historic Russian impulse to play more as a Pacific power, evident in – for example – Stalin's request for naval facilities from Mao Zedong in 1950 (a similar request apparently later being made by Khrushchev). But this, in the last analysis, is a limited ploy. Russia's far-eastern territories and interests weigh less in the balance than the European and the East Asian, and Pacific impulse has more often been reactive, powered by perceived threat or opportunism. Thus, Soviet military strength in the region was boosted to meet the challenge of China after the Sino-Soviet split at the beginning of the 1960s; and a *de facto* alliance with Vietnam in the 1970s had a similar intent.

What Russia has not yet achieved is the role of economic heavyweight in the Pacific basin. Indeed, its links with the growing East Asian economies are particularly weak, and its own role in the region rests too much on its 'mines and fish' (Segal 1990, p. 11) But there are possibilities for economic development, particularly as some of the political problems of the region diminish in the 1990s. The resources of Siberia and the East are tempting, if difficult to work. But the unfriendly bureaucratic and political culture of Russia may militate against this area being selected as a priority for investment by Pacific powers such as Japan when there are more friendly governments and cultures in the region.

Sino-Soviet economic relations have in the past been frustrated by political relations, but even before Gorbachev it was evident that there were Soviet moves to defuse the political tensions. Ambassadorial talks between the two countries resumed in 1982 and in consequence trade began to increase from 1984. Gorbachev mended fences with China in his speech of 1986 in Vladivostok, and in the late 1980s sought to resolve the conflicts with China over Cambodia, and over the delineation of the northern border between the two states. Much of this was formally sealed by his visit to Beijing in May 1989 at the time of the Tiananmen demonstrations. The way was open for the Soviet Union, with one foot in the Pacific, to benefit from the dynamism of that region, and in particular from its new relationship with China. Yet the likelihood of this producing, at present, much beyond a further increase in a reasonably healthy, and growing, trading partnership is doubtful. There is, after all, a limited economic complementarity here. China's textiles and agriculture trade for Russia's raw materials. China's basic needs – for capital, technology and relatively high-value markets, will not be, and cannot be, met by Russia.

Nonetheless, Gorbachev's initiative opened the way for nation-to-nation trade and cooperation, and for cross-border trade. Further, his decision to resolve major difficulties with China – especially making concessions on the long-running border dispute – has contributed to the more peaceful and settled Pacific that the Chinese seek in order to pursue economic development. The Chinese seem likely to reap more of the benefits initially; thus the door to renewed relations – albeit at a fairly low level – between China and Vietnam has been opened thanks to Gorbachev, and this in turn has enhanced the prospects for generally more harmonious relationships within the region.

Similarly, China's recognition of South Korea in August 1992, always a difficult issue for China given its ambivalent relationship with Kim Il-Sung's North Korea, was relatively straightforward, preceded for some years by the development of substantial economic ties, including South Korean involvement in joint ventures in China. Within a short time of recognition South Korea had moved into the top three or four nations in terms of importance in China's trade. The death of Kim Il-Sung in 1994 may shift the log-jam on the Korean peninsula, but it may nonetheless take some time to reassure the beleaguered north.

Beyond East Asia

In so far as China has a view of the general development environment in Asia, it clearly seeks stability and at least neutral political relationships with which to underpin its own development programme. The group of countries which have in the past been as resistant as any to China's blandishments have been those of South-east Asia, especially those nations grouped together in ASEAN, despite the fact that a number of them have significant Chinese populations. In fact these rather conservative, capitalist, regimes have long been afraid of China's political strength and ideological outlook. Interestingly, in the aftermath of Tiananmen, criticism from these states was quite low-key and probably reflective of some of their own authoritarianism. But since that time China has been making consistent efforts to woo the ASEAN member states, partly to underpin the 'open door' which still remains the heart of China's economic reforms, partly to establish good-neighbourly relations and limit the international cold shouldering that followed Tiananmen, and partly to demonstrate its importance in the resolution of Asian conflicts (see Chapter 20). As early as August 1990, Premier Li Peng toured South-east Asia. In July 1991 China's Foreign Minister attended a meeting of the ASEAN states for the first time. In the autumn China joined Asian Pacific Economic Cooperation. In January 1992 Chinese President Yang Shangkun visited the key state of Singapore and in July 1993 Chinese representatives attended a meeting of ASEAN held to discuss security issues. Singapore and others of the ASEAN states are amongst the fastest growing economies of the South-east Asia and Pacific regions and are potential trading partners for China in its wider regional strategy.

Towards a Greater China?

Recently there has been some discussion of the prospects for a 'Greater China', or a China which incorporates the highly desirable, and highly prosperous, territories of Hong Kong and Taiwan (*China Quarterly*, 1993). It is argued that cultural bonds and economic convergence will combine to ease the path towards this new entity. This, in my view, undervalues the political problems.

Hong Kong returns to China in 1997 (and Macao, Portuguese territory, the following year), when memories of Tiananmen will still be relatively fresh. Not only was it the irrational viciousness of those events which produced panic in Hong Kong, but also the casual attitude towards law and human rights displayed by the Chinese government – even though that had been a feature of the Chinese system for many years. What confidence could now be placed in China's commitment to 'one country, two systems', or in its declaration that China's life-style would remain unchanged for at least fifty years? Moreover, the little credibility that China still maintained after 1989 was surely dispelled by its implacability towards Governor Patten's proposals of October 1992 for a modest degree of democratisation in the colony. Admittedly, there is a substantial convergence and integration of the economies of Hong Kong and the Special Economic Zone of Shenzhen, which may indeed ease the process of reunification. Having made exceptions for Shenzhen, allowing it a freedom not permitted to many other parts of China, continuing to make those exceptions for the newly re-acquired Hong Kong may be a less painful political process for China's leaders. On the other hand, Shenzhen has never been anything other than a part of China, subject to its laws and its political system, and accepting the broad limits of social and political behaviour that were established in China after 1949. But Hong Kong has its own political and social understandings, and while there is a good deal of mass fatalism about a future life under the government of the People's Republic, there is also an active political class, radicalised by the 1989 events . After 1997, it will no doubt divide between those who wish to accommodate to, and those who cannot accept, the new limits. One suspects that the dissident minority will not be sufficiently large to create major political problems for China, but this is impossible to be sure of. China may maintain its authoritarian rule while the majority of the new Hong Kong–Chinese citizens concentrate on earning a living in a prosperous, enlarged, Shenzhen-Hong Kong economic zone. China's intent would no doubt be to bed Hong Kong down into a stable, conservative, prosperous regime on the Singapore model, but that is as unpredictable as were the Tiananmen events themselves.

Taiwan, too, separated from mainland China in 1949 when Mao Zedong's defeated enemies fled there, has developed its own political and social norms within a common Chinese culture. In recent years it has gone from low-level and indirect trading and political contacts with China to relatively normal economic and (mainly indirect) political relationships, although still remaining sensitive about high-level and direct political contact. This is understandable, given that neither state as yet formally recognises the other. For both parties there are mutual advantages in econ-omic development and a stable political environment in the Pacific. In recent years this has led to a fairly substantial transformation in their once bitterly hostile relationship. Taiwan has ceased, as of May 1991, to pretend that it is fighting Chinese communism and China has proclaimed, in a statement of August 1993, that it only wants 'peaceful reunification' with Taiwan. Yet in fact it is difficult to see that any political arrangement leading to reunification is feasible. Although a Chinese cultural entity of sorts, Taiwan remains a separate political entity (although not recognised as such by the outside world), and many political leaders see little benefit in reunification. More to the point, there is a degree of Taiwanese independence sentiment which can express itself relatively freely and set limits to what is possible in the way of moves towards reunification. Thus the continued development of economic ties seems unlikely to subdue or transmute political attachments. Indeed, it has been argued that the 'spillover' effect. (economic closeness engendering political closeness) may only work locally, perhaps bringing the Chinese province of Fujian (heavily, but not exclusively favoured by Taiwan investment) closer to Taiwan and in the process possibly weakening Fujian's attachment to the cen-tral People's government (Crane 1993, p. 76). Developments to date seem to give the best indications of the future course of events. Taiwan and the People's Republic will avoid, or downplay, political conflict and promote their best mutual economic interests, which are now significant – Crane (1993, p. 705) points out that two-way trade reached US$10 billion in 1993, ten times what it was in 1986. Investment, too, is very substantial, although for Taiwan only one of a number of investment location possibilities in Asia. But it remains to be seen whether this long game will not lead to frustration and a change of heart in Beijing about the peaceful strategy for the long-term goal of reunification. And for Taiwan, as for Hong Kong, Tiananmen remains a warning.

Conclusions

China is as yet only a potential economic giant. Yet it is that very potential which determines the attitudes of the states of the Pacific region towards China. In the short term there are economic benefits from trading and investment. In the long term, China's development strategy points towards a policy that seeks political stability, moderation and good relations with all states in the region. There is every incentive for China to seek to downplay political problems and seek harmonious regional coexistence. Its present unpredictability – changes of course in economic policy, domestic political conflict – can be borne by the outside world with a degree of fatalism, since a generational change in leadership may produce more amenable leaders, and the continued economic development of the country will make it increasingly dependent, in the long-term, on the goodwill of its neighbours. Trade and other economic conflicts may occasionally blow up, but these will be more than offset by the deradicalisation of a future China and its commercial value. These are perhaps tendentious predictions, but probably the best that can be made, and are the kind of assumptions that guide political leaders in the Pacific, although no doubt there is a certain hedging of bets in some capitals.

Chronology

1989

15 April	Former Party leader Hu Yaobang dies
24 April	Beijing students boycott classes
28 April	Beijing Students' Autonomous Federation created
4 May	Anti-government demonstrations on anniversary of Movement of 4 May 1919
13 May	Hunger strike by some of students in Tiananmen Square begins
15 May	Mikhail Gorbachev visits Beijing, first General Secretary of the Communist Party of the Soviet Union to do so since Khrushchev
16 May	Number of hunger strikers passes 3000
18 May	Premier Li Peng meets with student leader Wu'er Kaixi and other students
19 May	Martial law imposed in Beijing
21 May	End of hunger strike
23 May	Beijing Independent Intellectuals' Association established
25 May	Beijing Workers' Autonomous Federation established
29 May	Goddess of Liberty erected in Beijing
4–5 June	Suppression of Tiananmen demonstrations
August	Japanese Foreign Minister hopes that China will 'normalise' its domestic political situation and not repeat the killings
October	Law controlling mass rallies and demonstrations passed
1 October	Fortieth anniversary of the PRC
November	Deng Xiaoping resigns as Chairman of the Central Military Commission

1990

January	Martial law lifted in Beijing
April	National People's Congress adopts Basic Law for the governance of Hong Kong
April	Jiang Zemin becomes Chairman of the State Central Military Commission
April	Li Peng visits the USSR, the first Chinese Prime Minister to do so since 1964
June	'Dissident' Fang Lizhi is allowed to leave China with his wife
July	First symposium of mainland and Taiwanese businessmen opens in Beijing
August	Premier Li Peng's tour of SE Asia

September	General Vo Nguyen Giap of Vietnam visits Beijing ostensibly to attend the Asian Games.

1991

April	British Foreign Secretary Douglas Hurd visits Beijing
April	Jiang Zemin visits Moscow, highest level visit since 1957: agreement on eastern end of Sino-Soviet border signed
May	Taiwan formally ends 'period of mobilisation for the suppression of the communist rebellion'
July	Memorandum on the new Hong Kong airport is formally initialled in Beijing
July	Chinese Foreign Minister Qian Qichen attends ASEAN meeting for first time
July	Seventieth Anniversary of the founding of the Chinese Communist Party
August	Japanese Prime Minister Kaifu visits Bejing and raises arms control and human rights in speech

1992

January	Chinese Prime Minister Li Peng visits Italy, Switzerland, Portugal, Spain
January–February	Deng Xiaoping tours southern China and presses for further economic reform. '... ideology cannot supply rice ...'
January	Report from China that there are 20 million more men than women
January	President Yang Shangkun visits Singapore, first major visit since diplomatic relations established in October 1990
February	Chinese Foreign Minister visits Cambodia, first such contact since 1979
March	China accedes to Nuclear Non-Profileration Treaty.
August	Christopher Patten becomes Governor of Hong Kong
August	China establishes diplomatic relations with South Korea
October	14th Congress of the Chinese Communist Party
October	Nelson Mandela visits China
October	Emperor of Japan visits China
December	Boris Yeltsin visits China

1993

February	Tiananmen student leader Wang Dan released from prison
May	Chinese consular office opened in Hanoi
May	Chinese Foreign Minister makes extensive tour of Western Europe
August	China publishes White Paper on Taiwan which talks of 'peaceful reunification'

September   Chinese Foreign Minister makes tour of Eastern Europe
December   Wei Jingsheng (leader of 1978–9) Democracy Movement released from prison

1994

1 January   Extensive reform of the tax system comes into effect
March   National People's Congress amendments to the constitution to fully recognise the socialist market economy.
May   USA renews China's Most Favoured Nation (MFN) trading status, with President Clinton de-linking from China's human rights record
July   New labour law grants statutory rights to workers but also allows for redundancy, smashing the 'iron rice bowl'
July   New stricter laws on dissent made public
August   Deng Xiaoping's ninetieth birthday
September   President Jiang Zemin visits Russia
September   First fully democratic elections in Hong Kong, for district boards
December   Long prison terms handed out to dissidents

Further Reading

General and introductory works

There are a number of general historical introductions which one might recommend for anyone embarking on study of China. Perhaps two or three stand out: thus, J. Gray, *Rebellions and Revolutions – China from the 1800s to the 1980s* (Oxford University Press, 1990) and J. Spence, *The Search for Modern China* (Norton, 1990) are both remarkable syntheses of the complex modern history of China. Spence's book is a massive tome, but beautifully written, well illustrated and not expensive. In addition, J. K. Fairbank, *The Great Chinese Revolution, 1800–1985* (Picador, 1986) is shorter but packs a lot in. A more advanced text linking past and present in some very perceptive essays is B. Womack (ed.) *Contemporary Chinese Politics in Historical Perspective* (Cambridge University Press, 1991).

One should not forget the moving, personal view of twentieth-century Chinese history as related in the best-selling *Wild Swans* by Jung Chang (Flamingo, 1993)

A well-argued and stimulating text is W. Jenner, *The Tyranny of History: The Roots of China's Crisis* (Penguin, 1992).

Although of an earlier vintage both the following works address, in different ways, the problem of how we in the West have come to understand China and are recommended on those grounds: R. Dawson, *The Chinese Chameleon* (Oxford University Press, 1967); T. Kuo and R. Myers, *Understanding Communist China* (Stanford, 1986); see also D. Shambaugh, *American Studies on Contemporary China* (M. E. Sharpe, 1993) and D. Shambaugh, *Beautiful Imperialist: China Perceives America, 1972–1990* (Princeton University Press, 1991).

For reference one could perhaps not do better than Mackerras and Yorke (eds) *The Cambridge Handbook of Contemporary China* (Cambridge University Press, 1991).

Westview Press (Boulder, Co) produces an annual survey of recent events under the title, *China Briefing*.

For the student, the journals *China Quarterly* (Oxford University Press), *Modern China* (Sage) and the *Australian Journal of Chinese Affairs* need to be consulted regularly. For the non-specialist the quarterly magazine, *China Now* (from the Society for Anglo-Chinese Understanding, Cheltenham, UK) provides good short feature articles and information on contemporary events.

Politics and intellectual life

Although dealing with an earlier period than this book, the *Cambridge History of China* cannot be ignored. Volumes 14 (Cambridge University Press, 1987) and 15 (Cambridge University Press, 1991) cover most aspects of China's political, social, economic and diplomatic life in the period 1949–82. Both are extremely expensive. Forthcoming at the time of writing is a selection of chapters from the History, with an additional chapter to cover the 1980s, also from Cambridge University Press, and under the editorship of R. MacFarquhar.

Turning to more conventional texts, very full and informative, and a good starting introduction to the Chinese political system is June Teufel Dreyer, *China's Political System – Modernisation and Tradition* (Macmillan, 1993). Wider in scope but also up to date is B. Brugger and S. Reglar, *Politics, Economy and Society in Contemporary China* (Macmillan, 1994) and E. Croll's insightful, *From Heaven to Earth: Images and Experiences of Development in China* (Routledge, 1994).

John Gittings, *China Changes Face, The Road From Revolution 1949–1989* (Oxford University Press, 1990), a one-volume assessment of the People's Republic, displays the author's deep understanding of China and is extremely well-written.

Party history is well-treated in S. Uhalley, *A History of the Chinese Communist Party* (Hoover Institution Press, 1988).

More detailed, looking at the complexities of the political and bureaucratic system in action is K. Lieberthal and M. Oksenberg, *Policy Making in China: Leaders, Structures and Processes* (Princeton University Press, 1988). See also on China's National People's Congress (Parliament), K. J. O'Brien *Reform Without Liberalisation* (Cambridge University Press, 1990).

The life and times of Mao's successor, Deng Xiaoping, are covered in a special issue of the *China Quarterly* (September 1993, no. 135) and in R. Evans: *Deng Xiaoping and the Making of Modern China* (Hamish Hamilton, 1993). Note that other special issues of the *China Quarterly* deal with *China and Japan* (December 1990, no. 124) and *The Individual and the State* (September 1991, no. 127); *Greater China* (December 1993, no. 136).

Ideological issues are explored in B. Brugger and D. Kelly, *Chinese Marxism in the Post-Mao Era* (Stanford, 1990) and in A. Dirlik and M. Mesiner, *Marxism and the Chinese Experience* (M. E. Sharpe, 1989). A collection of essays by the dissident scholar, Su Shaozhi, is published under the title *Marxism and Reform in China* (Spokesman, 1993).

Perhaps too journalistic in style, but displaying a remarkable range of contacts amongst the Chinese leadership is Harrison Salisbury, *The New Emperors, Mao and Deng – A Dual Biography* (HarperCollins, 1993). To complement this is S. Schram, *The Thought of Mao Tse-tung* (Cambridge University Press, 1989).

A number of works appeared to celebrate the 40th anniversary of the People's Republic in 1989, or considered that forty-year span. A good general overview is D. Goodman and G. Segal (eds) *China at Forty – Mid Life Crisis?* (Clarendon Press, 1989). This volume was revised to appear as *China in the Nineties* (Clarendon, 1991). See also the special issue of the *China Quarterly*, on this theme – no. 119, September 1989. A more specific focus on the first decade of the post-Mao reforms is provided by R. Benewick and P. Wingrove (eds) *Reforming the Revolution* (Macmillan, 1989); G. White (ed.) *The Chinese State in the Era of Economic Reform* (Macmillan, 1991); and M. Dassu and T. Saich (eds.) *The Reform Decade in China* (Kegan Paul, 1992).

The literature on the Tiananmen events is now quite extensive. Some of the more useful volumes include original documents as well as commentary. Such are Han Minzhu (ed.), *Cries for Democracy, Writings and Speeches from the 1989 Chinese Democracy Movement* (Princeton University Press, 1990) and Mok Chiu Yu and J. F. Harrison (eds) *Voices from Tiananmen Square* (Montreal, Black Rose Books, 1990). More comprehensive are M. Oksenberg *et al, Beijing Spring 1989, Confrontation and*

Conflict, The Basic Documents (M. E. Sharpe, 1990) and J. Unger: *The Pro-Democracy Protests in China, Reports from the Provinces* (M. E. Sharpe, 1991).

A number of edited volumes appeared fairly soon after the June events, including G. Hicks: *The Broken Mirror: China After Tiananmen* (Longman, 1990); T. Saich (ed.) *The Chinese People's Movement, Perspectives on Spring 1989* (M. E. Sharpe, 1990). Appearing later, and more substantial, is S. Ogden *et al* (eds) *China's Search for Democracy: the Student and Mass Movement of 1989* (M. E. Sharpe, 1992).

Perspective and re-evaluation are the keynotes of a considered set of essays, J. Wasserstrom and E. Perry (eds) *Popular Protest and Political Culture in Modern China: Learning from 1989*, (Westview, 1992).

G. Black and R. Munro *Black Hands of Beijing* (Wiley, 1993) is a detailed and fascinating account of the lives of some of China's dissidents, plus a meticulous account of the Tiananmen events. A. Nathan, *China's Crisis* (Columbia University Press, 1990) contains some thoughtful essays from a capable scholar.

Little-documented, but important, is the Chinese political prison system, for which see H. Wu, *The Chinese Gulag* (Westview, 1992).

A key group in Chinese society, the intellectuals, can be heard speaking freely on the eve of Tiananmen in Perry Link's riveting *Evening Chats in Beijing* (Norton, 1992). More formal, but with a wider scope is M. Goldman *et al. China's Intellectuals and the State: In Search of a New Relationship*, (Harvard University Press, 1987). Goldman's monographs, particularly her most recent, *Sowing the Seeds of Democracy in China: Political Reform in the Deng Xiaoping Era* (Harvard, 1994) provide detailed accounts of intellectual and political dissent. Strictly speaking outside our brief, but engrossing reading, is A. Thurston, *Enemies of the People, The Ordeal of the Intellectuals in China's Great Cultural Revolution* (Harvard University Press, 1988). One of the most persistent internal critics of Chinese society is Liu Binyan who has written his own story in *A Higher Kind of Loyalty* (Methuen, 1990). A wide range of intellectual and dissident writing appears in G. Barme and J. Minford (eds) *Seeds of Fire: Chinese Voices of Conscience*, (Bloodaxe Books, 1989). S. M. Rai's *Resistance and Reaction* (Harvester Wheatsheaf, 1991) is full of original material on university politics.

For an up-to-date examination of foreign relations see T. Robinson and D. Shambaugh (eds), *Chinese Foreign Policy: Theory and Practice* (Oxford University Press, 1994). H. Harding has turned his considerable talents from China's domestic politics to look at Sino-US relations in *A Fragile Relationship – The United States and China Since 1972* (Brookings Institution, 1992). Another skilled sinologist has also turned to foreign policy and provided an excellent counterpart to Harding – see L. Dittmer, *Sino-Soviet Normalisation and its International Implications* (University of Washington Press, 1992). The past and future of Hong Kong are dealt with in two useful books – G. Segal, *The Fate of Hong Kong* (Simon and Schuster, 1993) and R. Cottrell, *The End of Hong Kong: The Secret Diplomacy of Imperial Retreat* (John Murray, 1993).

Economic and social

Although published some years ago, H. Harding *China's Second Revolution : Reform After Mao* (Brookings Institution, 1987) is still probably one of the most authoritative (and readable) introductions to the economic reform process. For a more contemporary view see M. Selden, *The Political Economy of China's Development* (M. E. Sharpe, 1993). Equally knowledgeable is G. White, *Riding the Tiger* (1993). A valuable view from the perspective of Chinese scholars is provided by Sheng Hua, *et al, China – From Revolution to Reform* (Macmillan, 1993). The economic role of the PLA is carefully examined by P. H. Folta in *From Swords to Plowshares? Defense Industry Reform in the PRC* (Westview, 1992).

Agriculture is still the foundation of China's economy. A fine background text which makes the frustratingly complex clear is F. Leeming, *Rural China Today* (Longman, 1985). The renowned Chen Village study has been updated to become *Chen Village under Mao and Deng*, R. Madsen and J. Unger (University of California Press, 1992). A broader, very intelligent, text is J. C. Oi, *State and Peasant in Contemporary China* (University of California Press, 1989).

One of the best of students of China's economy, N. Lardy, has written a fine study of the role of one of the key elements of the economic reforms, trade, in *Foreign Trade and Economic Reform in China, 1978–1990* (Cambridge University Press, 1992); and valuable texts are J. Howell, *China Opens Its Doors: The Politics of Economic Transition* (Harvester Wheatsheaf, 1993) and R. Garnaut and Liu Guoguang (eds), *Economic Reform and Internationalisation* (Allen & Unwin, 1992). Both set the economy in the wider context, while A. Takahara, *The Politics of Wage Policy in Post-Mao China* (Macmillan, 1992) reveals the complexity of reform.

Geographic factors and their interaction with the reform process are clearly and comprehensively discussed in T. Cannon and A. Jenkins (eds) *The Geography of Contemporary China, the Impact of Deng Xiaoping's Decade* (Routledge, 1990); more recent is F. Leeming, *The Changing Geography of China* (Blackwell, 1993). More focused on the environment are V. Smil, *China's Environment Crisis* (M. E. Sharpe, 1993) and R. L. Edmonds, *Patterns of China's Lost Harmony* (Routledge, 1994).

China's minorities, often neglected, receive proper treatment in T. Heberer, *China and Its National Minorities* (M. E. Sharpe, 1989).

Cultural

For useful critiques and samples of recent Chinese writing consult the following: W. Larson and A. Wedell-Wedellsborg (eds) *Inside Out: Modernism and Post-Modernism in Chinese Literary Culture* (Aarhus University Press, 1993); E. Widmer and D. Der-wei Wang (eds) *From May Fourth to June Fourth: Fiction and Film in Twentieth-Century China* (Harvard, 1993); *World Literature Today*, Summer 1991 (special issue on Chinese Literature); H. Zhao (ed) *The Lost Boat: Avant-garde Fiction from China* (Wellsweep Press, 1993).

Bibliography

Ash, R. (1992) 'The Agricultural Sector in China: Performance and Policy Dilemmas during the 1990s', *China Quarterly*, 131.

Bachman, D. and Dali L. Yang (eds) (1991) *Yan Jiaqi and China's Struggle for Democracy*, Armonk, New York, M. E. Sharpe.

Bachrach, P. and Botwinick, A. (1992) *Power and Empowerment: A Radical Theory of Participatory Democracy*, Philadelphia, Temple University Press.

Bakken, B. (1993) 'Crime, Juvenile Delinquency and Deterrence Policy in China', *The Australian Journal of Chinese Affairs*, vol. 30.

Banister, J. (1987) *China's Changing Population*, Stanford, Stanford University Press.

Banister, J. (1992) 'China: Recent Mortality Levels and Trends', paper presented to the Annual Meeting of the Population Association of America, Denver.

Barmé, G. (1992) 'Wang Shuo and Liumang (Hooligan) Culture', *The Australian Journal of Chinese Affairs*, July.

Beijing Review (1990) 'Chinese Judges Set Juvenile Courts', 23–29 April.

Benewick, R. (1991) 'Political Institutionalisation at the Basic Level of Government in China', in G. White (ed.), *The Chinese State in the Era of Economic Reform*, Basingstoke, Macmillan.

Black's Law Dictionary (1979) St Paul, Minnesota: West Publishing Co.

Blecher, M. (1991) 'Developmental State, Entrepreneurial state: The Political Economy of Socialist Reform in Xinji Municipality and Guanghan County', in White, G. (ed.) *The Chinese State in the Era of Economic Reform*, Basingstoke, Macmillan.

Blecher, M. and Shue, V. (forthcoming) *The Tethered Deer: Government and Economy in a Chinese County*.

Blecher, M. and Wang Shaoguang (1994) 'The Political Economy of Cropping in Shulu County, China, 1949–1990', *China Quarterly*.

Bo, Yibo (1991) *Several Important Policy-makings and Events in Retrospect*, Beijing, China, CCP Central Committee Party School Press.

Branson, L. (1990) Interviews reported in *Sunday Times*, London, 27 May.

Burns, J. P. (1988) *Political Participation in Rural China*, Berkeley and London, University of California Press.

Byrd, W. A. and Lin, Q. (eds) (1990) *China's Rural Industry*, Washington, DC, Oxford University Press for the World Bank.

Chan, A., Madsen, R. and Unger, J. (1992) *Chen Village Under Mao and Deng*, Berkeley and London, University of California Press.

Chang, G. H. (1988) 'A Symposium on Marxism in China Today: An Interview with Su Shaozhi, with comments by American scholars and a Response by Su Shaozhi', *Bulletin of Concerned Asian Scholars*, vol. 20, no 1.

Cheng Ming (1993) 'The Chen Faction Attacks Deng; Qiao Shi Returns Fire', Hong Kong, 1 August.

Cheung, Tai Ming (1993) 'The Tainted Millions: Corruption Raises its Ugly Head in the Army', in *Far Eastern Economic Review*, vol. 156, no 32.

China News Digest, 8 September 1993.

China Quarterly (1993) Special Issue – 'Greater China', no 136.

Chinese Education: A Journal of Translations, White Plains, New York, M. E. Sharpe.

Coale, A. J. (1984) *Rapid Population Change in China 1952–1982*, Report no 27, Committee on Population and Demography, Washington, National Academy Press.

Crane, G. (1990) *The Political Economy of China's Special Economic Zones*, Armonk, New York, M. E. Sharpe.

Crane, G. (1993) 'China and Taiwan: not yet "Greater China"', *International Affairs*, vol. 69, no 4.

Croll, E. (1978) *Feminism and Socialism*, London, Routledge & Kegan Paul.

Croll, E. (1987) 'New Peasant Family Farms in Rural China', *Journal of Peasant Studies*, vol. 14, no 4.

Croll, E., Davin, D. and Kane, P. (1985) *China's One-Child Family Policy*, Basingstoke, Macmillan.

Epstein, I. (1986) 'Children's Rights and Juvenile Correctional Institutions in the People's Republic of China', *Comparative Education Review*, 30, no 3.

Epstein, I. (1993) 'Child Labor and Basic Education Provision in China', *International Journal of Educational Development*, vol. 13, no 3.

Evans, H. (1992) 'Monogamy and Female Sexuality in the People's Republic of China', in S. Rai *et al* (eds) *Women in the Face of Change: the Soviet Union, Eastern Europe and China*, London, Routledge.

Feuchtwang, S. (1991) *The Imperial Metaphor: Popular Religion in China*, London, Routledge.

Gelatt, T. (1991) 'Lawyers in China: The Past Decade and Beyond', *Occasional Papers/Reprints Series in Contemporary Asian Studies*, no 6, University of Maryland School of Law.

Glaser, B. S. (1993) 'China's Security Perceptions: Interests and Ambitions', *Asian Survey*, vol. 33, no 3.

Goodman, D. S. G. (1992) 'China: The State and Capitalist Revolution', *The Pacific Review*, vol. 5, no 4.

Greenhalgh, S. (1992) *Negotiating Birth Control in Village China*, Working Paper no 38, Washington DC, The Population Council.

Harding, H. (1992) *A Fragile Relationship: Sino-American Relations Since 1972*, Washington DC, Brookings Institution.

Holberton, S. (1993) 'PLA seeks Cash for its Ploughshares', *Financial Times*, London, 9 July.

Hu Qiaomu (1982) 'Some Questions Concerning Revision of the Party Constitution', *Beijing Review*, no 39.

Hull, T. H. (1990) 'Recent Trends in Sex Ratios at Birth in China', *Population and Development Review*, vol. 16, no 1.

Hull, T. H. and Wen Xingyan (1992) 'Rising Sex Ratios at Birth in China: Evidence from the 1990 Population Census', paper prepared for the International Seminar on China's 1990 Population Census, Beijing.

Human Rights in China (1993) *Going Through the Motions: The Role of Defense Counsel in the Trials of the 1989 Protesters*, New York, Human Rights in China.

Jacka, T. (1992) 'The Public/Private Dichotomy and the Gender Division in Rural China', in Andrew Watson (ed.) *Economic Reform and Social Change in China*, London, Routledge.

Jefferson, G. H., Rawski, T. G. and Yuxin Zheng (1992) 'Innovation and Reform in Chinese Industry: A Preliminary Analysis of Survey Data', working paper.

Johansson, S. and Nygren, O. (1991) 'The Missing Girls of China', *Population and Development Review*, vol. 17, no 1.

Johnson, K. (1993) 'Chinese Orphanages: Saving China's Abandoned Girls', *Australian Journal of Chinese Affairs*, 30.

Jones, W. C. (1985) 'The Constitution of the People's Republic of China', *Washington University Law Quarterly*, LXIII.

Kane, P. (1987) *The Second Billion: Population and Family Planning in China*, Harmondsworth, Penguin Books.

Kane, P. (1988) *Famine in China 1959–61: Demographic and Social Implications*, Basingstoke, Macmillan.

Kaye, L. (1993) 'Congressional Record', *Far Eastern Economic Review*, 11 March.

Kelliher, D. (1991) 'Privatisation and Politics in Rural China', in G.White (ed.) *The Chinese State in the Era of Economic Reform*, London, Macmillan.

Kueh, Y. Y. (1992) 'Foreign Investment and Economic Change in China', *China Quarterly*, no 131.

Lardy, N. R. (1992) 'Chinese Foreign Trade', *China Quarterly*, no 131.

Lee, Kuen (1993) 'Property Rights and the Agency Problem in China's Enterprise Reform', *Cambridge Journal of Economics*, 17.

Leung, H. M., Thoburn, J. T., Chau, E. and Tang, S. H. (1991) 'Contractual Relations, Foreign Direct Investment, and Technology Transfer: The Case of China', *Journal of International Development*, June.

Leung, J. (1991) 'Social Welfare Provisions in Rural China: Mutual-help and Self-protection', *Hong Kong Journal of Social Work*, 24.

Leung, J. (1992) *The Transformation of Occupational Welfare in the PRC: From a Political Asset to an Economic Burden*, China Research Monograph, 3, Hong Kong, Department of Social Work and Social Administration, University of Hong Kong.

Li Wei (1993) 'China's Fewer Births and Greater Prosperity Cooperatives', *Women of China*, Beijing, November.

Lieberthal, K. (1992) 'The Collapse of the Communist World and Mainland China's Foreign Affairs', *Issues and Studies*, September.

Lieberthal, K. and Oskenberg, M. (1988) *Policy Making in China: Leaders, Structures and Processes*, Princeton, Princeton University Press.

Lin Zhun (1992) Vice President of the Supreme People's Court of PRC, 'Juvenile Justice in China', paper delivered at International Seminar on Prevention, Adjudication and Rehabilitation of Juvenile Delinquency.

Lo, Dic (1993) 'Explaining Chinese Industrialization under Reform: A Structuralist Perspective on Growth and Retrenchment', paper presented at the symposium on *The Chinese Economy in the Period of Rectification and Readjustment, 1989–91*, University of Leeds.

'Mayor's Report' (Chen Xitong) (1989) *Report on Checking the Turmoil and Quelling the Counter-Revolutionary Rebellion*, Beijing, New Star Publishers, 30 June.

McMillan, J. and Naughton, B. (1993) 'How to Reform A Planning Economy: Lessons from China', *Oxford Review of Economic Policy*, vol. 8, no 1.

Minford, J. (1985) 'Picking up the Pieces', *Far Eastern Economic Review*, 8 August.

Naughton, B. (1990) 'Economic Reform and the Chinese Political Crisis of 1989', *Journal of Asian Economics*, vol. 1, no 2.

Naughton, B. (1991) 'Why has Economic Reform Led to Inflation?', *AEA Papers and Proceedings*, May.

O'Brien, K. (1990) 'Implementing Political Reform in China's Villages', unpublished manuscript.

Pateman, C. (1989) *The Disorder of Women*, Cambridge, Polity Press.

Perkins, D. (1991) 'Price Reform vs. Enterprise Autonomy. Which Should Have Priority?', *China's Economic Dilemmas in the 1990s: The Problems of Reform, Modernization, and Interdependence*, vol. 1 pp 160–6, Joint Economic Committee, Congress of the United States.

Population and Development Review, vol. 15, no 4.

Potter, S. H. and Potter, J. M. (1990) *China's Peasants*, Cambridge, Cambridge University Press.

Qian, Yingyi and Chenggang Xu (1993) 'Why China's Economic Reforms Differ: The M-Form Hierarchy and Entry/Expansion of the Non-State Sector', in *The Economics of Transition*, forthcoming.

Research of the Industrial Events of the People's Republic of China (1991) Hanoi Press.

Rocca, J.-L. (1984) *La Déliquence Juvenile et le Controle Social dans la Chine Contemporaine*, Paris, Ecole des Hautes Etudes en Sciences Sociales.

Saich, T. (1983) 'Party and State Reforms in the People's Republic of China', *This World Quarterly*, vol. 5, no 3, July.

Saich, T. (1986) 'Political and Ideological Reform in the People's Republic of China: An Interview with Professor Su Shaozhi', *China Information*, vol. 1, no 2.

Saich, T. (1991) 'Much Ado About Nothing: Party Reform in the 1980s', in Gordon White (ed.) *The Chinese State in the Era of Economic Reform: The Road To Crisis*, Basingstoke, Macmillan.

Saich, T. (1992) 'The Fourteenth Party Congress: A Programme for Authoritarian Rule', *China Quarterly*, 132.

Saich, T. (1993) *Discos and Dictatorship: Party-State and Society Relations in the People's Republic of China*, Leiden.

Schwartz, B. (1957) 'On Attitudes Toward Law in China', in American Council of Learned Societies, *Government Under Law and the Individual*, Washington, DC; reprinted in J. A. Cohen (1968), *The Criminal Process in the People's Republic of China, 1949–1963: An Introduction*, Cambridge, Mass, Harvard University Press.

Segal, G. (1990) *The Soviet Union and the Pacific*, London, Unwin Hyman.

SFPC/CSP (1990) State Family Planning Commission of China and Child Survival Project, Australian National University, *Infant and Child Mortality in Shanghai and Hunan: Levels, Trends and Differentials*, Division of Demography and Sociology, Australian National University.

Shambaugh, D. (1992) 'China's Security Policy in the Post-Cold War Era', *Survival*, vol. 34, no 2.

Shirk, S. L. (1993) *The Political Logic of Economic Reform in China*, Berkeley and Los Angeles, California, University of California Press.

Stacey, J. (1983) *Patriarchy and Socialist Revolution in China*, Berkeley, California, University of California Press.

State Statistical Bureau (1992) *China Statistical Annual Report*, Beijing, State Statistical Publishers.

State Statistics Bureau (1993) *Statistical Yearbook of China*, Beijing, China Statistics Press.

Stephens, T. B. (1992) *Order and Discipline in China*, Seattle, University of Washington Press.

Summary of World Broadcasts (SWB) (1993) FE/1722 B2/8, 23 June.

The Criminal Law and the Criminal Procedure Law of China, (1984) Beijing, Foreign Languages Press.

The Mirror (1993) Hong Kong, 1 November.

The Records of Industrial Events of the People's Republic of China (1991) Hunan, China, Hunan Press.

Thoburn, J. T., Leung, H. M., Chau, E. and Tang, S. H. (1990) *Foreign Investment in China under the Open Policy: The Experience of Hong Kong Companies*, Aldershot, Avebury.

Thoburn, J. T., Leung, H. M., Chau, E. and Tang, S. H. (1991) 'Investment in China by Hong Kong Companies', *Institute of Development Studies Bulletin* (University of Sussex) vol. 22, no 2.

Thøgersen, S. (1990) *Secondary Education in China after Mao: Reform and Social Conflict*, Aarhus, University Press.

US Foreign Broadcast Information Service, Daily Report: China. (FBIS).

Unger, J. (ed.) (1991) *The Pro-Democracy Protests in China: Reports from the Provinces*, New York, M. E. Shaula.

Unger, R. M. (1976) *Law in Modern Society*, New York, The Free Press.

Wang, Xiao-qiang (1994) ' "Groping for Stones to Cross the River": China's Price Reform versus Big-bang', in Gang, Yang and Cui, Zhiyuan (eds) *A Reformable Socialism? The Chinese Alternative to Shock Therapy and Mass Privatization*, Oxford University Press.

Wang Ningjun (1993) 'Insurance in China', *Women of China*, Beijing, June.

Wasserstrom, J. and Powy, E. (eds) *Popular Protest and Political Culture in China: Learning from 1937*, Newport, Conn., Westview Press.

White, G. (1988) 'The New Economic Paradigm: Towards Market Socialism', in R. Benewick and P. Wingrove (eds), *Reforming the Revolution*, Basingstoke, Macmillan.

White, G. (1993) *Riding the Tiger: The Politics of Economic Reform in Post-Mao China*, Basingstoke, Macmillan.

White, T. (1992) 'Rural Politics in the 1990s: Rebuilding Grassroots Institutions', unpublished manuscript.

Woodward, D. (1992) 'The Role of the People's Liberation Army', in Watson, A. (ed.) *Economic Reform and Social Change in China*, London, Routledge.

World Bank (1991) *World Development Report*, Beijing, China Finance and Economics Publishers.

World Bank Report (1992) 'Strategies for Reducing Poverty in the 1990s', Washington.

Wu, H. H. (1992) *Laogai: The Chinese Gulag*, Boulder, Colorado, Westview Press.

Xiao Ming (1993) 'Going to the Sea', *Women of China*, Beijing, September.

Xiao Xie (1993) 'Rolls-Royce's Sales are Gathering Speed', *China Daily*, 3 July.

Yangcheng Wanbao (1992) 'Qingnian nongmin qiyejia Chen Jinyi', 31 October.

Young, S. (1991) 'Wealth but not Security: Attitudes Towards Private Business in China in the 1980s', *Australian Journal of Chinese Affairs*, no 25.

Yuan Lili (1993) 'From Office Worker to Chief Manager', *Women of China*, Beijing, November.

Zhang, Baohui (1992) 'Markets, the State, and the Transition of the Chinese State Socialist Economy', paper presented at the 1992 Annual Meeting of the American Political Science Association, Chicago.

Zhang, L. Y. (1994) 'Location-specific advantages amd direct foreign investment in South China', *World Development*, January.

Zhang, Junzuo (1992) 'Gender and Political Participation in Rural China' in S. Rai *et al.* (eds) *Women in the Face of Change: the Soviet Union, Eastern Europe and China*, London, Routledge.

Zweig, D. (1991) 'Internationalizing China's Countryside: The Political Economy of Exports from Rural Industry', *China Quarterly*, no 128.

Index